Determinants of Foreign Direct Investment in Emerging Markets

STUDIEN ZU INTERNATIONALEN WIRTSCHAFTSBEZIEHUNGEN

Herausgegeben von Prof. Dr. Michael Frenkel

Band 5

PETER LANG

Frankfurt am Main · Berlin · Bern · Bruxelles · New York · Oxford · Wien

Torsten Wezel

Determinants of Foreign Direct Investment in Emerging Markets

An Empirical Study of FDI Flows from Germany and its Banking Sector

PETER LANG
Europäischer Verlag der Wissenschaften

Bibliographic Information published by Die Deutsche Bibliothek
Die Deutsche Bibliothek lists this publication in the Deutsche Nationalbibliografie; detailed bibliographic data is available in the internet at <http://dnb.ddb.de>.

Zugl.: Vallendar, Wiss. Hochsch. für Unternehmensführung, Diss., 2004

ISSN 1618-503X
ISBN 3-631-53343-8
US-ISBN 0-8204-7658-7

www.peterlang.de

Vorwort

Die vorliegende Arbeit wurde im Herbstsemester 2004 an der Wissenschaftlichen Hochschule für Unternehmensführung – Otto-Beisheim-Hochschule – Vallendar als Dissertation angenommen.

Ganz selbstverständlich möchte ich zunächst meinem Doktorvater, Prof. Dr. Michael Frenkel, großen Dank aussprechen für die im wissenschaftlichen als auch zwischenmenschlichen Sinne vorzügliche Betreuung meines Promotionsvorhabens. An dessen erfolgreichem Abschluss hatte ich nicht zuletzt dank seiner stets zielführenden und ermutigenden Ratschläge nie ernsthafte Zweifel, was unter externen Doktoranden gewiss eine Ausnahme darstellt.

Herrn Prof. Dr. Jürgen Weigand danke ich genauso herzlich für seine Bereitschaft, das Zweitgutachten für diese Arbeit zu übernehmen.

Meinem langjährigen Freund Dr. Ralf Fendel möchte ich für die ausdauernde Unterstützung in fachlicher und moralischer Hinsicht besonders herzlich danken, ebenso dem übrigen Forschungsteam des Lehrstuhls bestehend aus Katja Funke, Isabel Koske, Dr. Günter Schmidt und Christoph Swonke. Nicht unerwähnt bleiben sollen die vielen anregenden Diskussionen während und am Rande der Doktorandenkolloquien sowie überhaupt die herzliche Atmosphäre am Lehrstuhl, die mir das häufige Pendeln mehr als Vergnügen denn als Last erscheinen ließen.

Ein Großteil dieser Arbeit entstand während meines Aufenthalts im Volkswirtschaftlichen Forschungszentrum der Deutschen Bundesbank. Wertvolle Unterstützung erhielt ich seinerzeit von dessen Leiter Dr. Heinz Herrmann sowie von meinen Kollegen Dr. Christoph Fischer, Dr. Alexander Lipponer, Fred Ramb, Dr. Christian Upper und Dr. Thomas Werner. Michael Dear war eine stete Hilfe beim Redigieren des englischsprachigen Manuskripts. Ihnen allen gilt mein spezieller Dank.

Entscheidenden Anteil am Gelingen des Forschungsprojekts hatten auch Prof. Dr. Jörg Breitung (Universität Bonn), der mir in kniffligen ökonometrischen Fragen jederzeit mit Rat und Tat zur Seite stand, und Prof. Dr. Claudia Buch (Universität Tübingen), deren Ideen oft neue Gesichtspunkte zu Tage förderten.

Ich widme dieses Werk meinen Eltern.

Torsten Wezel — Frankfurt am Main, im November 2004

Table of Contents

Index of Tables

Index of Figures

Index of Boxes

Chapter I: General Introduction to the Investigation

1 Motivation

Most economists agree that foreign direct investment (FDI), involving a long-term interest in and significant management influence over a foreign affiliate, is beneficial for both the investor and the country receiving the capital flow. Foreign investors gain access to valuable natural resources or take advantage of low foreign labor costs to either re-import foreign-produced goods or sell directly to the rapidly growing markets of these economies. As modern growth theory has it, host countries themselves can profit from the "integration effect" associated with FDI – supply of modern production technology, quality control practices and up-to-date management techniques. If both parties were able to reap these benefits without frictions, there would be no need for research in this field. Indeed, if unrestricted FDI leads to a more efficient allocation of resources across economies and within a host country not showing signs of market distortions, there is little reason to restrict the entry of foreign investors into domestic markets. However, this is heavily predicated on the existence of institutions which ensure that markets work efficiently. Typically, greatly-needed building blocks such as competition policy and equitable legal systems are non-existent or extremely weak in the least developed countries, or are on the rise, if still incomplete, in many of the transition economies or fast-growing countries elsewhere – this, incidentally, is why the term "emerging markets" appears just appropriate. Knowing about the deficiencies still prevalent in the institutional setting, governments in these countries erect barriers to FDI for fear that multinational corporations might exploit their proprietary advantages to the detriment of the host economy by, for instance, engaging in anticompetitive practices. Hence, under certain circumstances there will likely be conflicts of interest between investor and host country. Yet the case for government intervention must still be made, and investment barriers should be imposed only if they actually overcome a given market failure and thus lead to an improvement in national welfare.[1]

What makes emerging markets so interesting to study is that, in spite of institutional imperfections, they receive substantial amounts of FDI inflows, feature relatively well-developed banking systems and are often even able to place sovereign bond issues of their own in the international capital markets.

---

[1] See UNCTAD (2003), p. 104.

The impressive rise in FDI inflows to emerging markets throughout the 1990s occurred in parallel with decreasing concessional bilateral aid, lessons learned from several severe financial crises leaving behind a growing preference for stable long-term flows on the part of recipient countries, and fading concerns about giving non-residents widespread access to national resources thanks to improved behavior of foreign investors.[2] Many governments of emerging market economies, realizing that they need to be more responsive to the challenges of the globalizing economy, have come a long way in updating regulatory systems and diminishing economic as well as political risks.

The specific aim of this investigation is to examine whether emerging markets that consistently had a better investment profile or were capable of improving it over time did attract higher FDI inflows from Germany and, in particular, its outwardly expanding banking industry. It also addresses the question of whether FDI in especially risky countries can be promoted by involving multilateral development banks in investment projects of the German banking sector.

The remainder of this introductory chapter is devoted to presenting the wide array of institutional impediments in the context of foreign direct investment and to familiarizing the reader with the structure of the following empirical investigation.

2 Obstacles to Foreign Direct Investment

The attitude of governments in emerging market economies towards FDI over the last few decades has not been static. As early as the 1970s, host countries, perceiving a mismatch between objectives of foreign investors and their own, resorted to implementing investment measures aimed at directing the behavior of foreign affiliates. These manipulative policy regulations, which the *United Nations Conference on Trade and Development* (UNCTAD) calls "host country operational measures" (HCOMs), comprise restrictions on the operating life of foreign affiliates (such as mandatory joint ventures, domestic content rules and export requirements) as well as, in a broader sense, investment incentives and cumbersome administrative procedures. When, in the following two decades, FDI turned out to be a relatively reliable source of private capital, governments started providing more attractive business environments, abolishing many of the HCOMs previously enacted while retaining specific ones to enhance national welfare and achieve stated development goals.

[2] See UNCTAD (2003), p. 85.

The principal investment restrictions will be presented in the following paragraphs along with the set of relevant administrative barriers and political risks, the significance to German FDI flows of which is to be examined in the empirical chapters of this study.

2.1 Restrictions on the Mode of Entry

As UNCTAD (2001) puts it, restrictions and conditions imposed by host country governments before or at the time of entry are to be distinguished from the genuine HCOMs. However, since these restraints on foreign ownership subsequently affect the operating life of multinationals abroad, they ought to be mentioned under this heading. The most severe restriction on FDI possible is, of course, not to allow foreign entry into the entire economy or certain sectors of strategic importance at all, which a sovereign state has the absolute right to do under international law. More commonly, though, investors are granted freedom to establish operations in emerging markets subject to certain equity participation limits (i.e. prohibition on wholly-owned affiliates) or the forced taking of stakes by local firms (i.e. requirement to form joint ventures).[3]

These requirements constitute in the author's opinion restrictions to entry since they are usually imposed on investors prior to the establishment of a physical presence abroad. The pre- and post-entry regulations are actually closely intertwined. The limits and requirements imposed by the authorities abroad may, after all, apply both as a condition to establishment and as a requirement necessary for the continued operations of the foreign affiliate. By the same token, outright restrictions on operations, such as limits on the import of capital goods, are likely to determine the ability of investors to enter a market and withstand competitive pressures. Moreover, performance requirements (e.g. technology transfer) may be imposed as preconditions already at the time of the investment, thus influencing the decision on whether to select a particular host country.[4]

2.2 Operational Requirements

At the beginning of the emerging markets boom in the late 1980s and early 1990s, some host countries thought that the imposition of investment restrictions ("non facere" obligations) and specific performance requirements ("facere"

[3] See UNCTAD (2003), p. 102.

[4] See UNCTAD (2001), p. 56.

obligations) would prevent market failures and generate positive spillovers in the domestic economy (for a list of operational requirements see Table 1, Appendix to this chapter). As regards restrictions, there was the underlying concern that multinational companies might resort to anticompetitive practices, try to avoid paying local taxes through transfer pricing, crowd out local firms and products, and gain too much influence on the domestic economy.[5] Host country governments hoped that necessitating positive action in the form of performance requirements would allow local firms to achieve efficiency gains via imitation or reverse-engineering of shared foreign technologies ("demonstration effect"), encouraging entrepreneurship of workers trained by foreign investors ("labor turnover effect") or creating a base of supplier firms around foreign production plants ("linkage effect"). This view, however, neglects other welfare considerations: if foreign firms pay a wage premium to keep workers from transferring technology to local start-ups, as has been shown to be the case empirically, this transfer may not necessarily be optimal for the domestic economy.[6]

Anecdotal evidence gained over the past decade points to a number of failed attempts to attract large-scale production that would be fully integrated into a multinational corporation's global network. Doing so would have required the establishment of wholly-owned subsidiaries free from specific local content requirements and from the forced sharing of technology. Many host governments did not allow for such prime investment conditions, instead requiring foreign investors to enter into joint ventures or have part of the output produced by local suppliers. Computer companies which faced these obstacles in some countries of Latin America, for instance, reacted by using small joint venture plants as "cash cows" in protected markets to reap a second round of oligopoly rents from dated technologies which local partners would not able to exploit for their own advancement.[7] No wonder, then, that local suppliers to sub-scale foreign plants never achieved the economies of scale necessary to produce competitively with advanced materials. In other parts of the world, prominently Southeast Asia, where wholly-owned subsidiaries are more commonplace, unencumbered foreign investors chose – out of self-interest – to form production partnerships with prime local suppliers ("contract manufacturing"), thus creating tangible externalities for the domestic economy.

[5] See UNCTAD (2001), p. 11, and UNCTAD (2003), p. 88.

[6] See Hoekman and Saggi (1999), pp. 10-11.

[7] In fact, U.S. computer manufacturers Hewlett Packard and Compaq even lobbied against liberalizing trade and investment in the Mexican IT sector; see Moran (2002), p. 7.

In recent times, emerging market economies have been moving towards more market-friendly FDI policies, offering investment incentives and actively marketing themselves as secure and profitable locations. Even so, the degree of liberalization varies between industries. While few restrictions on admission and establishment remain in the manufacturing sector, FDI in natural resources and some parts of the service sector (media, financial services) is still subject to a high level of government control.[8]

Some changes were brought about by the *WTO Agreement on Trade-Related Investment Measures* (TRIMs; entered into force on January 1, 1995), which, among other things, outlaws local content and trade-balancing requirements (see Chapter V for more details). However, as market structures are weaker than in industrialized countries, emerging market economies must remain concerned about preserving their national policy space for direct investment so as to address specific needs arising from the development process.[9]

2.3 Investment Incentives

It may come as a surprise to the observer that the aforementioned operational measures and investment incentives – defined by UNCTAD as measurable economic advantages granted to encourage specific investor behavior, such as subsidies, tax holidays, special economic zones etc. – are not mutually exclusive. Indeed, they often go hand in hand within a single host country and are based on the same economic rationale.

Yet operational requirements and investment incentives operate in a different manner. While HCOMs are designed to *prescribe* a certain behavior for multinational investors in order to realize certain results, investment incentives are hoped to *induce* investors to act in a certain way. Many times, governments offer incentives to attract FDI and then apply HCOMs to introduce some degree of conditionality, which is presumably needed to align the investment with national development goals.[10] The scope and rationale of investment incentives will be described in greater detail in the concluding chapter.

---

[8] See UNCTAD (2003), p. 103.

[9] Ibid, p. 86.

[10] See UNCTAD (2001), pp. 11, 56.

2.4 Administrative Procedures

The influence of HCOMs is part of a wider framework of regulations that foreign investors have to cope with. Some obstacles to FDI – those relating to the quality of the bureaucracy – are less visible at first glance since they usually crop up only after the signing of the written agreement between investor and state.

Administrative procedures do exist in all countries, industrialized and developing. Yet it is in the latter group where they are most pronounced and cumbersome. Excessive regulation of foreign entry can entail significant extra costs and delays, sometimes inducing investors to terminate their operations in such a country or locate somewhere else in the first place. Bureaucratic barriers include (1) entry approvals (legal, statistical, labor, pension, and fiscal registration and application for investment incentives), (2) difficult access to land, site development, and utility connections, and (3) operational requirements over and above pure HCOMs (such as import-export permits and on-site inspections).[11] See Table 2 in the appendix to this chapter for a more detailed list of procedures.

The economics of such administrative barriers are, then, not always clear-cut. At times, such barriers are erected simply to protect incumbent domestic enterprises from competition by more efficient foreign firms. However, a government that chooses to rely on excessive regulation in dealing with foreign investors may cause them to stay away, resulting in dwindling revenues. This negative fiscal effect brings about a sub-optimal state and low public utility. Even if these barriers do not deter investors, the fiscal accounts may still suffer if, given widespread corruption, bureaucrats engage in private rent-seeking. As Morisset and Neso (2002) find, high levels of corruption are associated with higher administrative costs and longer delays for foreign investors. The reason is that governments in corruption-ridden countries can no longer collect fiscal revenues through regular channels and therefore feel impelled to apply otherwise distortionary administrative procedures in an attempt to sustain public spending. In the "governance" literature, much research effort has been devoted to the causes and effects of corruption. A review of the findings as they are relevant to the empirical investigation in this study will be provided in Chapter II.

The discrepancy between countries with and without adequate production environments to attract FDI points to a strategy that Moran (2002) has termed

[11] See Morisset and Neso (2002), pp. 5-6.

"build up". This approach to fostering entry of foreign firms features a *macro* component aimed at low inflation and a realistic exchange rate, a *micro* component regarding good infrastructure and education, and an *institutional* component which addresses legal and regulatory consistency combined with fighting red tape and corruption. If these qualities are lacking, even a host country that is located in an otherwise attractive region (such as Eastern Europe) and has joined a regional investment agreement may find it difficult to convince investors to settle there.[12]

2.5 Elements of Non-Commercial Risk

Administrative barriers are themselves only a subset of political risk, i.e. the set of non-commercial risks beyond the well-known uncertainties that are at the heart of private business (i.e. financial and operational risks) and, at the macroeconomic level, swings in the business cycle as well as disruptions caused by fiscal and external imbalances. What distinguishes political risks from the aforementioned HCOMs is the inability of investors to anticipate harmful events instigated by the host country authorities such as nationalizations in all sectors, specific takings (expropriation) or, more broadly, frustration of contracts. It is interesting to note that outright takings of foreign property can be lawful if they are (1) for a public purpose, (2) non-discriminatory and (3) give rise to the payment of compensation. While there are already many issues in determining whether all three conditions are fulfilled in a given case, "creeping" expropriations, where incremental but cumulative infringements on recognized ownership rights lead to the effective negation of the investor's interest in the property, or "regulatory takings", in which the exercise of governmental regulatory power diminishes the economic value of the affiliates' assets without denying formal ownership, are even harder to pin down.[13] Chapter IV provides more insight into these specific issues.

These by and large unlawful acts may be committed by the same administration that signed the investment agreement, suddenly facing a difficult economic situation, or by a new administration, having risen to power democratically or in an unconstitutional manner, that displays a less favorable attitude towards FDI.

[12] Bulgaria, neither having pursued privatization vigorously nor showing a stable political or macroeconomic environment, is a case in point. Despite having concluded an association agreement with the EU and having been fully liberalized externally as early as 1992 according to the classification of Kaminsky and Schmukler (2003), the country has attracted relatively little FDI; see Hoekman and Saggi (1999), p. 15.

[13] See UNCTAD (2003), pp. 110-111.

Some of these after-the-fact changes are not necessarily evil-minded because notions about the fairness of the previously agreed terms are notoriously subject to revision. The fundamental problem is that the life of an FDI project is typically much longer than the electoral cycle, thereby causing an incongruity between the assurances that the investor is given by the administration and the inability of the latter to ensure that these promises will be fulfilled beyond its term in office. Foreign direct investors may be confident that the incumbent host government will honor its obligations but they must be vigilant about the commitment of future administrations to adhere to these responsibilities. Investors are therefore naturally vulnerable to policy changes.[14]

One could resort to concluding implicit agreements on good conduct of the parties to a written contract. These so-called *self-enforcing contracts* involve a certain optimal behavior (subgame perfect equilibrium) according to a game-theoretic perspective.[15] However, unless there is symmetric information at the time of signing the contract, in which case reaching an implicit agreement maximizing the joint surplus is not a problem, host governments will have to make explicit assurances, however credible, to the investor with a view to bridging the information gap. Turning to public or private risk insurers can alleviate some of these uncertainties, but such political risk insurance usually comes at a high cost. As the analysis in Chapter IV illustrates, project finance can be structured such that prominent potential victims – multilateral development banks – are introduced as financial partners. This can act as a deterrent to inimical government behavior and has indeed become a strategic risk mitigation mechanism.

In Chapter II the risks pertaining to expropriation and payment restrictions are grouped with administrative barriers – i.e. the quality of the bureaucracy and the level of corruption. These risks are deemed to affect the investor directly and are separated from the "macro-level" risks of political instability, weak enforcement of law and order, and the prevalence of armed domestic conflict. In Chapter III yet another form of macroeconomic instability is examined, namely the occurrence of banking crises that are every so often caused by imprudent policies of the host country's authorities. Returning to outright political risk, Chapter IV illustrates how the perceived likelihood of expropriation or similarly detrimental action influences investors' locational choices and explores whether institutional safeguards other than political risk insurance can mitigate that particular risk.

---

[14] See Mistry and Olesen (2003), pp. 26-27, and Schnitzer (1999), p. 1127.

[15] See Schnitzer (1999), pp. 1119.

3 Course of the Investigation

The following empirical investigation comprises three individual studies woven together by a common thread: obstacles to foreign direct investment (of the whole economy and, in particular, the banking sector) such as country/political risk, the danger of financial crises or the threat of expropriation as well as special "drivers" that are commonly considered crucial for FDI such as labor costs, barriers to trade, agglomeration effects, the existence of financial centers or co-financing provided by multilateral development banks. The analysis moves from the economy-wide level, examining the determinants of aggregate German FDI flows, to the industry and the firm level, where the factors relevant for foreign equity participations of the banking sector and its willingness to commit more risky equity when teaming up with multilateral development banks are scrutinized.

The analysis conducted in *Chapter II* makes a contribution to the still relatively sparse literature on FDI exclusively in emerging markets by estimating determinants of German FDI flows to Latin America and Asia during the past decade. Using data contained in a newly available Bundesbank microdatabase, an FDI flow variable, constructed from year-to-year differences in FDI stocks adjusted for certain otherwise distorting factors, is subjected to econometric testing, using several exogenous variables previously found to be significant in the literature. These include so-called non-traditional factors such as country risk and agglomeration effects which are widely regarded as influential for FDI in emerging market economies. The analysis in that chapter therefore focuses on estimating the effects of various risk measures. In principle, it would have been preferable to include in the quantitative analysis information on the extent of FDI liberalization in the sample emerging markets. This could have meant accounting simply for the existence of bilateral investment treaties Germany has entered into with certain host countries, or these countries' accession to the OECD or WTO. Similarly, one could have included specific barriers to entry or performance requirements these countries maintain as well as incidents of expropriation or payment restrictions. However, doing so would have brought about the problem of having to translate characteristics of investment regimes into variables, where in addition exceptions or reservations to the investment agreements would likewise have to be incorporated.[16] While surveying all of

[16] See also the criticism raised by Hallward-Driemeier (2003, p. 3) regarding the use of dummy variables to account for the existence of *bilateral investment treaties* (BITs) in empirical studies: "Too much attention has been placed on whether or not a BIT exists than on the strength of the property rights actually being enshrined in these agreements".

these multi-faceted investment measures is a daunting task in itself, using dummy variables for each treaty or membership would, apart from overburdening the relatively small data set, have tended to misrepresent the actual degree of non-commercial risks within the sample of emerging market economies. Unfortunately, no single index of harmful investment measures covering both the country and time dimension of the sample was available at the time of writing;[17] the Heritage Foundation's index of openness to capital flows and foreign investment only runs from 1994 to 2001 (it is used, though, in Chapter III since that sample has a later starting date). As a consequence, only the effects of administrative barriers and political risk at large are examined, based on two independently published commercial indices of aggregate country/political risk and, more specifically, a separate measure of administrative impediments. In addition, an index comprising five categories of structural reforms in Latin American countries is also subjected to empirical testing. The methodology used in that chapter is the Seemingly Unrelated Regressions (SUR) procedure, which allows for appropriately incorporating the contemporaneous correlation of disturbances as well as first-order auto-correlation of the time series disturbances and cross-sectional heteroskedasticity. In arriving at a parsimonious regression for each region, an Extreme Bounds Analysis (Leamer, 1983 and 1985) is performed to select individual variables robust to the inclusion of other explanatory variables. Making empirical use of German firm-level data, additional estimations are performed for direct investment of the manufacturing sector and three of its sub-sectors. Concluding the empirical analysis of this chapter, the hypothesis that capital-intensive industries react particularly strongly to the changes in the institutional environment of the host country is tested.

Chapter III takes a closer look at an individual sector by addressing German FDI in foreign banking markets. Most studies in this strand of the literature find a strong relationship between FDI and bilateral trade linkages as well as the decision of non-banks to enter emerging markets, a phenomenon that is commonly called the "follow the client" motive. Other factors that have been

[17] Recently, a new index of financial liberalization, also incorporating information on capital account liberalization, was published by Kaminsky and Schmukler (2003). The authors evaluated for 28 countries (14 developed and 14 emerging) in the period 1973-1999 the existence of (a) regulations on offshore borrowing by domestic financial institutions and by non-financial corporations, (b) multiple exchange rate markets, and (c) controls on capital outflows (scales 1, 2 and 3 for "fully liberalized", "partially liberalized" and "repressed", respectively). Capital account liberalization is depicted by factors (a) and (b). Unfortunately, the index is not useful for this study because it does not measure a country's openness to the entry of foreign corporations via equity participation.

shown to exert a positive influence on direct investment are host country income, the level of development of the financial sector abroad and its openness to foreign bank entry as well as the profit margin to be had there. A number of studies also stress that foreign multinational banks are deterred by a high degree of country and/or political risk. A limitation of the previous work in this field is that most studies are only concerned with banking FDI between developed countries and, thus, do not consider the distinctive framework concerning various risk factors which is prevalent in emerging markets. Another drawback is that many studies use relatively dated time series, which prevents the analysis of the changed financial market conditions in the aftermath of the Asian crisis. The analysis in this chapter seeks to close this gap by focusing on FDI flows into emerging markets exclusively and using data from the mid-1990s onward. It analyzes the factors crucial to the locational decisions of multinational German banks in selected emerging markets in central and eastern Europe, Latin America and Asia. Emphasis is placed on testing variables of macroeconomic and financial sector risk along with measures of bank-client integration, host country market characteristics and banking market openness. As an innovation in this strand of FDI research, a variable taken from the literature on "early warning indicators" which measures the backing of short-term banking deposits by international currency reserves is put to econometric testing. After estimating results using ordinary least squares (OLS) for the data set as a whole, it is disaggregated first by region (European transition economies, Latin America, Asia) and then by time period (pre- and post-Asian-crisis) to check whether the results for each sub-sample are driven by distinct factors.

Spurred by the observation that even large multinational financial conglomerates occasionally seek the support of a multilateral development bank (MDB) when establishing a presence in high-risk environments, *Chapter IV* investigates whether the availability of co-financing by such agencies as the International Finance Corporation (IFC) or the European Bank for Reconstruction and Development (EBRD) has prompted German banks that obtained such support to invest more "risk-adjusted" equity capital in selected emerging banking markets during 1998 and 2001 than did ordinary investors. In the literature, this particular topic has not yet attracted much attention. Econometric evaluation of the impact of participation in reform programs has typically been confined to assessing the effectiveness of IMF country programs. Evidence on the "treatment" effects of multilateral agencies' support at the firm level is still scarce, however. Building on a theoretical model by Asiedu and Villamil (2000), the analysis starts from the assumption that the presence of an official investor in an FDI project gives the recipient country a stronger economic incentive to honor its contractual obligations. High-risk countries do not themselves have at their disposal devices with which they can improve their standing with international investors in the short run. Here, using the instruments multilateral development banks are offering – loan subsides, technical assistance and, most importantly, provision of co-financing – may work to lower a host country's required threshold of political safety that needs to be crossed for it to receive FDI at all. Essentially a coalition of stakeholders, the multilateral agency may threaten to suspend its loans to the non-cooperative country altogether. This should lead its government to weigh its options carefully if the expected future stream subsidized lending that would be lost after a default represents a significant portion of the country's external financing. Therefore, participation of a multilateral agency can be thought of as a deterrent to expropriation or similarly detrimental events such as payment restrictions or denial of access to investors' property. In order to measure the extent to which IFC/EBRD participation increased German banks' willingness to enter high-risk environments, the empirical part of that chapter uses an innovative dependent variable which measures investors' equity capital that, given a country's risk profile, can be deemed "at risk". This "exposure", aptly called *capital-at-risk,* is a product of the absolute amount of investment multiplied by the country's probability of sovereign default which in turn is derived by linking the sovereign risk rating of the country to global historical five-year default rates on government bonds. For the econometric estimation of the treatment effect, which would consist of a significantly higher volume of risk-adjusted FDI, propensity score matching is used. This evaluation technique handles the problem of selection bias that will occur if treated banks exhibit systematic differences in their reactions to reform. It does so by identifying the relevant "counterfactual" outcome among members of a comparable control group that participants would hypothetically have realized if they had not participated. Based on an estimation which translates observable project characteristics relevant to the development banks' decision-making process into a probability of participation in the co-financing program (known as "propensity score"), every treated bank is "paired" with at least one non-treated project which before the treatment is as similar as possible regarding the combined characteristics. From interviews five regularly-applied selection criteria emerged: lack of financial market development in the host country, the quality of its banking supervision, the investor's experience in emerging markets as well as the target bank's equity capitalization and return on assets. Assuming that all characteristics relevant to the selection are accounted for and that unobservable factors do not create a bias between the two groups of projects, it is then possible to estimate the average treatment effect by subtracting the counterfactual capital-at-risk from the one that "sponsored" banks did realize.

Upon summarizing the main results of the empirical investigation, the concluding *Chapter V* first describes how international financial institutions and regional trade blocs have addressed barriers to foreign direct investment, ranging from unilateral measures and bilateral investment treaties to joint efforts within the framework of the *Organisation for Economic Co-operation and Development* (OECD) and the *World Trade Organisation* (WTO). Thereafter, the set of initiatives that has been initiated by multilateral organizations, notably the *International Monetary Fund* (IMF) and the *World Bank*, to combat corruption (particularly by deriving standards and codes) and strengthen financial system stability (using early warning systems) are reviewed and further steps suggested. Finally, options for lowering the risk of expropriation and improving dispute settlement procedures are discussed. The study closes by pointing out policy implications for the collaboration of international organizations and wages an outlook on the next line of research on FDI in emerging markets.

Appendix to Chapter I

Table 1: Summary of Selected Host Country Operational Measures

Restrictions on the mode of entry	*Limitations on operations ("non facere")*	*Performance requirements ("facere")*
• Requirements to establish a joint venture with domestic participation • Requirement for a minimum level of domestic equity participation • Restrictions on long-term leases of land and real property • Restrictions on employment of key foreign professionals or technical personnel	• Restrictions on access to local credit facilities or foreign exchange • Restrictions on repatriation of capital and profits (i.e. case-by-case approval, additional taxation or remittances) • Requirements on imports of capital goods, spare parts, manufacturing inputs, or restrictions/conditions on access to such items available locally • Operational permits and licenses • Advertising restrictions for foreign firms • Restrictions related to national security • Linking export quotas to domestic sales	• Sourcing/local content performance requirements • Manufacturing performance requirements • Technology transfer requirements • Employment performance and training requirements • Export/foreign exchange earning requirements • Trade-balancing requirements

Source: UNCTAD (2001), pp. 8-9, and, regarding classifications, p. 11.

Table 2: Summary of Host Country Administrative Procedures

Entry approvals	*Land, site development, utility*	*Operational requirements (beyond HCOMs)*
• Company and investment code registration • Initial bank deposits • Residence and working permits • Tax office and statistical office registration • Foreign investment licensing • Business and trading permits • Existence, conformity, and opening reporting • Health care and pension plans • Social security registration	• Access to land (owned by the state) • Town planning certificates • Site inspections and general approvals • Building permits • Electricity, power, water and sewage connection • Access to post and telephone/fax/internet lines	• Import-export intention and permits as well as clearance process • Fiscal situation certificate ("quitus") • Health and safety inspections • Labor inspections • Social welfare plan payments

Source: Morisset and Neso (2002), p. 6.

Chapter II: Determinants of German Foreign Direct Investment in Latin American and Asian Emerging Markets in the 1990s

1 Introduction to Chapter II

With hindsight, the 1990s were the decade of initial emerging market exuberance and subsequent disillusionment. Foreign direct investment flows to prospering regions such as Latin America and, most prominently, Asia grew by leaps and bounds – from about the mid-1980s to the second half of the 1990s average annual worldwide FDI flows to developing countries increased eightfold[18] – nourishing hopes for sustainable growth by transforming the host countries' infrastructure and enhancing their ability to withstand global economic downturns. As a matter of fact, German FDI stocks (at book values) in the six largest Latin American economies more than doubled between end-1989 and end-1997, while those of German subsidiaries in the eight largest markets in Asia almost quadrupled during that period. However, when the Asian crisis broke out, the long-held belief of these fast-growing economies' invulnerability was shattered, and it became apparent that warning signs such as real overvaluation of the currency, high short-term foreign indebtedness of the country as a whole or of individual sectors, as well as the absence of long-overdue structural reforms may not have been heeded by a majority of foreign enterprises.

The question then is: were those "red flags" in the sense of worsening country and/or political risk assessments – representing a subjective probability of certain adverse outcomes[19] – perceived by international investors? This study aims at identifying the determinants of German FDI in the emerging economies of Latin America and Asia throughout the past decade, and, in particular, those relating to "governance" aspects, measured by indices of country or political risk. Governance issues have consistently been, and still remain a major challenge for emerging market economies. Despite having undertaken substantial stabilization or liberalization efforts[20] and pursuing appropriate fiscal and monetary policies, many of these countries are suffering from a wide range

[18] See Nunnenkamp (2001b), p. 4, who presents UNCTAD data.

[19] Definition by Lehmann (1999), p. 22.

[20] Lora (2001) provides cross-country evidence on the extent of trade, tax, labor and financial market reforms as well as privatization in Latin America (see section 2.2.2.5).

of political and regulatory deficiencies which need to be tackled to appease investors. At first glance, emerging market economies feature proper investment regimes when in fact obscure licensing procedures and discretionary administrative regulations characterize the true nature of the country's investment policy. Even willing governments are often unable to convey credible signals to foreign investors.[21]

Most empirical research using German FDI data[22] has been undertaken with respect to industrialized economies. Only a few studies are devoted exclusively to the investment behavior of German enterprises in developing or emerging economies. Hubert and Pain (1999) find in regressions confined to non-EU countries, i.e. mainly developing countries, that only stocks of research & development, unit labor costs in Germany relative to the host country and real exchange rate volatility turn out to be significant with the expected signs. Similarly, only some German FDI studies employ political risk variables. Agarwal et al. (1991), in a very comprehensive study of the traditional and risk-related determinants of German investment abroad, generally find no deterring effect of political risk (composite risk and, separately, strikes and lockouts) on FDI flows to developing countries in the 1980s. Moore (1993) identifies an index of labor unrest in the 17 OECD countries examined. Surprisingly, the number of days lost in strikes is mildly significant and *positively* correlated with FDI flows. Jost and Nunnenkamp (2002) run cross-section and pooled OLS regressions for German FDI in more than 60 developing countries between 1989 and 2000. Apart from the usual results for host country per-capita GDP and population, they find good scores for country risk as measured by the Euromoney index and an openness measure (adjusted for country size) as well as, in separate regressions, low political risk and a skill variable (rate of secondary schooling) to exert a strong positive influence on FDI stocks.[23] Interestingly, the importance of country risk and a skill variable is shown to rise during the last decade.

This chapter is organized as follows. The subsequent section first explains how the FDI flow variable used in this study is derived. It then gives an overview of the literature on determinants of FDI in emerging markets, and, particularly,

---

[21] See Lehmann (1999), p. 21.

[22] For a good overview of German studies on FDI, see Fischer (2000).

[23] It is quite likely, however, that most of the series containing the FDI stocks are non-stationary – a phenomenon that is not appropriately accounted for in the purely static estimation. The authors additionally examine flow data from the German balance of payments (note that the openness measure turns insignificant, p. 63) which is doubtful considering the conceptual shortcomings (see section 2.1.1, second indentation mark).

those factors relating to risk aspects. Section three provides details on the econometric approach and the selection process used for identifying robust variables among a pool of exogenous variables. The regression results are presented in section four, with a distinction being made between the country, sector and sub-sector level. Section five has the concluding remarks.

2 Data

2.1 Definition of the FDI Variable Used

There is no unanimously agreed method of measuring FDI. Different studies proceed in different ways. Therefore, it seems important to make as clear as possible how FDI is defined here and why this particular definition is chosen. In this study, the endogenous variable is the net inflow (or outflow) of direct investment capital of German investors into (or from) emerging market economies during a given calendar year. Depending on how one looks at it, foreign direct investment may be understood purely as a flow variable or as a stock variable. The *IMF Balance of Payments Manual* does not exclusively recur to the cumulative stock of FDI capital but defines direct investment as comprising "not only the initial transaction establishing the relationship between the investor and the enterprise but also all subsequent transactions between them and among affiliated enterprises, both incorporated and unincorporated".[24]

The direct investment capital flows used in the estimations are derived from the direct investment stock statistics compiled by the Deutsche Bundesbank since 1976 as an annual complete survey and published on a partly aggregated basis in Special Statistical Publication No. 10 ("*Kapitalverflechtung mit dem Ausland*" – "International capital links"). These data are now also available in the form of a computer-aided microdatabase for the years 1989 to 2002.[25] During the sample period, German enterprises reported minority interests (of at least 10% but less than 50%) in foreign enterprises if the balance-sheet total of the investment target exceeded DM 10 million (in 1999: €5 million). Controlling interests (50% or more) had to be reported if the investment target's balance-sheet total exceeded DM 1 million (in 1999: €0.5 million). In 2002 the threshold for both

[24] IMF (1997), p. 86. "Direct investment capital transactions include those that create or dissolve investments as well as those that serve to maintain, expand, or reduce investments"; ibid., p. 88.

[25] In the reporting year 1989 methodological changes were made which eliminated the comparability of the stocks with those in the years 1976 to 1988. At the time this chapter was written, only data up to 1999 were available.

categories became €3 million. Indirect participating interests likewise must be reported if a "dependent" (i.e. majority-owned) foreign subsidiary itself holds a stake of at least 10% in another enterprise abroad. It should be stressed, therefore, that foreign direct investment merely represents the provision of financial capital – in this case by German enterprises to their foreign subsidiaries.[26]

The direct investment stocks included in the database are book values and are calculated as the sum of the investor's share in the nominal capital of the investment target, the capital reserves, and the retained profits/profits brought forward (cumulative reinvested earnings). Loans granted by the capital owners or affiliated enterprises are added to this equity capital. To finally obtain the direct investment stock pursuant to the IMF's "directional principle", the subsidiary's lending to or claims on the parent company must be subtracted.[27] It should be noted that the stock data quoted in foreign currency by the enterprise subject to reporting requirements have to be converted into German currency at the current exchange rate on the individual balance-sheet date (as mandated by the OECD Benchmark Definition).[28]

[26] Thus, the term "direct investment" has to be clearly distinguished from the neo-classical concept of investment which is based on the change in value of capital goods (i.e. property, plant & equipment) on the assets side of the balance sheet; see also Lehmann (1999), p. 10, Jost (1999), p. 141, Hausmann and Fernández-Arias (2001), p. 33, or Razin (2002), p. 2.

[27] See Lipponer (2003), p. 219. The "directional principle" requires the direct investments to be separated according to the direction of the capital flow. Loans from subsidiaries to the investor therefore have to be deducted from the direct investment capital; see IMF (1997), p. 81. This practice contrasts with the "asset liability principle", which presents such assets as autonomous – counterbalancing – direct investments.

[28] There is also the question of whether or not the stock data and thus also the FDI stock differences (which, after suitable correction, are interpreted as flow data), should be adjusted for inflation in the host country – as is done by Moore (1993), who deflates the stock differences using foreign price indexes for capital goods – or for exchange rate effects as recommended by Wagner (1991), who eschews Bundesbank stock data for these implicit effects. Accordingly, previous-year FDI stocks or, more correctly, the stocks of fixed assets and other long-term assets, would have to be adjusted for both inflation and the change in the bilateral exchange rate in the reporting year. Alternatively, one might rightfully assume that relative purchasing power parity holds and the inflation differential between Germany and the host country in question is absorbed by the exchange rate, having both distorting factors cancel each other out. To be sure, most empirical studies do not test nominal values but either deflate the FDI variable or relate it either to GDP or some other scaling factor (see section 2.1.3).

2.1.1 Stocks Versus Flows

The use of stock data for estimating a flow variable is an imperfect approach due to several distorting factors. Here is why this is and how the distortions are minimized:

- In the Bundesbank's stocks statistics the acquisition of assets is recorded in the form of balance-sheet book values. Nevertheless, in the case of takeovers, an additional amount (goodwill) is frequently paid on top of the pure book value of the assets. These additional sums were particularly significant in recent years in cases of technology company takeovers. Therefore, evaluating the transaction data, which are recorded at market values in the balance of payments, would be preferable – yet this raises other problems (see below). However, as advanced developing countries rather than industrialized countries are at the heart of this study, it may be assumed that, owing to the relatively uncertain profit expectations and a political environment which is often difficult to gauge, the difference between market and book values may not be substantial. In the case of newly established subsidiaries (i.e. greenfield investment) these problems do not arise anyway.

- While transaction-based balance of payments data in this respect seem superior for studying FDI flows, they have other serious shortcomings. For one, the FDI flows in the German balance of payments statistics do not list the individual recipient abroad which is a precondition for the sectoral analysis in section 4.2 of this chapter. Worse still, only immediate direct investment relationships (as to equity capital) are recorded under participating interests in the German balance of payments statistics, but not indirect ones, i.e. those held via a holding company, which likewise compulsorily fall under the FDI definition. Reinvested earnings stemming from indirect capital links are not included, either. On balance, and leaving accounting issues aside, merely considering balance of payments data means failing to use a fully consolidated system encompassing indirect ownership and, therefore, in all likelihood greatly understating actual FDI capital.[29] Therefore, in measuring the investment activity of German multinationals, the only "relevant" flow variable should be derived from (adequately modified) differences in stocks and not by using flows recorded in the balance of payments. Accordingly, this study uses a modified FDI "flow" variable, i.e. the difference in FDI stock from one year to another, adjusted for actual participation rates, deviating

[29] See OECD (1996), p. 11.

reporting years, balance-sheet depreciation and repatriated profits.[30] This variable nevertheless corresponds – apart from the distortions mentioned above – to the basic definition of direct investment capital transactions contained in the IMF's Balance of Payments Manual.[31]

- The balance-sheet values are shown in the stock statistics at the respective reporting date of the direct investment enterprise concerned, which sometimes differs from the end of the calendar year. For practical reasons, the unadjusted figures are not divided between the two calendar years included in the reporting year of such enterprises.[32] Instead, all balance-sheet values of enterprises whose reporting dates are *prior to* June 30 – i.e. whose reporting year therefore mostly does not coincide with the current reporting year of the stock statistics – are included in the preceding calendar year.

2.1.2 Adjustment for Participation Rates, Balance-Sheet Depreciation and Repatriated Profits

The FDI microdatabase contains participation rates for indirectly owned interests (usually held via a holding company) which need to be adjusted for the share of FDI capital that German investors effectively hold. That is, the "real" participation rate is calculated as the product of the vertical ownership shares. Doing so is necessary to account for multiple ownership in holding companies. For example, if a holding company has a 50% stake in a direct investment company and is itself equally owned by two German investors, the adjusted participation will be 25% for each parent.

As the assets are recorded as book values and are depreciated by a certain rate mandated by foreign tax regulations, the left-hand side of the balance sheet does not correspond to the actually existing (historical) capital stock. This pure

[30] For a good methodological overview see Bellak (1999), p. 120-122.

[31] "The components of direct investment capital transactions ... are equity capital, reinvested earnings, and other capital associated with various intercompany debt transactions"; IMF (1993), p. 87. Hausmann and Fernández-Arias (2001) explicitly adhere to the flow concept: "FDI is defined as the increase in the equity position of a non-resident owner..." (p. 33).

[32] This applies to 2,923 of 32,240 reports (9.1%) for the 14 emerging markets considered here. Theoretically, it would be possible in these cases to include the balance-sheet values in the previous year linearly with the period not coinciding with the year under review (for example, if May 31, 1999, were the reporting date, seven-twelfths of the balance-sheet values originally included in 1999 would be assigned to the 1998 reporting/calendar year, with the value for 1999 being adjusted accordingly). For technical reasons – this breakdown would require a "matching" of the reporting numbers of the investor and the investment target over all of the sample years at the microdata level, which is not feasible – this is not an option.

taxation effect needs to be removed. Accordingly, by using a perpetual inventory model,[33] FDI stocks are adjusted for the original tax depreciation undertaken when calculating the profit of the subsidiary; the aim of this adjustment is to determine which fixed assets are available for production each year. To this end, the net capital stock (fixed assets) of the investment target is marked up for each year using a notional depreciation rate of 8%,[34] which is multiplied by the share of FDI capital in total assets. The resulting gross capital stock of the following period is adjusted for increases or decreases in productive capital. By contrast, write-downs of financial assets, especially those of service providers, are not adjusted because the depreciation rate is uncertain. The inflow of direct investment capital in a given period therefore is the difference of the stocks[35] between the current year's stocks and preceding years' stocks plus the imputed depreciation of the adjusted capital stock.[36]

The resulting flow variable still includes the total annual surplus rather than merely the profits remaining in the investment target after transferring the parent company's share of the profit – i.e. reinvested profits. Accordingly, the profits of the previous year repatriated in the current year would need to be deducted from this flow variable.[37] As this information cannot be extracted directly from the FDI stock statistics, a suitable approximation is called for: In the case of *direct* participating interests, the item "income from dividends and other profits" relating to German outward FDI (as recorded in the German balance of

[33] This adjustment is recommended by Bellak (1999), p. 125.

[34] The rate of 8% is used by Chennells and Griffith (1997), p. 92, and is calculated as the average of economic depreciation rates for "industrial buildings" (3.6%) and for "industrial plant and machinery" (12.3%).

[35] In this connection it should be noted that, in the case of direct participating interests, those in dependent holding companies which themselves hold at least a 10% stake in another company have to be excluded from the stock of direct investment capital in order to avoid double counting – these own participating interests are recorded separately as indirect FDI. This approach is not applied to dependent holdings without participating interests required to be reported or to minority-owned holdings with their own participating interests; see Lipponer (2003), p. 218, and Jost (1999), p. 144.

[36] To give an example, the inflow (exclusive of repatriated profits) for the year 1991 is calculated as follows:

$$\text{FDI Flow}_{1991} = \Delta \text{FDI}_{1991} + (\Delta \text{FA}_{1991} + (\Delta \text{FA}_{1990} + \text{FA}_{1989} \cdot (1+\delta)) \cdot (1+\delta)) \cdot \delta,$$

where

ΔFDI = difference between the "original" direct investment stocks in the reporting year and the previous year,

FA = fixed assets * percentage share of assets (i.e. investor's share of capital),

δ = notional depreciation rate (8%).

[37] As was done, for instance, by Singh and Jun (1995), p. 11.

payments statistics[38]) is used. Unfortunately, for *indirect* participating interests no such information is available.[39] For simplicity, a full profit transfer from the investment target to the holding company (by virtue of a corresponding agreement) is assumed.[40] Accordingly, total profits are subtracted from the indirect FDI capital in each year, yielding reinvested earnings as the difference between the following year's retained profits/profits brought forward and those of the current year. This difference is already reflected in the variation of FDI stocks across years.[41] A comparison of the flows derived from "raw" and adjusted differences in FDI stocks illustrates that while these deviations may not dramatically alter the econometric outcome, they can cause individual variables to gain or lose significance.[42]

2.1.3 Absolute and Normalized FDI Flows

The study uses a principal endogenous variable, *FDIGDP*, defined as outflows of German foreign direct investment to a given host country as a percentage of its GDP (both in nominal values). The countries comprise the largest emerging market economies[43] in Latin America (Argentina, Brazil, Chile, Colombia, Mexico and Venezuela) as well as South and Southeast Asia (People's Republic of China, India, Indonesia, Republic of Korea, Malaysia, the Philippines, Singapore and Thailand). Given that larger economies have consistently been shown to receive larger FDI inflows (see section 2.2.1.1), the above

[38] Deutsche Bundesbank, Statistical Supplement No. 3, Table 5b "Factor income – income from direct investment", column 2.

[39] See Jost (1999), p. 133.

[40] This adjustment was carried out for 993 out of 2941 positions (or 33.7%) at the sector-aggregated level.

[41] In principle, retained profits/profits brought forward would have to be subtracted in the case of newly acquired direct investment companies. However, it is only for 1997-1999 that such positions can be identified in the microdata by checking whether an investment target surfaces in the database the following year. This is no longer possible for the years 1989-1996 as data prior to 1996 have already been rendered anonymous. Therefore, in order to avoid additional bias due to incomplete adjustments, these equity positions are left unchanged.

[42] Referring to regressions in section four, at the country level (Latin American sub-sample) the trade taxation variable drops from a 1% level of significance (unadjusted flows) to the 5% level (adjusted flows) while the reverse is true for the agglomeration variable. Similarly, at the sector level (Asian sub-sample), country risk and exchange rate volatility now lose their respective weak significance (otherwise significant at the 10% level if unadjusted), and trade barriers suddenly matter somewhat.

[43] Selection criterion: $\frac{1}{2} \cdot (\text{real GDP}_{i,1990} + \text{real GDP}_{i,1999})$, at constant 1995 US dollars (World Development Indicators). The cut-off point was arbitrarily set at an average GDP of US$ 60 billion (next in line were Pakistan ($58.4 billion) and Peru ($50.0 billion)). Taiwan and Hong Kong were excluded owing to data insufficiencies.

normalization is performed to eliminate size effects and thus to determine the linkage between FDI flows and the variations in external factors over and above absolute market size as implied by GDP. Correspondingly, estimations are centered on deviations from an implied average value of FDI flows and size of host countries. In addition, a related alternative variable, *FDIFLOW*, is defined in absolute values, adjusted for inflation differentials and nominal exchange rate changes, i.e. the FDI inflows are measured in constant 1990 US dollars.[44] In anticipation of quantitative results in section four, note that in the tentative regression for *FDIFLOW* (see Table 12, Appendix II) size effects contained in the exogenous variables clearly govern the econometric outcome: for Latin America, only absolute real GDP, in addition to country risk, tested significant. The Asian sample also exhibits fewer significant variables than if the other and arguably more meaningful variable *FDIGDP* is used. Also, both regressions using *FDIFLOW* exhibit a comparatively low R-Squared. Therefore, *FDIFLOW* is not used henceforth.

Apart from log-linearizing FDI stocks, the use of normalized FDI variables (FDI inflows as share of GDP) is relatively widespread in the literature on foreign direct investment. Froot and Stein (1991), Singh and Jun (1995), Barrell and Pain (1999), Hausmann and Fernández-Arias (2001), Nookbakhsh et al. (2001), Mody and Murshid (2002) and Razin (2002) use the FDI-to-GDP ratio proposed in this study. Similarly, Pistoresi (2000), Chakrabarti (2001) and Nunnenkamp (2001b) link their FDI variable to host country population, i.e. per-capita FDI, while Lehmann (1999) computes country shares in total U.S. capital expenditures as an investment variable. Wheeler and Mody (1992) relate FDI in a given sample country to investment in an arbitrarily chosen numeraire country. Desai et al. (2003), while incorporating absolute GDP in their regressions, do not even bother to report the estimates for the market size variable due to the intuition that larger economies tend to receive greater volumes of FDI.

2.1.4 Descriptive Statistics

As Figure 1 shows, developments in the build-up of German FDI positions differed markedly between the two regions. Emerging from a small base, Asia experienced a pronounced, yet stable inflow of direct investment in the 1990s that eventually almost closed the huge initial gap to Latin America, which, partly due to the 1995 Mexican crisis, displays more volatile FDI flows. This fact corresponds to the fluctuations of global FDI flows to both regions.[45] The

[44] According to the adjustment method proposed by Pain (2003), p. 112.

[45] See Fernández-Arias and Hausmann (2001), p. 96.

fast recovery from the Asian crisis, at least as far as FDI inflows are concerned, has to be credited to hurried liberalization efforts on the part of crisis countries in the region. For example, South Korea, formerly hesitant to allow foreign investors to exert a controlling influence, swiftly opened the economy to FDI after the crisis had hit. Other countries set in motion a wide range of structural reforms.[46]

Figure 1: German FDI Stocks and Flows

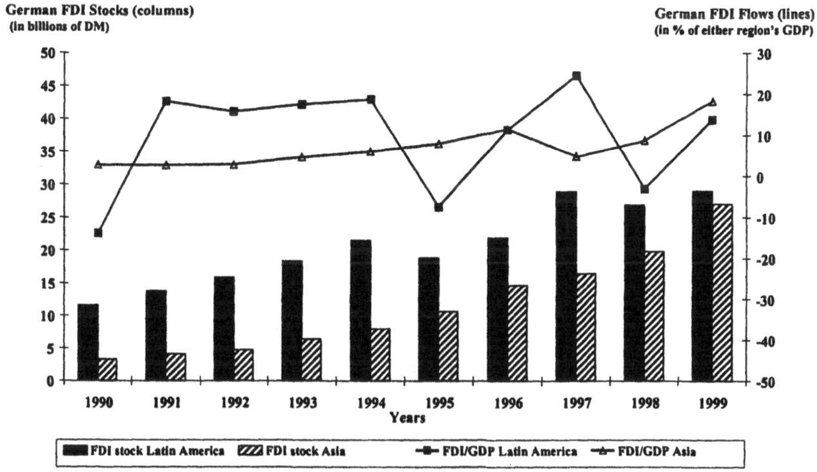

More importantly, though, reform *expectations* might have been the driving force behind rebounding FDI flows: Thompson and Poon (2000), surveying multinational companies operating in the ASEAN countries, show that investors anticipated that reforms would bring about operational benefits at the firm level, likely making the region a more attractive location for sales and production over the longer term. The long-term orientation of foreign investors taking controlling stakes in host country firms is the unique quality of FDI, according to Mallampally and Sauvant (1999), who observe that overall FDI flows to the five most affected Asian countries declined only slightly in 1997, contrasting sharply with negative flows for bank lending and portfolio investment. Mody and Murshid (2002) furnish evidence of the resiliency of FDI flows going to those emerging markets temporarily in distress. For flows to 60 developing countries between 1981 and 1998, they report a significantly positive coefficient

[46] For example, Singapore: strengthening of competitiveness, Malaysia: reform of banking system, Thailand and Indonesia: institutional and regulatory reforms; see Thompson and Poon (2000), pp. 2-3. Since 1999, worldwide (and German) FDI flows to Asia have leveled off, while those to Latin America have declined strongly.

for a crisis dummy that captures the interaction between lagged crises and FDI inflows which points to the persistence of FDI inflows in the aftermath of a crisis relative to other flows.[47]

Within the regions, Latin America displays a relatively stable distribution of German FDI stocks throughout the 1990s, with Brazil's startling dominance reaching its maximum of two-thirds of total German FDI in the mid-1990s and receding thereafter (Figure 2).

Figure 2: Distribution of German FDI Stocks Across Latin America (in % of sample country total)

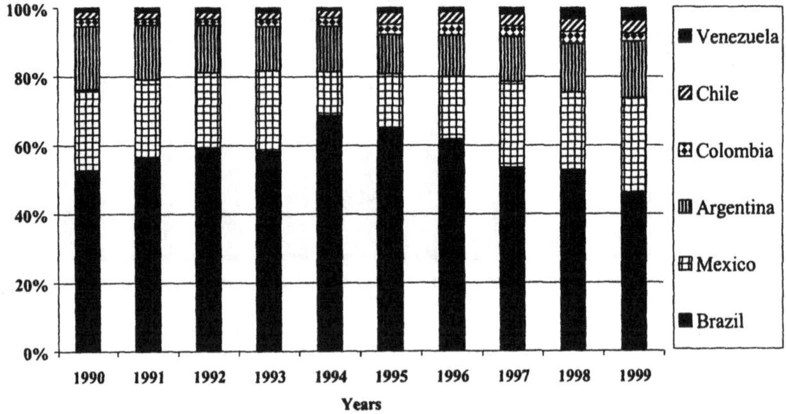

In the Asian emerging markets, Singapore's traditional supremacy gradually gave way to China's FDI boom in the latter part of the decade (Figure 3). In both regions, the distribution of FDI stocks is generally quite uneven across countries. This is especially true for Latin America where Brazil, Mexico and Argentina comprise roughly 90% of German FDI stocks.

[47] See also Nunnenkamp (2001a), pp. 19-21, who reports much higher volatilities of portfolio and other investment (mostly bank loans) relative to FDI flows to 13 Latin American and Asian nations in the 1980s and 1990s.

Figure 3: Distribution of German FDI Stocks Across Asia
(in % of sample country total)

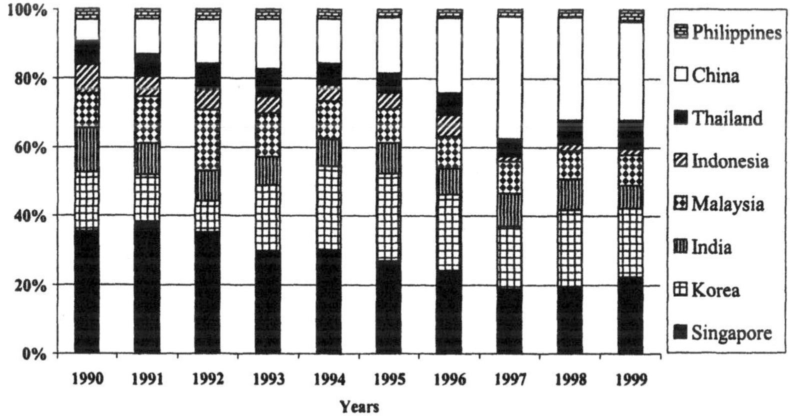

2.2 Exogenous Variables Considered for FDI at the Country Level

In the vast FDI literature a great many explanatory variables are employed to explain cross-border capital flows. Over time, however, a distinctive set of factors frequently used in econometric modeling has emerged. Lim (2001), surveying the FDI literature, comes up with a list of seven important factors: size of the host market, agglomeration effects, factor costs, fiscal incentives, business/investment climate, trade barriers/openness, and economic distance/transport costs. The last factor can be neglected in this study as the host countries included are all located overseas and thus more or less equally far away from the country of FDI origin, Germany. Theory and empirical evidence on the determinants cited above are reviewed in the following section (for details on the variables used see Table 13, Appendix II).

2.2.1 Traditional Variables

2.2.1.1 Market Size and Level of Income

Among the traditional variables, GDP or GDP per capita is widely used in the literature as a proxy for market size or purchasing power. Lim (2001) finds market size in terms of the size of the whole economy (absolute real GDP) or the level of income (GDP per capita) to be the most robust determinant, although both factors depict quite different market characteristics. In virtually all the studies surveyed, either indicator of market size is highly positively significant. This finding is validated by Chakrabarti (2001) for 18 studies in the past 30 years.

Since the endogenous variable is already scaled to GDP and as absolute real GDP, by virtue of favoring large populations, is a rather poor indicator of market potential, the study includes GDP per capita, *GDPCAP*, following Chakrabarti (2001) who finds this variable strongly positively related to scaled (per-capita) FDI in an *Extreme Bounds Analysis* (see section 3.2) for 135 countries in 1994.

2.2.1.2 Wage Competitiveness

Cost competitiveness – especially relevant for efficiency-seeking FDI – is probably best expressed by productivity-adjusted real wages, assuming that labor is largely immobile internationally and labor costs therefore differ across countries, while other cost drivers such as capital and intermediate goods are traded on international markets with price-equalizing effects.[48] Moreover, measuring capital productivity is more difficult than deriving unit labor costs, due to the widespread unavailability of capital stocks at market values and capital goods price indices as suitable deflators.[49]

Among empirical studies, Barrell and Pain (1996) find a much smaller long-run elasticity for relative capital costs than for relative labor costs. Using unit labor cost indices, the authors also detect a positive relationship between U.S. unit labor costs relative to those abroad and the level of outward FDI, i.e. a negative impact of rising relative labor costs seen from the angle of the host countries. Hubert and Pain (1999) argue that unit labor costs already include – apart from deviations from average productivity levels – differences in labor quality. For this reason, Lehmann (1999) negates the necessity of including an educational attainment or "skill" variable when testing unit labor costs in his regressions. Mody et al. (1999) find for Japanese FDI in Asia that it is mainly driven by high-quality labor and not merely by cheap labor abroad, the coefficients of which are, in fact, insignificant. Measuring labor quality by secondary schooling rates may, as they argue, be misleading, as quality is more related to industrial experience – i.e. on-the-job performance – rather than formal educational

[48] See Turner and Golub (1997), p. 7.

[49] See Lipsey (2002), p. 36. Barrell and Pain (1996) were forced to leave out the Latin American region due to lack of reliable time series data on indigenous costs (p. 203).

attainments.[50] Also, it is difficult to estimate the time lag with which improvements in school enrollment are manifested in a more productive workforce. Testing for effects of secondary school enrollment on FDI inflows to 36 developing countries, Noorbakhsh et al. (2001) report strong significance for this skill variable – but only if productivity-adjusted wages are excluded from the regression. While educational attainment does seem to matter, this particular finding leads to the conclusion that a skill variable may not add a great deal of new information in the presence of labor productivity measures. By contrast, Wheeler and Mody (1992) and Wei (2000) find a positive relationship between wages (not productivity-adjusted) and FDI inflows to developing countries.

In the analysis in this chapter, the wage variable is *unit labor costs, ULC,* which is defined as the *labor costs per worker in manufacturing divided by the gross value added per worker in manufacturing.*[51] Ideally, weighted labor costs for all sectors of the economy should be used, but it is only for the manufacturing sector that data are available across all countries in the sample. Still, such a generalization is not uncommon in FDI research.[52] Barrell and Pain (1999) also use manufacturing unit labor costs for their *country-level* estimations, and later in their paper run a separate regression for Japanese FDI flows to *manufacturing* sectors abroad.

2.2.1.3 Trade Barriers/Openness of the Economy

Traditionally, direct investment was used by foreign firms to circumvent trade barriers ("tariff-hopping") and, thus, to establish market presence by physically erecting production facilities or buying existing ones abroad. It has been argued that host country governments will be more likely to establish trade barriers if a particular domestic industry facing import penetration is still at an infant stage

[50] Survey results reported by the authors allegedly indicate that, despite lower secondary enrollment rates, labor quality in Thailand is higher than in the Philippines.

[51] This measure conforms to the definition recommended by the German Federal Statistical Office (Statistisches Bundesamt). Yet, there are also other definitions. For example, Turner and Van 't dack (1993, pp. 87, 136-137) compute unit labor costs on the basis of total earnings of labor in manufacturing expressed in US dollars divided by value added in manufacturing at current prices expressed in constant purchasing power parity (PPP) rates. This ratio allows for relating labor costs to output per unit of time, with the resulting unit labor costs being expressed in terms of a common currency. The merit of this approach is that currency fluctuations influencing the value added are excluded. However, computing unit labor costs on this basis would require data on pure host country output (i.e. units produced per year) which is generally not available for less developed countries; see Turner and Van 't dack (1993), p. 91.

[52] Unit labor costs are not widely available for services despite that sector's growing importance in emerging markets; see Turner and Golub (1997), p. 7.

or if the product life cycle is already beyond the hump.[53] On the other hand, incipient trade restrictions may prompt anticipatory or "quid pro quo" direct investment. In that sense, the possibility of FDI, or "threat of FDI", may limit the level of trade protection that the government can impose.[54] In the past, import protection instituted by host governments promised such high rates of return to foreign investors that the efficiency of the subsidiaries was not viewed as a major concern. However, as the majority of emerging economies have chosen to ease restrictions on imports, so-called "market-seeking" or "horizontal" direct investment is likely to have fallen over time[55] (greater openness coinciding with lower FDI inflows), giving way to "efficiency-seeking" or "vertical" direct investment that requires a liberal trade environment. This newer form of direct investment aims at exploiting sources of competitiveness such as lower (unit) labor costs, a skilled workforce or a more conducive business environment.[56] A high degree of openness is required for stimulating vertical FDI which relies on substantial flows of intermediate inputs and goods in and out of the host country. In sum, the overall impact of trade barriers is uncertain and depends on the nature of FDI (horizontal versus vertical) undertaken in each case.

While the case for trade barriers fostering FDI inflows appears quite convincing, the relationship between traditional openness measures and FDI is less clear. The "natural" openness or outward orientation of an economy can be thought of as the trade intensity absent any interventionist policy measures. The ordinary openness proxy, trade intensity in terms of either share of imports or exports (or both) in GDP, constitutes a trade flow outcome measure and is confirmed as being influential for FDI inflows to developing countries by, for example, Noorbakhsh et al. (2001) and Hausmann and Fernández-Arias (2001). However, Pritchett (1997), Lehmann (1999), and Jost and Nunnenkamp (2002) propose that this type of openness measure be adjusted for structural, non-policy determinants of trade intensity such as geographic size, per-capita income or

[53] See Stehn (1992), p. 73.

[54] See Konishi et al. (1999), pp. 290-291.

[55] As Nunnenkamp (2001b) notes, FDI was formerly preferred to trade by resource-abundant countries for accessing large amounts of capital necessary for resource extraction and foreign technical skills unavailable at home. With the advent of trade liberalization and more integrated financial markets, "resource-seeking" FDI may have decreased in importance relative to joint ventures or arm's-length trade deals that make use of growing domestic expertise (p. 11).

[56] See Nunnenkamp (2001b), pp. 12-13, and also Mallampally and Sauvant (1999) who, in addition, list a third category: "resource/asset-seeking" FDI trying to capture host country advantages in raw materials, skilled labor, innovative assets or physical infrastructure.

resource endowment.[57] Doing so, Lehmann as well as Jost and Nunnenkamp (2002) find a significantly positive impact of trade openness in panel estimations for developing countries, whereas Wheeler and Mody (1992) report a negative correlation of their openness measure (index by *Business International*) with relative FDI inflows to manufacturing sectors. At any rate, the overall flow of trade relative to domestic activity does not reveal the degree of trade distortion caused by other factors.[58]

Furthermore, non-tariff barriers, existing in the form of quantitative restrictions, subsidies to domestic producers, standards and regulations on import good characteristics, government purchasing policies and arbitrary customs procedures (commonly known as "red tape") act in a trade-distorting manner. Evidently, many of the aforementioned incidents are difficult to measure quantitatively;[59] in particular, a cross-country comparison would appear "forbidding".[60] While price-impact measures (tariff equivalents, subsidy measures, effective rates of protection) undertaken by international organizations such as the OECD might provide an answer, there are numerous data and information problems in isolating the immediate impact of non-tariff restrictions, largely relating to the influence that market imperfections and exchange rate fluctuations exert on the price differentials surveyed.[61] Even if it were possible to comprehensively quantify non-tariff barriers to trade, the severity of the distortions would not be determined as those restrictions are generally not transparent in their operation.[62]

Pritchett (1997) cautions that none of those openness measures can compare trade policies both across countries and over time because each of them was constructed to compare countries during a different time period. This implies that they cannot plausibly be used in a panel setting. Therefore, this study uses the *share of taxes on international trade in current government revenue, DUTY*,

[57] The aforementioned authors suggest the use of residuals from a trade intensity regression which employs structural country characteristics indicating the amount by which a country's openness differs from that expected for a country of its size; see, for example, Pritchett (1997), p. 312.

[58] See Pritchett (1997), p. 327.

[59] Barrell and Pain (1996) rightfully note in this context that "such barriers are notoriously difficult to measure, especially as the most effective barriers are those that are anticipated but not yet (if ever) implemented" (p. 202).

[60] See Pritchett (1997), p. 311.

[61] See Baldwin (1989), pp. 9-12.

[62] See Pritchett (1997), p. 309.

as a measure of the burden on trade activity,[63] whereby a positive coefficient can be expected for horizontal FDI. This very definition is used by Singh and Jun (1995), who report it as significantly positively correlated to relative FDI inflows for a set of 31 developing countries. A similar measure, namely the average level of tariffs (UNCTAD data), is tested by Pritchett (1997) in regressions for 72 developing countries. It is the only variable to be significantly correlated to both the openness measure by Leamer (1988)[64] and an indicator of non-tariff barriers.[65] In addition, this investigation checks the validity of a *conditioned openness variable*, *OPEN*, i.e. modified trade intensity measured by the residuals of regressing the logs of GDP per capita and population on a given host country's trade intensity (imports and exports as share of GDP). The coefficient should be positive for vertical FDI.

2.2.1.4 External Indebtedness

Despite being an important indicator of a country's solvency often foreshadowing an imminent financial crisis, measures of foreign indebtedness are used in FDI research less often than for analyzing other capital flows. At the theoretical level, Ghura and Goodwin (2000) argue that a rising external debt ratio, indicating a debt overhang, induces economic agents to anticipate future tax liabilities to service the debt. If the integration of capital markets is rather low, the ensuing capital flight would then raise the domestic cost of capital. Apart from conceivable political reverberations, this effect is likely to negatively impact the overall profitability of foreign subsidiaries. Arguments from corporate finance theory[66] may be transposed to the macro level in the sense that a relatively high degree of risky debt may weaken a country's ability to realize growth possibilities via new investment. A valuable real option may be forgone if the additional investment and payments to bondholders (in case the option is exercised) exceed the value of the investment. On the other hand, if the debt level of the host country is still below a certain level perceived critical by

[63] This, of course, can only be regarded as a proxy, because in a situation of extremely high tax rates international trade may be obstructed, rendering the share of taxes in GDP inadvertently low.

[64] Leamer (1988) constructs both an openness and a trade distortion index that measure deviations from trade flows predicted by a modified Heckscher-Ohlin-Vanek model, using data from 1982.

[65] See Pritchett (1997), pp. 318, 320, 324-325. The author uses as indicator of non-tariff barriers the import-weighted percent of tariff codes lines covered by various types of non-tariff barriers (licenses, quotas, prohibitions) as a percentage of all tariff code lines within the aggregate (p. 314).

[66] See, for example, Myers (1977), and there in particular pp. 155, 164-165.

investors, this consideration may not apply and FDI flows may actually increase with rising external indebtedness.

The aforementioned profitability argument is also put forward by Agarwal et al. (1991) who in addition advance the notion that unbearable indebtedness may lead to an arbitrary default on sovereign debt and, subsequently, to expropriations and restrictions on the capital account. The authors test their hypotheses empirically by including in their estimations for German FDI to developing countries in the 1980s a variable that proxies debt overhang. For lack of data on market valuation of emerging market debt, they, methodically questionably, employ the change in undifferentiated country risk[67] throughout the decade and find that, unlike foreign investors as a whole, German firms did not restrict their exposure when country ratings plummeted. Among the few empirical studies to consider the level of external debt, Pistoresi (2000) reports a significantly negative coefficient for emerging markets' foreign debt per capita which is especially relevant for the Latin American sub-sample.

As the measure of external indebtedness carries only a minor weight in the composite PRS country risk rating (5%), a separate variable, *DEBT*, measuring the ratio of host country external debt to GDP, was added to the regressions in recognition of the postulated impact of rising indebtedness on FDI outcomes.

A further issue in the area of public finances relates to taxation. The case for measuring the negative influence of high corporate tax rates abroad appears clear: by depressing after-tax investment returns, high tax rates discourage FDI inflows. The problem with using statutory tax rates or the share of corporate tax receipts in GDP is that the former is generally biased upward because of numerous tax exemptions (apart from not being a good variable in a panel setting because of little variation from year to year) while the latter effectively measures government collection of taxes in a given year that may differ from the year in which German companies actually pay their taxes. Moreover, in the taxation literature effective marginal tax rates incorporating data on statutory corporate tax rates, inflation rates, depreciation allowances for assets and discount rates for financing are increasingly utilized. The obstacle to an empirical investigation of the distorting effects of fiscal policy on FDI is that these marginal tax rates are readily available only for industrialized or at best OECD countries as the computation of marginal tax rates for developing

[67] The risk index used is by *Institutional Investor*. To differentiate the supposed debt overhang variable from the one used for measuring country risk, in that estimation only sample countries with initially favorable index ratings were included; see Agarwal et al. (1991), p. 81.

economies for cross-section applications is seriously hampered by data scarcity.[68] Hence, a taxation variable is omitted in this study.

2.2.2 Non-Traditional Variables

This section gives an overview of the literature on non-traditional factors, with emphasis on the research previously undertaken in the area of governance.

2.2.2.1 Country Risk/Political Risk

Most studies reviewed here control for specific measures of host country political risk. Only some refer to a broader definition of country risk, as is the case in the aforementioned study by Jost and Nunnenkamp (2002). For example, Mody and Srinivasan (1998) find a strong correlation between country safeness (measured by the *Institutional Investor* index) and host country share of U.S. FDI outflows by means of the within estimator. The authors argue that "while country risk measures do not affect the long-run choice of countries, they do affect the *timing* of the investment" (p. 787).

The issue of political risk has attracted more interest among researchers. In a pioneering paper, Schneider and Frey (1985) furnish evidence that in emerging markets political and socioeconomic factors are relevant on top of the "classical" macro factors. As the authors show, estimation results for FDI inflows into industrial as well as developing countries are significantly improved if also controlling for governance variables such as political instability and the ideological thrust of government. Similarly, Beyer (2002) in a study of transition countries shows that the fit of his regressions improves when combining both economic and political variables relating to the base year of transition. The author finds political factors depicted by the *Freedom House Economic Freedom Index* or the efficacy of privatization bureaus to have great explanatory power. Stevens (2000), investigating plant and equipment spending of U.S. corporations in Mexico, Brazil and Argentina, shows that the inclusion of political factors detrimental to the operations and earnings of U.S. investors, such as an occasional hostile attitude of government towards FDI, intentional devaluations in a fixed-exchange-rate system and the existence of exchange controls or repatriation restrictions, improves the regression's goodness-of-fit for Argentina greatly (R-squared rises from 0.19 to 0.90).[69]

---

[68] See Easterly and Rebelo (1993), p. 6, and Mendoza et al. (1994), p. 2.

[69] The regression for Brazil shows a lesser improvement; for Mexico the adjustment is only marginally positive.

"Headline" political risk, or rather the absence thereof, is found to be a driving factor of developing country FDI inflows by Singh and Jun (1995), who subject a composite variable merging six internal causes of political risk to econometric testing. Brunetti and Weder (1997) examine the most prominent uncertainty measures in investment regressions using the same specifications while holding constant the sample of 60 countries as well as the time period (1974-1989). They find a number of categories (with individual variables) – government instability (revolutions), political violence (political executions/war casualties), political uncertainty (black market premium on foreign exchange, variation of real exchange rate distortion) – that are consistently significant at least at the 5 percent level and thus robust to changes in specification. However, indicators of enforcement uncertainty – rule of law, corruption – lose their very strong significance (decrease from the 1 to the 10 percent level) when a variable measuring openness to trade is added to the regression. From the results the authors draw the (frankly unrealistic) conclusion that Nigeria would have been able to increase the investment rate by five percentage points had it been able to reduce the level of corruption to that of Hong Kong. Comparable insights are related by Pfeffermann et al. (1999) who evaluate survey data covering nearly 4,000 enterprises in 74 countries and isolate a number of influential factors for FDI inflows: the unpredictability of the judiciary, availability of financing, labor and tax regulations, crime and theft, and corruption.

Within the set of political risk measures, one can distinguish between corruption alias administrative deficiencies and governmental instability in the host country. The question of how devastating corruption can be is investigated by Wei (2000) who evaluates OECD data on industrial countries' FDI flows to 45 economies. Higher taxation and higher corruption are shown to reduce inward FDI by 4.8% and 26%, respectively (using the *Business International* risk index). The author asserts that corruption and political stability are negatively correlated, arguing that corruption may breed public discontent which may eventually topple the government or alternatively induce short time horizons among officials. In a study of both industrial and developing countries, Mauro (1995) finds that a one-standard-deviation increase in the corruption index used (Business International), meaning less corruption, leads to an improvement in the investment rate of 2.9% of GDP. He reports an increase of 4.75% for an identical marginal gain in the bureaucratic efficiency index. Both indices are found to be highly robust against the inclusion of other explanatory variables. Box 1 provides more information on the manifold causes and effects of corruption.

Box 1: Causes of Corruption and Relevance for FDI

Far from being a new concept, the issue of corruption has attracted a great deal of attention among researchers, policy-makers and the media in recent years. Corruption is defined by the World Bank as "the abuse of power for private benefit". While the definition seems to connote simplicity, corruption is a complex phenomenon that can almost never be explained by a single cause. Also, it is notoriously difficult to detect because acts that represent corruption tend not to take place in broad daylight.

Ever since the end of the Cold War, developing countries have been impelled to pursue more transparent and accountable policies in the race for private foreign capital. While, previously, official bilateral donors had virtually ignored governance issues, developing countries all of a sudden found themselves exposed to strict market discipline: sound macroeconomic and regulatory policies were joined by greater institutional transparency and the protection of investors' rights as vital prerequisites for prompting FDI inflows. Propelled by the IMF and the World Bank, the privatization process, while in itself routinely messy, often put an end to the practice of a few privileged bureaucrats selfishly exploiting public institutions. Meanwhile, both investing and receiving countries have become more aware of the fiscal and social costs of corruption, and the construction of indicators and indices of corruption has enabled countries with governance problems to be pinpointed. Also, democratic practices (unencumbered elections, free and active media) are more widespread in many regions. Yet at the same time, the incidence of corruption peaked in the mid-1990s, fueled by high taxes, large increases in public spending and a growing maze of regulations and controls on economic activity. These circumstances also highlight the relationship between big government and low-level corrupt practices. Corruption becomes endemic when it ceases to shock the public and then becomes widely tolerated. To a large extent it is the government that, by pursuing ill-conceived, non-transparent policies coupled with ineffective controls, creates the opportunities and incentives for corruption. *Opportunities* exist because of discretionary areas of government policy (complex tax customs systems, various regulations on the private sector, discretion over allocation of public expenditure), whereas *incentives* facing the bureaucrats include meritocratic recruitment and promotion practices as well as a general lack of transparency in government operations. Of course, if there is a receiving party, there also must be one that is paying. Intense competition between multinationals seeking to tap new markets has led managers to pay large bribes to host country officials in order to close contracts.

Research on corruption, originally primarily concerned with analyzing weaknesses in public institutions and distortions in economic policies which have given rise to rent-seeking by public officials, has increasingly turned to economic aspects such as public spending and wage policy. A large body of research has analyzed why high-corruption countries have bloated public sectors where low wages are paid. In an established environment of high bribes and costly detection, it may be cost-efficient for the government to pay wages below reservation wages to attract mostly dishonest employees instead of raising wages to high levels that would deter sleaze. Effectively, wage levels are traded against the number of civil servants on the payroll. By not enforcing rules or even encouraging corruption, such a government may offer "implicit contracts" to its cronies that make up for low wages. If monitoring costs or corruption-eliminating wage levels are very high, this informal extra income can be far more lucrative than the official pay. This informal arrangement will also help the government stay in office because of the many complacent bureaucrats that are a "trademark" of high-corruption countries.

Sources: Abed and Gupta (2002), pp. 1-4, Tanzi (2002), pp. 19-25, 49-52, and Dabla-Norris (2002), pp. 114-115.

Studying the impact of wide-spread corruption on the rate of private investment in developing countries, Everhart and Sumlinski (2001) find an indirect negative effect of corruption via the quality of public investment. Put differently, any given level of public investment will be characterized by a higher quality than would be the case with a higher degree of corruption present.[70] The authors also stipulate that this indirect effect leads to a lesser crowding out of private investment in an environment of low corruption. As Lehmann (2002) argues, poor governance introduces asymmetric information, thereby raising agency costs of market participants incurred in dealing with supervisory agencies. Consequently, increasing capital costs obstruct inflows of FDI substantially. Again, Nigeria serves an example for unexploited reforms – were the country to improve its governance structure to those of Singapore, the expected required rate of return could be diminished by more than 13 percentage points.

Bubnova (2000) studies the interaction between the way a country is governed and the risks facing private infrastructure investment (measured by spreads of infrastructure bonds). The author contends that corruption acts to prevent democratic development and results in poor infrastructure. In relating governance to risks facing private infrastructure investment (measured by spreads of emerging market infrastructure bonds) she identifies four clusters of strongly positive relationships in the set of explanatory variables: in addition to economic performance and religion-induced tensions, which play a lesser role in the sample countries here, political factors include regulatory risk (corruption/ bureaucratic delays/contract enforceability) and political disorder risk (domestic conflict/expropriation risk). Corruption and autocracy risk account for most of the bond spread variation. For a subset of weak-governance countries the

[70] See also Tanzi and Davoodi (2000), p. 12, who argue that poor public infrastructure due to corruption is likely to reduce private productivity and thus depress a country's growth prospects. Interestingly, the authors find that of 53 countries in the 1990s, those with high corruption tended to have a higher ratio of lawyers to engineers. Thus, they conclude: "Ceteris paribus, it would seem that a more corrupt society needs more lawyers" (p. 13).

political risk measure has the largest influence on the bond spread, and the R-squared is significantly higher than for the set of stable countries. The author concludes that "governance frameworks, and specifically the associated presence or absence of political and regulatory risks, are crucial factors at the initiation of private infrastructure bond financing" (p. 47).

By contrast, Singh and Jun (1995) and Hubert and Pain (1999) fail to find significance for the occurrence of strikes[71] in developing and non-EU countries, respectively. The same goes for German FDI flows to developing countries in the 1980s, as shown by Agarwal et al. (1991). Singh and Jun (1995) do, however, report a significantly negative coefficient for strikes in a sub-sample of "low FDI countries" where standoffs are more frequent.

In light of this overwhelming evidence, the bottom line of research on governance issues is that high country/political risk does represent an obstacle to higher inflows of FDI capital. Accordingly, *several measures of country and, more specifically, differentiated political risk* are used here. The risk data were obtained from two professional providers of country risk estimates, the *Political Risk Services Group* (in short: PRS) with its *International Country Risk Guide* (ICRG)[72] – variable: *PRSCRISK* – and the business magazine *Euromoney* with its bi-annual country risk surveys – variable: *EMCRISK*.[73] Both indices assign high scores to "safe" countries. Far from being the only sources of country risk information,[74] these publications enjoy a good reputation among researchers

---

[71] Industrial and civic strife (Singh and Jun) or number of work days lost in each of the host countries through strikes (Hubert and Pain); see Singh and Jun (1995), p. 16, and Hubert and Pain (1999), p. 173.

[72] The PRS Group uses estimates based on information collected by its own staff, which results in the publication of 22 variables in three subcategories for 140 countries on a monthly basis; see www.prsgroup.com/commonhtml/methods.html#_International_Country_Risk for more information, and, more specifically, www.icrgonline.com/page.aspx?page=icrgmethods.

[73] See, for example, Euromoney (2000), pp. 106-109. As a political risk rating was added only in September 1992, no such variable could be derived from the Euromoney data. The country risk score is calculated using nine individual, weighted categories; for explanation of the different categories see Euromoney (1997), pp. 60-62 and Table 14, Appendix II. The individual scores are based on a survey of economists at leading financial and economic institutions.

[74] As already hinted at, there are in fact many more, such as *Freedom House*, *International Investor* and *Transparency International*, to name just a few professional ones. Furthermore, risk indices have been developed by academics and international development institutions (such as the *World Bank's Country Policy Institutional Assessment*). Some of the risk indices could not be used in the first place, either because the period covered did not match this study's time frame or because the index did not report data for all of the emerging markets examined in this study.

(ICRG[75] used by Brunetti and Weder (1997), Lehmann (1999), Wei (2000), and Everhart and Sumlinski (2001); Euromoney data used by Ramcharran (1999) and Jost and Nunnenkamp (2002)) and supply continuous data for the relevant time period. Inevitably subjective, the survey data often provide the best information available on the less visible aspects of governance, and such perceptions are frequently as important as hard-to-obtain evidence.[76]

Figure 4 illustrates how country risk in both regions evolved throughout the last decade. After strengthening throughout the first half of the 1990s thanks to higher macroeconomic and political stability, the Asian crisis of 1997 caused both indices to fall sharply with respect to the Asian countries in the sample, and, with a contagion-induced delay of one year, the Latin America sub-sample got under pressure as well. Interestingly, the Euromoney experts seem to have been more euphoric initially than those of the PRS Group and consequently needed to reconsider their assessments even more strongly in the aftermath of the crisis. Note that both country risk measures include the respective political risk rating.

To isolate genuine macroeconomic risk, which, incidentally, could also be picked up by the variation in other variables, the variable *PRSERISK* was formed. Following the approach of Bubnova (2000) described above, in this study the political risk dimension is further divided into subcategories of orderly business dealings, i.e. corruption and autocracy risks, called *PRSADMIN*, and of political disorder risks, *PRSSTAB* (see Figure 5 for average political risk scores).[77]

[75] For example, Brunetti and Weder (1997) find PRS' corruption measure more comprehensive (and more significant) than that of Business International because the former does not focus on narrow business transactions but rather "asks whether high government officials are likely to demand special payments and whether illegal payments are generally expected throughout lower levels of government" (p. 14). Conversely, Wei (2000) criticizes that PRS does not reveal how the ratings are derived (p. 3). The PRS Group itself – at www.icrgonline.com/page.aspx?page=icrgmethods – asserts that its measure of corruption is "more concerned with actual or potential corruption in the form of excessive patronage, job reservations, 'favor-for-favors', secret party funding, and suspiciously close ties between politics and business".

[76] See Bubnova (2000), p. 11. Inherent subjectivity makes comparisons of individual risk assessments difficult, inspiring Kaufmann et al. (1999) to embark on aggregating indicators from several sources into a meta index.

[77] Other subcategories of PRS' political risk measure – external conflict, socioeconomic conditions, military in politics, religion in politics, ethnic tensions, democratic accountability – were omitted because they largely pertain to developing countries and do not seem to play a decisive role in the countries assessed in this study.

Figure 4: Country Risk in Emerging Latin America and Asia
(regional averages)

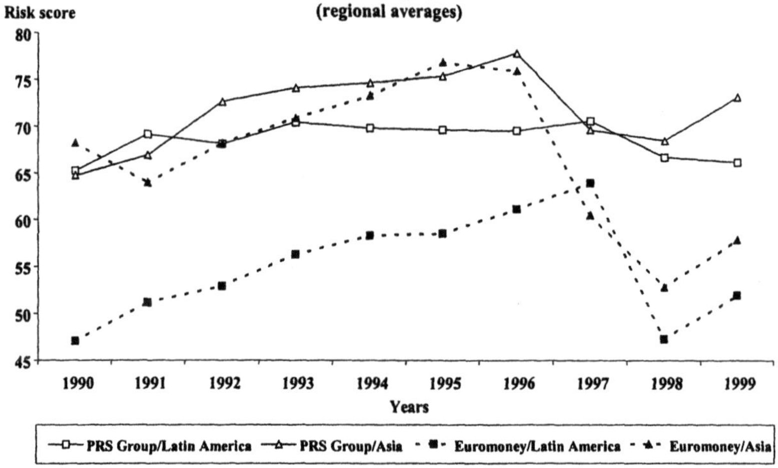

Grouping corruption and "red tape" due to their connectivity was brought up by Mauro (1995) as a more precise measure of corruption than corruption alone.[78] Accordingly, the variable *PRSADMIN* can be thought of as a measure of administrative uncertainty surrounding official decisions that immediately affect foreign investors (at the "micro-level"). It involves subjective assessments of the degree of *corruption* (with a high rating meaning a low degree of "sleaze"), the *quality of the bureaucracy* (high score for countries where the bureaucracy has the strength and expertise to govern without drastic changes in policy or interruptions in government services), and the so-called *investment profile* (measuring the risk of expropriation, restrictions on profit repatriation[79] and payment delays; again with high points for low-risk countries). This exact specification was tested by Pistoresi (2000) who, as expected, finds a significantly negative relationship between FDI inflows to a similar set of

[78] Wide-spread corruption may lead to further bureaucratic delay as a result of officials "dragging their feet" until receiving the expected bribe.

[79] The issue of repatriation restrictions facing multinational enterprises, a specific facet of political risk, is touched upon by Ihrig (2000) in a case study of US subsidiaries in Brazil between 1977 and 1991. The model she employs is able to capture the effect of such restrictions on capital investment and technology transfer to the Brazilian subsidiaries. Partial remittance restrictions are shown to cause multinationals to remit funds to the home country, whereas full blocking, logically, prompts reinvestment of funds. However, the Brazilian case suggests that countries who notoriously impose restrictions or threaten to do so can increase foreign capital investment if they credibly abolish these restrictions.

emerging markets and this combined administrative quality variable, which, in that case, depicts an inefficient and undependable bureaucracy.

The same result holds true in Pistoresi's estimations for a measure of political instability.[80] In this study, the corresponding variable *PRSSTAB* is composed of "macro-level" factors foreign firms have to put up with: the stability of the government (assessing both the government's ability to carry out its declared programs and its ability to stay in office), the aspect of law and order (evaluating the strength and impartiality of the legal system as well as the degree of popular observance of the law), and the prevalence of internal conflict (the highest rating being given to countries without armed opposition to the government and lacking arbitrary governmental violence against its own people; lowest rating given to a country embroiled in an on-going civil war).

Figure 5 describes the development of political risk scores and their sub-components across regions. Again, the risk scores for both sub-samples first rose and then fell after the Asian crisis, but the swings were more moderate compared to the composite country risk ratings. Note that the political risk assessments for Asia recovered in 1999 (*PRSSTAB* already in 1998), while those for Latin America deteriorated further.

Figure 5: Political Risk and its Components (regional averages)

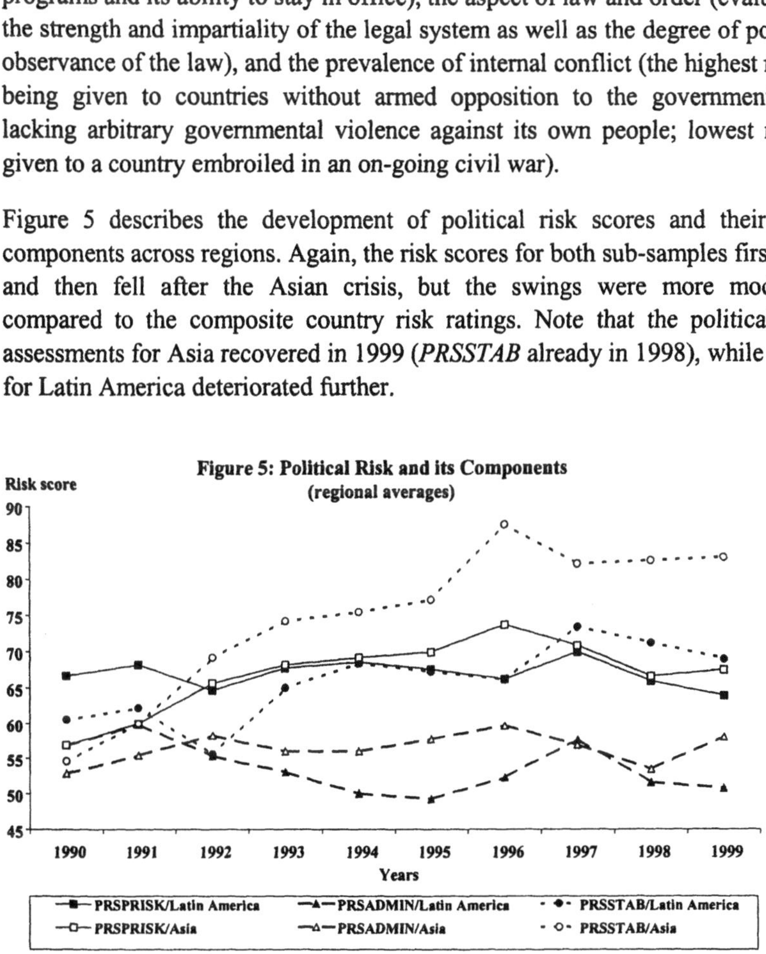

[80] Made up of six *Business International* indices, see Pistoresi (2000), p. 41.

2.2.2.2 Agglomeration Effects

There is considerable disagreement in the literature as to what exactly constitutes agglomeration. Some authors equate clustering effects of that kind with the size of the existing FDI stock (perhaps lagged) or "herding" of foreign firms, whereas others perceive the quality of the host country's infrastructure as a suitable proxy.[81] Positive spillover effects through the widespread establishment of foreign subsidiaries play a prominent role. Commonly, once a large multinational corporation sets up shop in one location, others will follow ("follow the leader" effect; see also Chapter III as to this concept). This is because foreign firms unable to enter in the same period as the leader will incur a large welfare loss compared to a scenario where all firms enter more or less simultaneously. In the extreme, potential late entrants may not get a foothold in the market because of the productivity advantage already attained by the first mover.[82] Well-known examples of such positive agglomeration effects are typified by automobile production in Mexico or the Asian electronics industry[83] as well as high-tech manufacturing FDI in Ireland.[84]

In an innovative study on that issue, Wheeler and Mody (1992) check both factors – clustering of FDI inflows and quality of the infrastructure – on their validity for 42 developing *and* industrialized countries. Both coefficients are of the same magnitude and highly significant for the manufacturing sector. The quality of infrastructure seems especially important for developing countries, and specifically the electronics industry. Mody and Srinivasan (1998) examine data on U.S. FDI to 35 countries and posit that the stock of past FDI is strongly positively correlated with current FDI inflows in all estimations, whereas the infrastructure variable (output of electricity per GDP) is found to be significant only if measured by the "between" estimator, having the authors conclude that only major infrastructure investment may act to attract investors. Lehmann (1999) uses lagged U.S. total investment as proxy for agglomeration and finds it to be significantly positive in all regressions. A first-mover effect is observed by Mody et al. (1999) in a strong partial correlation between a Japanese firm's plans to invest in elsewhere in Asia and its expectation of competitors having similar plans. Braunerhjelm and Svensson (1996) examine agglomeration effects

[81] See Lim (2001), p. 7. As an example for quality-of-infrastructure proxies, Razin (2002) finds a positive significance of developing country telephone density for FDI inflows (p. 10).

[82] See Markusen (1990), p. 2.

[83] See Lim (2001), pp. 5-6.

[84] Respondents to a survey among foreign investors in several technology-oriented manufacturing industries stated that their location decision was influenced by the fact that other key markets were already located in Ireland; see Barry and Bradley (1997), p. 1804.

at the industry level, using the relative share of a particular industry in total manufacturing employment. The results of a Tobit estimation imply that in terms of agglomeration "the more important the industry of the investing firm is in the host country, the more the firm's affiliate will produce in that country" (p. 837) or, interpreted differently, the higher the probability that FDI has occurred. Agglomeration effects are found to be most pronounced in high-tech industries.

The agglomeration variable used here, *AGGLO*, is defined as the *moving-three year average of contemporary and lagged total FDI inflows relative to respective host country GDP*. Note that this is not simply a partially lagged endogenous variable since it recurs to FDI flows from the rest of the world and not just Germany. The variable aims at capturing both first-mover advantage effects (by including contemporary flows) and the magnitude of privately supplied infrastructure abroad over the past couple of years.

2.2.2.3 Corporate Financing Conditions

Rarely used in empirical research, the varying availability of relatively low-cost financing generated within the firm should intuitively play a fundamental role in the magnitude and timing of corporate investment decisions, particularly with respect to efficiency-seeking FDI. Cushman (1985) includes a corporate cash flow variable which he lags by one year and finds significantly positively correlated to U.S. FDI in industrialized countries. Barrell and Pain (1996) add to their regressions for outward U.S. FDI lagged corporate profits (also significantly positive).

The relevance of the level of corporate profits for Germany is underscored by Heiduk and Hodges (1992) in a case study of the investment activity of German multinationals. The authors purport that, given the higher volatility of foreign compared to domestic investment, German firms facing financial distress tend to trim FDI before they decrease domestic investment.

As using cash flows generated within the firm is arguably the most inexpensive way of financing investment, this study incorporates the *lagged aggregated cash flow of German firms normalized to total corporate assets*, *CFLOW*. Note that there is logically no variation across host countries such that the variable can be rendered significant only by fluctuations over time. Put differently, *CFLOW* resembles a time dummy of changeable magnitude.

2.2.2.4 Real Exchange Rate (Volatility)

There are opposing views on the impact of the real exchange rate (RER) on FDI inflows. An upward movement in the host country's RER may stir fear of protectionism among foreign investors and lead them to invest abroad in anticipation of additional trade barriers.[85] Conversely, Froot and Stein (1991) show that under credit rationing, i.e. imperfect capital markets, a (real) exchange rate depreciation induces foreign investors' wealth to rise, enabling them to outbid their competitors abroad for information-intensive assets having monitoring costs. Therefore, aggregate FDI flows will increase in proportion to a depreciation of the domestic currency.[86] Razin (2002) illustrates a similar wealth effect: foreign firms would be put at an advantage over domestic borrowers by being able to post more valuable collateral in borrowing from domestic banks.[87] Yet, as Ghura and Goodwin (2000) point out, the overall impact of a real depreciation is uncertain, as imported inflation raises the price of investment goods and consequently depresses investment.[88] In the arguably most relevant empirical investigation on exchange rate movements with respect to this study, Goldberg and Klein (1997) find that a depreciation in the bilateral RER of large Asian countries to the yen attracts FDI inflows from Japan while FDI from the U.S. falls. Interestingly, U.S. flows do not react to changes in the bilateral RER to the dollar,[89] nor are there significant effects for the Latin American sub-sample. To avoid collinearity with the unit labor cost variable,[90] the main model forgoes a particular exchange rate variable in levels. However,

[85] See Kosteletou and Liargovas (2000), p. 139.

[86] See Froot and Stein (1991), p. 1202. This shift in relative wealth is caused by nominal exchange rate movements that are not matched by domestic price level adjustments, rendering deviations from purchasing power parity possible.

[87] This effect naturally applies mostly to mergers and acquisitions and less to greenfield investment. However, the latter can be expected to grow, too, as (nominal) exchange rate depreciations – according to the "relative labor cost theory" – give foreign production a competitive edge in labor costs over domestic output and will thus lead to higher FDI inflows; see Kosteletou and Liargovas (2000), p. 139, and Goldberg and Klein (1997), p. 12.

[88] Generally speaking, a widely-perceived deviation of the real exchange rate from its estimated equilibrium level may affect long-run investment decisions via a shift in relative production costs; see Barrell and Pain (1996), p. 202.

[89] This may be due to the fact that real and nominal exchange rates of the sample countries were closely related as the observed weight of the US dollar in Asian currency baskets was often between 90 and 100 percent; see Goldberg and Klein (1997), p. 21. Hence, movements in RER to the dollar were either caused by very strong shifts in exchange rates to other currencies within the basket or by bilateral inflation differentials.

[90] This would expressly apply to those countries with fixed exchange rate regimes or de facto nominal exchange rate stability over the sample period.

the significance of the *bilateral real exchange rate, RER,* is tested in a separate regression excluding labor costs.

It is, however, quite justified to look beyond pure *level* effects. The expectation of short-term changes in exchange rates may influence the timing of investment transactions: for example, firms may precipitate payments in currencies expected to appreciate.[91] In the area of bilateral exchange rate *volatility*, several theoretical studies show that higher variability is positively correlated with FDI inflows (Cushman (1985), Aizenman (1991, 1992)[92], Goldberg and Kolstad (1995), and Sung and Lapan (2000)). In a theoretical model based on the view taken in the real options literature, Sung and Lapan (2000) demonstrate that by erecting more than one production facility, i.e. opening another plant abroad, and postponing the decision as to where to produce, a multinational firm acquires a real option whose value increases with greater exchange rate fluctuations.[93] They posit that more volatile exchange rates induce a rise in the relative value of opening the foreign plant. This contradicts the traditional view that firms would then reconsider foreign investment to reduce their risk exposure.[94] Depending on the degree of volatility, firms will open only the foreign plant or both.[95] Therefore, high exchange rate variability will promote FDI outflows to alternative production sites.

This hypothesis is confirmed by several empirical studies. Stockman and Vlaar (1996) observe that higher volatility in the bilateral exchange rate significantly increases the growth rate of Dutch FDI outflows.[96] A similar result is found by Hubert and Pain (1999) who test both real and nominal exchange rate fluctuations separately for German data and find that nominal exchange rate volatility negatively impacts FDI outflows, whereas the reverse holds for the real exchange rate. The latter finding is, as the authors point out, consistent with the production shifting hypothesis. Love and Lage-Hidalgo (2000), testing

[91] See Barrell and Pain (1996), p. 205.

[92] Aizenman (1992) shows that under a flexible exchange rate higher volatility of monetary shocks induces disparities in the real wage at home and abroad, and thus induces geographic diversification via foreign direct investment, while concurrently lowering aggregate investment (pp. 909, 914).

[93] The real option's value is calculated as the expected value of additionally opening the plant abroad, i.e. value of the firm with both plants exclusive of the value of merely the home plant, minus the sunk cost incurred by opening the foreign plant. It is shown that the differential profits increase with higher exchange rate volatility; see Sung and Lapan (2000), p. 415, and, similarly on the real options argument, Aizenman (1992), p. 897.

[94] See Goldberg and Kolstad (1995), pp. 856-857.

[95] See Sung and Lapan (2000), p. 415.

[96] The authors do not specify whether they test nominal or real exchange rate fluctuations.

whether past volatility in the US$-peso rate affects FDI flows to Mexico, also report a strongly positive coefficient.[97]

In this study, exchange rate volatility is therefore modeled along the lines of Hubert and Pain (1999) by constructing a *two-year moving average of past real exchange rate fluctuations*. It is important to note that, contrary to some of the previously mentioned studies that simply use first differences of exchange rates, here volatility is measured as the variance of the real exchange rate over past years, i.e. regardless of the direction of the individual change:

$$(1) \quad RERVOL_{i,t} = \sqrt{0.5 \sum_{k=1}^{2} \log \left(\frac{RER_{i,t-k} - RER_{i,t-k+1}}{RER_{i,t-k+1}} \right)^2}$$

where $RER_{i,t}$ is the real exchange rate between Germany and the ith country in a given year.[98]

2.2.2.5 Structural Reforms

Recent studies have increasingly incorporated structural reform measures in FDI host countries. The intuition is that current or envisaged reforms in the regulatory realm will positively affect investment conditions for foreign firms over the longer term. However, during such adjustment periods, FDI flows may actually dwindle, as Tuman and Emmert (1999) show for Japanese FDI in 12 Latin American countries for the period 1979-1992. During a given year of implementing economic adjustments, the sample countries received an average of roughly $30 million less in FDI. Agarwal et al. (1991) fail to find a positive impact of lagged World Bank adjustment loans on total German FDI flows to developing countries.

[97] Furthermore, Barrell and Pain (1996) find that an expectation of a depreciation in the host country's currency will postpone US investment. Cushman (1985) reports rising U.S. FDI to G7-countries in response to an increase in the standard deviation of the expected change in the real exchange rate. By contrast, Sin and Leung (2001) do not find a strong impact of the nominal exchange rate on flows to developing countries up to 1992.

[98] Real exchange rates computed using consumer price indices. The RER itself is normalized to base year 1990. An increase in the RER denotes a real appreciation of the host country's currency. The variances are measured as the squared annual differences relative to the previous year. One could have used unit labor costs as indicator of the real exchange rate, as proposed by Hubert and Pain (1999, p. 174), but doing so would mean neglecting changes in the nominal exchange rate and thus a greater degree of noise; see Barrell and Pain (1996), p. 202.

A genuine measure of structural reforms has been developed by Lora (2001, drawing on earlier work of 1997). This unique meta-index for Latin American countries consists of five subcategories (trade, financial, tax and labor market reforms, and privatization) measured by individual indices and covers the period from 1985 to 1999. Lora himself does not subject his data to econometric testing, but Fernández-Arias and Montiel (2001) do so, exploring how structural effects, which the index measures, relate to growth in Latin America up to 1995. Reassuringly, they find that Lora's structural policy index contains independent information not already captured by four other stabilization regressors.[99] In fact, the index's coefficient is significantly positive and eliminates the unexplained excess of Latin American growth (low growth despite reforms)[100] observed in their baseline regressions. To test whether this holds true for the impact of structural reforms on FDI flows, Lora's recently updated index, here termed *STRUCT*, is included in the estimations for the Latin American sub-sample.

3 Methodology

In the following sections, the estimation method selected for the study is described, followed by a presentation of the procedure for selecting robust variables.

3.1 Estimation Method

In principle, the parameters for each country could be estimated, although inefficiently, by ordinary least squares (OLS). Given the geographic proximity of the countries to one another in each region, it would be a strong assumption that the countries in either cross section behave entirely independent of one another, particularly given the fact that the model assigns the same parameter vector to all units (i.e. countries).[101] Therefore, the error terms in the FDI equations are likely to include factors common to all countries in either sub-

[99] These are: lower public consumption (relative to GDP), lower inflation, financial deepening (broad money to GDP), exchange rate unification (black market premium), and, allegedly, trade intensity (imports and exports to GDP, estimates not given); see Fernández-Arias and Montiel (2001), pp. 526, 529.

[100] This often-voiced "puzzle" is discarded by the authors "in the sense that unidentified region-specific factors depressed growth in Latin America during the 1990s, offsetting the large positive growth impetus of the reforms". They conclude that "the growth response of recent reform in Latin America – that is, its marginal effect – was adequate"; Fernández-Arias and Montiel (2001), pp. 543, 535.

[101] See Greene (2003), p. 333.

sample and thus to be correlated between cross sections at a given time. This supposition renders a pooled analysis of FDI data using the *Seemingly Unrelated Regressions* (SUR)[102] procedure more efficient than applying OLS to each country separately since the common, immeasurable influences are accounted for. The SUR technique allows for integrating contemporaneous correlation by estimating the full variance-covariance matrix of the system's disturbance vector. This, of course, requires that the panel be balanced. Another prerequisite for using SUR estimation is that T (years) be greater than N (countries), otherwise the (feasible) *Generalized Least Squares* (GLS) estimator, which is needed to obtain the initially unknown covariance matrix, cannot be calculated.[103]

To obtain general results for each region, only one coefficient per regressor is estimated (and the subscript of ß dropped). Thus, in the stacked form, the regression model is:

$$(2)\quad \begin{bmatrix} \mathbf{y}_1 \\ \mathbf{y}_2 \\ \vdots \\ \mathbf{y}_M \end{bmatrix} = \begin{bmatrix} \mathbf{X}_1 & \mathbf{0} & \cdots & \mathbf{0} \\ \mathbf{0} & \mathbf{X}_2 & \cdots & \mathbf{0} \\ & & \ddots & \\ \mathbf{0} & \mathbf{0} & \cdots & \mathbf{X}_M \end{bmatrix} \boldsymbol{\beta} + \begin{bmatrix} \boldsymbol{\varepsilon}_1 \\ \boldsymbol{\varepsilon}_2 \\ \vdots \\ \boldsymbol{\varepsilon}_M \end{bmatrix} \quad or \quad \begin{bmatrix} \mathbf{y}_1 \\ \mathbf{y}_2 \\ \vdots \\ \mathbf{y}_M \end{bmatrix} = \mathbf{X}\boldsymbol{\beta} + \boldsymbol{\varepsilon}.$$

Under the assumption that the disturbances are uncorrelated across observations, the disturbance system becomes:[104]

$$E\left[\boldsymbol{\varepsilon}_m \boldsymbol{\varepsilon}_n' \mid \mathbf{X}_1, \mathbf{X}_2, \ldots, \mathbf{X}_M\right] = \sigma_{ij}\mathbf{I} \qquad or$$

$$(3)\quad E\left[\boldsymbol{\varepsilon}\boldsymbol{\varepsilon}'\right] = \mathbf{V} = \begin{bmatrix} \sigma_{11}\mathbf{I} & \sigma_{12}\mathbf{I} & \cdots & \sigma_{1M}\mathbf{I} \\ \sigma_{21}\mathbf{I} & \sigma_{22}\mathbf{I} & \cdots & \sigma_{2M}\mathbf{I} \\ \vdots & \vdots & & \vdots \\ \sigma_{M1}\mathbf{I} & \sigma_{M2}\mathbf{I} & \cdots & \sigma_{MM}\mathbf{I} \end{bmatrix}$$

where *n* and *m* denote the *n*th and *m*th equation, respectively, and **I** is the T×T identity matrix. As can be inferred from (3), the individual equations are linked

[102] For a good overview on SUR techniques see Dielman (1989), pp. 29-47, Judge et al. (1988), pp. 444-468, or Greene (2003), pp. 340-362.

[103] See Greene (2003), p. 322. Larger sets of countries will therefore usually preclude using the SUR technique which fortunately is not the case in this study as T=10 (years) and N=6 or N=8 (countries). In STATA, SUR estimation with only one coefficient per regressor produces virtually identical results as GLS estimation accounting for cross-sectional correlation.

[104] See Greene (2003), p. 341.

only by their disturbances, hence "seemingly unrelated regressions." An efficiency gain exists, because the pooling approach takes account of correlation between the error vectors and uses information on explanatory variables included in the system but excluded from the individual equation.[105] The greater the correlation of the disturbances, the greater the efficiency gain obtained by applying GLS. The GLS estimator in the SUR case, therefore, is:

$$(4) \quad \hat{\boldsymbol{\beta}} = \left[\mathbf{X}'\mathbf{V}^{-1}\mathbf{X}\right]^{-1} \mathbf{X}'\mathbf{V}^{-1}\mathbf{y}.$$

In addition, the SUR estimation with STATA provides for including a first-order autoregressive (AR(1)) process. In this case, the original data are transformed by adding to the residuals a lagged and weighted error term such that

$$(5) \quad \varepsilon_{i,t} = \rho_i \, \varepsilon_{i,t-1} + u_{it}$$

which amounts to multiplying the variance-covariance matrix **V** by the transformation matrix $\mathbf{P}_i$ that removes the autocorrelation of the errors. Alternatively, only one common AR(1) coefficient ρ may be estimated. With these, the SUR estimation method does, in a sense, contain dynamic elements which would substitute for a full-fledged dynamic estimation if, say, the common AR(1) coefficient were sufficiently small (less than 0.2, for example). Therefore, FDI panel data may be estimated by a static model if the influence of lagged coefficients and thus the dynamics of the source data are shown to be weak.

To test whether the off-diagonal elements of **V** are indeed non-zero, a likelihood ratio test, which is based on the likelihood ratio statistic[106]

$$(6) \quad \lambda = -2(\log L_r - \log L_u) = T(\log|\hat{\mathbf{W}}_r| - \log|\hat{\mathbf{W}}_u|)$$

is used, where $\mathbf{W}_r$ and $\mathbf{W}_u$ are the residual sums of squares and cross-product matrices using the constrained and unconstrained estimators, respectively. The

[105] See Judge et al. (1988), p. 450.

[106] See Greene (2003), p. 349. A similar test of the null hypothesis of homoskedasticity is performed for each regression based on: $\lambda = -2\left(\ln L_0 - \ln L_1\right) = n \ln s^2 - \sum_{g=1}^{G} n_g \ln s_g^2$ where $s^2 = \frac{\mathbf{e}'\mathbf{e}}{n}$ and $s_g^2 = \frac{\mathbf{e}_g'\mathbf{e}_g}{n_g}$, with g being the number of groups across which heteroskedasticity may occur; see Greene (2003), p. 236.

likelihood ratio statistic is asymptotically χ^2-distributed with degrees of freedom equal to the number of imposed restrictions.

In sum, the SUR model allows for contemporaneous correlation of disturbances as well as first-order autocorrelation of the time series disturbances and cross-sectional heteroskedasticity. The log likelihood function is instrumental in arriving at the correct specification of the final model, as section four shows.

3.2 Selection of Exogenous Variables

Section 2.2 illustrates that a wide variety of potential exogenous variables has been tested in the literature. While the merits of using a theoretical model as a basis for estimating determinants of direct investment are obvious, this study nonetheless employs an ad-hoc estimation, which tests an array of variables that in the literature have been found to be crucial for FDI flows. The problem of converting structural approaches to modeling FDI into testable hypotheses lies primarily in the scarcity of economic data of developing countries, both across years and types of determinants. This shortcoming has led authors pursuing such an approach (*inter alia*, Lehmann (1999) and Stevens (2000)) to simplify their models, as the variables contained in the structural models were not readily available and thus needed to be substituted by proxy variables in the subsequent regressions. Hence, while most researchers would agree that apart from classical macroeconomic variables one has to account for locational factors such as agglomeration effects or idiosyncratic "political" risks pertaining to the maintenance of property rights, it is less clear exactly which of these factors belong in the true regression in any one case.

Although ad-hoc estimations are used here, the approach to selecting the model variables is nonetheless structural in the sense that only those variables that are found to be robust in an iterative procedure based on the *Extreme Bounds Analysis* (EBA), originally suggested by Leamer (1983, 1985), are included in the final model. This test, as modified by Levine and Renelt (1992), defines those variables of interest, z, as robust if, in a regression of the form

$$(7) \quad \gamma = \alpha_j + \beta_{yj} \cdot y + \beta_{zj} \cdot z + \beta_{xj} \cdot x_j + \varepsilon \ ,$$

they are always significant when combined with each of the other variables, with y being a vector of fixed ("free") variables that are always included and x_j a vector of up to three variables taken from the pool of N variables.

As Figure 6 shows, the EBA performs alterations in this subset x_j to find the widest range of coefficient estimates of the variable of interest z, which is then defined as *robust* if the lower extreme bound, being the lowest value of $\beta_{zj}-2\sigma_{zj}$ (slope parameter minus two times the standard deviation), and the corresponding upper extreme bound, $\beta_{zj}+2\sigma_{zj}$, are either both negative or both positive.[107]

Figure 6: An Example of the Extreme Bounds Analysis

Variables: *(1) GDP, (2) CRISK, (3) ULC, (4) DUTY, (5) DEBT, (6) AGGLO, (7) CFLOW, (8) RERVOL*

|----------y---------| z |-------------------x_j-------------------|

FDI = α+*GDP*+*CRISK (1,2)*+β_3 *ULC* + *DUTY+DEBT+AGGLO (4,5,6)*

+β_3 *ULC* + *DUTY+DEBT+CFLOW (4,5,7)*

(check: is β_3 *higher (lower) than the upper (lower) extreme bound so far? If so, adjust bound)*

+β_3 *ULC* + *DEBT+CFLOW+RERVOL (5,6,7)*

+β_3 *ULC* + *AGGLO+CFLOW+RERVOL (6,7,8)*

+β_4 *DUTY* + *CRISK+DEBT+AGGLO (3,5,6)*

⇓ *and so on until:*

+β_8 *RERVOL*+ *DEBT+AGGLO+CFLOW (5,6,7).*

In other words, a statistical relationship between the FDI flow variable and a variable of interest z is deemed robust if the latter remains statistically significant at the five percent level with an unchanged sign when the conditioning set of variables is subjected to changes. Otherwise, one has reason to lack confidence in the relationship with the endogenous variable. Such a variable of interest is to be called "fragile" because it does not display enough independent variation to explain cross-country differences in FDI.[108]

The method used in this study to arrive at the regression y differs from the proposed approach in that there is no vector of commonly used (fixed) variables

107 See Sala-i-Martin (1997), pp. 2-4. The author criticizes this test as too strong because only one regression in which the coefficient sign changes suffices to reject the variable in question, thereby almost guaranteeing that all of the variables tested are labeled as non-robust. He suggests considering the distribution of the β_z and using the fraction of the cumulative distribution function lying of each side of zero as robustness criterion. In the present study, however, the Extreme Bounds Analysis turns out to work nicely in accepting only a narrow number of truly robust variables.

108 See Chakrabarti (2001), pp. 93-95.

in FDI research,[109] with the exception of market size, usually proxied by GDP or GDP per capita. The lack of universally acknowledged standard regressors thus calls for preselecting fixed variables, much in the same fashion as proposed for choosing the variables of interest, *z*.

Accordingly, the set of fixed variables must first be determined by running the EBA solely with the variable of interest and the conditioning information set. In some cases this initial procedure will turn out only one robust variable in the "first round", which is then set as a fixed variable in the next round of regressions in order to find another variable that by virtue of this inclusion now becomes robust as well. Now having a "critical mass" of regressors in place, these *two* variables – not three, given the rather limited number of conditioning factors – will then be used in a "full" EBA to detect more robust factors.

Because of the normalization of the endogenous variable by relating it to GDP, market size has effectively been rendered negligible and thus *GDPCAP* is included to control for purchasing power in the host country. Even so, this variable should not routinely be assumed to be one of the fixed variables but must also be subjected to the Extreme Bounds Analysis.

4 Econometric Results

4.1 Country Level

Following a "general-to-specific" approach, first a model that includes all explanatory variables is estimated. Subsequently, the list of variables is narrowed down to the ones found robust in the Extreme Bounds Analysis. In addition, alternative variables for risk, cost, and openness are estimated separately. The estimation outcome contains standardized coefficients $\beta_j^* = \beta_j\ (s_{xj}/s_y)$ with s_{xj} being the standard deviation of the jth exogenous variable and s_y the standard deviation of the endogenous variable.[110] As a double-log linear model allowing the coefficients to be interpreted as elasticities was not feasible due to the occurrence of negative FDI flows, this standardization allows for comparing the "weights" with which the individual variables enter the equation. The measure

---

[109] Mauro (1995) applies the Levine-Renelt approach and a similar one by Barro (1991) to growth rates of investment to GDP and includes as fixed variables GDP, population growth and secondary education. The two latter ones are, however, clearly non-standard in the FDI literature. Garibaldi et al. (2002) use a version of Leamer's Extreme Bounds Analysis in their regressions for FDI in transition countries.

[110] For further reference see Pindyck and Rubinfeld (1981), pp. 90-91.

of goodness-of-fit has to be derived from the Wald test statistic and is therefore usually called "pseudoR^2".[111]

The regression results for Latin America in Table 3 provide a number of valuable insights.

Table 3: Estimations for Latin America at the Country Level

FGLS estimation with individual country effects, adjusted for heteroskedasticity & cross-sectional correlation
Dependent variable: *FDIGDP*; number of observations: 60

	(1)	(2)	(3)	(4)
GDPCAP	-0.086	-0.084	-0.572	
	(-0.62)	(-0.56)	(-2.23)**	
PRSCRISK	0.294		0.222	0.273
	(5.75)***		(3.28)***	(6.02)***
EMCRISK		0.265		
		(2.55)**		
ULC	0.118	0.159		
	(1.05)	(1.12)		
RER			-0.090	
			(-0.71)	
DUTY	0.174	0.202		0.225
	(2.09)**	(2.45)**		(4.12)***
OPEN			0.269	
			(1.04)	
DEBT	0.028	0.038	-0.304	
	(0.38)	(0.35)	(-1.95)*	
AGGLO	0.183	0.168	0.361	0.182
	(2.31)**	(2.08)**	(2.94)***	(6.63)***
CFLOW	0.028	0.084	-0.039	
	(0.41)	(1.72)*	(-0.56)	
RERVOL	0.076	0.105	-0.044	
	(1.23)	(1.49)	(-0.66)	
PseudoR^2	0.65	0.41	0.40	0.54

Note: z-values in parentheses; *** = significant at the 1% level, ** = significant at the 5% level, * = significant at the 10% level

Most importantly, it is shown that country risk clearly matters in the region. Both risk indices, *PRSCRISK* in (1) and *EMCRISK* in (2), are strongly

[111] See Greene (2003), p. 97, for derivation. Verbeek (2001), p. 182, discussing alternative measures to R^2, makes use of the likelihood ratio statistic (LR) which is asymptotically equivalent to the Wald test statistic (W). The Wald (or F-) statistic is related to pseudoR^2 as follows: $F \approx \frac{n}{K-1} * \frac{R^2}{1-R^2}$ *and* $(K-1) * F \approx W \approx LR$. *Therefore,* $R^2 \approx \frac{W}{n+W}$.

significant with the expected sign and carry the greatest weight among the explanatory variables. Further decomposition of the risk aspect reveals that the economic risk measure, *PRSERISK*, if chosen instead of headline country risk is strongly positively significant and robust (coefficient = 0.3132, z-ratio = 4.68); upper bound = 0.0156, lower bound = 0.0068) as opposed to *PRSPRISK* (ß = 0.0606, z = 0.84). Among the political risk components, the index of administrative quality, *PRSADMIN* (replacing headline political risk) is significant and correctly signed (ß = 0.2084, z = 2.37), whereas *PRSSTAB*, measuring domestic stability, is negatively correlated with FDI inflows.

Second, German FDI in that region seems to have been geared towards tapping markets protected against imports[112] over the sample period, since the tariff variable, *DUTY*, is robustly positively significant while *ULC*, an indicator of efficiency-seeking FDI, is not. In addition, agglomeration effects have clearly spurred German FDI flows with a view to securing market access in the face of strong competition from abroad. An alternative model (3) using the real exchange rate, *RER*, and the conditioned openness measure, *OPEN*, instead of unit labor costs and taxation of trade, respectively, worsens the fit of the regression compared to (1) as both alternative variables end up being insignificant.

An unexpected result is found for Lora's structural reform index: contrary to the intuition, *STRUCT*, turns out to be significantly negative (z-value = -4.75) if added to regression (1), and its inclusion improves the regression's fit considerably (pseudoR^2 rises to 0.75), leaving room for interpretation. Coinciding with the results of Tuman and Emmert (1999), current crisis conditions might overshadow structural reforms whose beneficial impact may only take root in later periods.[113] However, lagging *STRUCT* by one period does not change the picture greatly (it remains significantly negative at the 1 percent level). Closer inspection of the data series reveals that there is a persistent improvement in index scores for almost all of the Latin American sample countries which contrasts sharply with the relatively high volatility of German FDI flows to the region. The negative correlation between FDI and the reform index could also owe something to the fact that index scores rose excessively in the early 1990s when a wave of privatization set in. This is true of all sample countries with the exception of Chile, whose privatization had already begun in

112 For additional evidence (on the strategy of the German automobile industry) see Nunnenkamp (1998), p. 22.

113 On the other hand, as illustrated in section 1, even *expectations* of structural reforms suffice to prompt investment decisions. Therefore, one can expect actual reforms depicted in the index to contemporaneously affect decision-making.

the early 1980s.[114] Soaring scores are, however, not mirrored by German FDI flows to the region in the early 1990s, presumably because German firms participated less in the privatization process than did investors from other nations.[115]

The parsimonious "final" regression (4) shows that of the eight original variables, only three are robust for the Latin American sub-sample according to the Extreme Bounds Analysis (see Table 4).

Table 4: Extreme Bounds Analysis at the Country Level

Fixed variables: Latin America – *PRSCRISK, AGGLO*; Asia – *ULC, DUTY.*
Regressions include the fixed variables plus one of those listed below (variables of interest) and three of the pool of remaining variables at a time. Bounds are derived from non-standardized coefficients.

LATIN AMERICA			ASIA		
Variable	Upper bound	Lower bound	Variable	Upper bound	Lower bound
ULC	0.3739	-0.1769	*PRSCRISK*	0.0645	-0.0015
DUTY †	0.0236	0.0016	*GDPCAP*	0.0876	-0.0197
DEBT	0.0026	-0.0057	*DEBT*	0.0033	-0.0003
GDPCAP	0.0934	-0.5008	*AGGLO*	0.0045	-0.0420
CFLOW	0.0244	-0.0272	*CFLOW* †	0.0313	0.0019
RERVOL	0.2164	-0.0890	*RERVOL*	0.0700	-0.0454

† denotes robust variable as defined by the Extreme Bounds Analysis (in addition to the fixed variables listed above)

PRSCRISK and *AGGLO* having been selected by the initial procedure[116] as the two fixed variables, the following EBA produces only one more robust variable, namely *DUTY*. For Asia, the case is more clear-cut: *ULC* and *DUTY* test robust in the initial procedure, and subsequently *CFLOW* is found to be the only truly robust variable in addition.

Regarding country risk, the outcome of the estimations for Asia paints a similar picture to the Latin American case (Table 5). Again, both risk measures are

[114] See Birch and Braga (1993), pp. 122-123 and 126.

[115] See Nunnenkamp (1998), pp. 25-26.

[116] In fact, in the "first round" only *PRSCRISK* is found to be robust, while *AGGLO* (upper bound = 0.0525, lower bound = -0.0069 with *PRSCRISK* as the free variable) is the variable clearly "next in line" in terms of consistency. *AGGLO* is nonetheless a robust variable since an EBA using *PRSCRISK* and *DUTY* as fixed variables to bring about a critical mass of regressors now yields two positive bounds for *AGGLO* (upper = 0.0486, lower = 0.0021).

significantly positive, with *EMCRISK* in this case being marginally more significant but likewise worsening the fit of the regression slightly. However, *PRSCRISK* is not a truly robust variable (minor violation of EBA, see Table 4) and is thus omitted from the parsimonious regression in (8).

Table 5: Estimations for Asia at the Country Level

FGLS estimation, with individual country effects, adjusted for heteroskedasticity & cross-sectional correlation
Dependent variable: *FDIGDP*; number of observations: 80

	(5)	(6)	(7)	(8)
GDPCAP	0.096 (1.42)	0.093 (0.63)	0.289 (2.85)***	
PRSCRISK	0.199 (2.54)**		0.119 (2.78)***	
EMCRISK		0.231 (2.87)***		
ULC	-0.194 (-3.44)***	-0.219 (-3.30)***		-0.221 (-6.61)***
RER			0.382 (10.45)***	
DUTY	-0.234 (-3.69)***	-0.228 (-3.28)***		-0.234 (-5.25)***
OPEN			0.153 (2.74)***	
DEBT	0.247 (2.61)**	0.250 (2.67)***	0.436 (6.14)***	
AGGLO	-0.409 (-3.50)***	-0.009 (-1.67)*	-0.289 (-3.28)***	
CFLOW	0.117 (7.01)***	0.121 (5.00)***	0.060 (2.80)***	0.125 (4.60)***
RERVOL	0.042 (2.10)**	0.013 (1.17)	0.066 (3.16)***	
PseudoR^2	0.79	0.70	0.86	0.75

Note: z-values in parentheses; *** = significant at the 1% level, ** = significant at the 5% level, * = significant at the 10% level

The question as to what accounts for the non-robustness is answered by testing for the other risk sub-components. Even though *PRSERISK* is at first glance as significant as in (1) with ß = 0.2936 and z = 4.70, it fails the EBA by a small margin (upper = 0.0085, lower = -0.0002) and as a result is, strictly speaking, non-robust. Headline political risk is again insignificant (*PRSPRISK*: ß = 0.0059, z = 0.98) while its sub-component *PRSADMIN* carries the expected positive sign (ß = 0.2324, z = 7.45) and, as opposed to Latin America, tests robust (upper = 0.0061, lower = 0.0009). Lastly, aspects of political stability cannot be shown to play a major role in the Asian sample countries (*PRSSTAB*: ß = -0.0597, z = -1.21).

Another important finding is that for Asia the signs of the coefficients for *ULC* and *DUTY* are reversed in comparison to Latin America, as both are significantly (robustly) negative. These results are clearly in line with the efficiency-seeking hypothesis as FDI in the Asian emerging markets was indeed driven by low costs and open borders to trade (*OPEN* significant and correctly signed). This interpretation is backed by the strong results for *CFLOW*, implying that the availability of low-cost financing does matter for investments in emerging Asia. Interestingly, *AGGLO* carries an unexpected negative sign. Evidence from the data series suggests that German multinationals tended to exhibit a counter-cyclical investment behavior. In some country cases they were the front-runners, well ahead of investments by the rest of the world. In others, they apparently "missed the boat", gaining access to markets much later than the average foreign investor. Finally, German companies reacted to the Asian crisis in a much more volatile manner than did other investors. At any rate, the agglomeration variable is not robust against the inclusion of other variables in the Asian case. The positive coefficient of *DEBT* should not come as a surprise considering the arguments put forward in section 2.2.1.4, because foreign debt ratios were lower on average and thus less critical than in Latin America.

Specification tests for the imposed restrictions – individual country effects, heteroskedastic error terms, cross-sectional correlation and within-group autocorrelation – were run one by one, with each additional restriction being compared to the one marginally less restrictive (e.g. merely heteroskedastic error terms). The statistics of the likelihood ratio test (see section 3.1 for derivation) of no individual country effects, solely homoskedastic error terms and no cross-sectional correlation consistently exceeded the critical values for the χ^2-distribution, thus rejecting the null hypotheses. However, the hypothesis of no autocorrelation could not be rejected, corresponding to the result that ρ was generally less than 0.10.

To check whether regional country sample ought to be estimated separately, a t-test is applied to the Latin American (1) and Asian (2) sub-samples. To test the null hypothesis that the two coefficients are identical, the t-statistic

(8) $t = \frac{\hat{\beta}_j^1 - \hat{\beta}_j^2}{\sqrt{\sigma^2(\hat{\beta}_j^1) + \sigma^2(\hat{\beta}_j^2)}}$ is applied.[117]

If the absolute t-ratio is larger than 1.96, the null hypothesis of equal coefficients is rejected, implying that separate, i.e. region-wide, testing is called for.

The finding that the test statistics for four out of eight variables are strongly significant (see Table 6) indicates that estimating FDI flows to the two continents separately is indeed the appropriate procedure.

Table 6: Testing for Joint Estimation of Coefficients

Variable	t-ratio
GDPCAP	-0.80
PRSCRISK	3.20*
ULC	2.90*
DUTY	2.97*
DEBT	-0.76
AGGLO	3.87*
CFLOW	-1.57
RERVOL	0.70

* denotes rejection of hypothesis

The clearly insignificant t-ratios for three of the remaining variables are due to non-robustness of the variables themselves in both regional cases (*GDPCAP*, *DEBT*, *RERVOL*) and should be disregarded accordingly.

4.2 Sector Level

Making use of the firm-level data available in the Bundesbank FDI database, the above country-level regressions are re-estimated for the manufacturing sector and several of its sub-industries (dependent variable: *FDISEC* – sectoral FDI divided by sectoral GDP), and in the case of sub-sectors, the relationship between capital intensity and political risk. While it would have been interesting

---

117 The general expression for the t-ratio is: $t_k = \frac{b_k - \beta_k}{\sqrt{s^2 S^{kk}}}$; see Greene (2003), p. 51.

to investigate other sectors of the economy such as agriculture or services, data on labor costs in those sectors are available only for some sample countries.

4.2.1 Manufacturing Sector

Inevitably, econometric work on individual emerging market industries suffers from scarcity of comparable sectoral data. The unit labor costs already utilized in the previous regressions and sector-specific cash flows of investing German manufacturers are the only readily accessible data at the industry level. As there was no compelling reason to exclude individual country-level factors, the whole set of remaining "global" variables was included to control for economy-wide effects. Again, an Extreme Bounds Analysis was performed to identify robust variables (see Table 7).

Table 7: Extreme Bounds Analysis for the Manufacturing Sector

Fixed variables: Latin America – *GDPCAP, PRSCRISK*; Asia – *GDPCAP, AGGLO.*
Regressions include the fixed variables plus one of those listed below (variables of interest) and three of the pool of remaining variables at a time. Bounds are derived from non-standardized coefficients.

LATIN AMERICA			ASIA		
Variable	Upper bound	Lower bound	Variable	Upper bound	Lower bound
ULC	1.4634	-3.6386	*PRSCRISK* †	0.0036	-0.0102
DUTY	0.1184	-0.0866	*ULC* †	-0.1963	-0.9032
DEBT	2.5657	-3.0846	*DUTY* †	-0.0047	-0.0278
AGGLO	0.4667	-0.0701	*DEBT*	0.1113	-0.4024
CFLOW	0.1125	-0.2455	*CFLOW* †	0.1012	0.0393
RERVOL	1.4781	-0.3341	*RERVOL*	0.0063	-0.3311

† denotes robust variable as defined by the Extreme Bounds Analysis (in addition to the fixed variables listed above)

By and large, the estimation results for the whole manufacturing sector (see Table 8) do not differ greatly from those found at the country level. Again, the PRS country risk variable turns out to be robustly positive for the Latin American sub-sample, being joined in this respect by *GDPCAP* (significantly negative), while *AGGLO* and *DUTY* lose their previous significance. For Asia, all variables found robust at the country level as well as *AGGLO* and *GDPCAP* pass the robustness check for the manufacturing sector. Interestingly, while *PRSCRISK* and *RERVOL* now display a negative sign for that region, *GDPCAP* becomes highly significantly positive, carrying by far the greatest weight in the regressions. The joint significance of unit labor costs and per-capita GDP indicates that while "cheap labor" is an important determinant of FDI flows from Germany, the Asian manufacturing market is an attractive location for German investors in its own right.

Specification tests yielded results comparable to those at the country level, except for the one on autocorrelation in the Latin American sample. For regressions (9) and (10), the hypothesis of no autocorrelation in the residuals was rejected – a logical result given a common AR(1) coefficient of $\rho = -0.201$. Accordingly, the estimations for the Latin American sample include the aforementioned adjustment mechanism to incorporate first-order autocorrelation.

Table 8: Estimations for the Manufacturing Sectors of Latin America and Asia

FGLS estimation, with individual country effects, adjusted for heteroskedasticity and cross-sectional correlation

Dependent variable: *FDISEC*; number of observations: 60 / 80

	LATIN AMERICA		ASIA	
	(9)	(10)	(11)	(12)
GDPCAP	-0.435 (-2.32)**	-0.109 (-2.48)**	1.206 (13.72)***	0.984 (8.34)***
PRSCRISK	0.218 (3.13)***	0.160 (3.97)***	-0.094 (-3.90)***	
ULC	-0.221 (-1.39)		-0.092 (-3.87)***	-0.153 (-5.72)***
DUTY	0.076 (0.83)		-0.301 (-6.95)***	-0.161 (-3.24)***
DEBT	-0.019 (-0.24)		-0.098 (-2.60)**	
AGGLO	0.214 (2.03)**		-0.412 (-5.82)***	-0.419 (-5.18)***
CFLOW(sec)	-0.072 (-1.22)		0.138 (7.09)***	0.138 (6.09)***
RERVOL	0.048 (1.05)		-0.096 (-6.31)***	
PseudoR^2	0.32	0.32	0.97	0.86

Note: z-values in parentheses; *** = significant at the 1% level, ** = significant at the 5% level, * = significant at the 10% level

4.2.2 Sub-Sectors in Manufacturing

It has been argued that capital-intensive industries – measured by fixed investment per employee – are more sensitive to shifts in political risks because of considerable plant-specific sunk costs. Agarwal et al. (1991, p. 85) contend that "the risk of selective expropriation is related to the technological diversity of FDI that renders industry-specific factors important for the expropriation decision." Lehmann (1999, p. 20), studying the capital expenditures of U.S. affiliates in the chemical and electronics sectors of lower-income countries, finds that the coefficient of political risk is larger for the relatively capital-intensive chemical industry. This finding along with other evidence[118] appears to be consistent with the real option theory that stipulates the negative influence of an restrictive investment regime on investment decisions of foreign investors.

According to Lehmann's model, investors face an incentive to delay an investment abroad the greater the taxes on local production and the higher the probability of a reversal of initial investment liberalization. Therefore, a credible policy with regard to maintaining a favorable investment environment is needed to stimulate firm owners to go ahead with sizable capital expenditures. Viewed from this angle, it is clear that political risk will exert a negative stimulus to investment in cases of large entry costs in terms of outlays for plant construction.[119] On the other hand, so-called footloose industries such as electronics with comparatively low set-up costs and, correspondingly, high locational flexibility will favor a cost-efficient production environment, i.e. good infrastructure and low labor costs. In turn, as such investment is vertical in nature and re-export of assembled products is intended, host country market size or purchasing power should be of secondary importance.[120]

German firm-level investment data confirm Lehmann's observation of sizable differences in capital endowment per worker (measured in thousands of Deutsche Mark (DM), Germany's currency preceding the Euro), as can be inferred from the following table.

[118] Among studies of sectoral FDI flows, Froot and Stein (1991) find negative correlations between FDI inflows to 13 separate U.S. industries and the real value of the US dollar. The result for the (capital-intensive) chemical industry turns out to be the strongest within the manufacturing sector.

[119] See Lehmann (1999), p. 9.

[120] See Wheeler and Mody (1992), p. 69.

Table 9: Capital Intensity of German Manufacturing Sectors (Sample Countries)

Region	Industry	Fixed assets per worker (1990-99 average; in DM 1000s)
Latin America	Chemicals (CHE)	71,230
	Information/communication technologies (ICT)[121]	33,632
	Machinery and equipment (MAE)	43,586
Asia	Chemicals (CHE)	73,012
	Information/communication technologies (ICT)[121]	35,553
	Machinery and equipment (MAE)	29,449

The chemical sector is compared to each of the other two industries in terms of the significance of the appropriate political risk variable. Here, *PRSADMIN* is selected because it depicts the occurrence of unfavorable action by the host country's authorities to the *immediate detriment* of investors. Worsening scores should act as a deterrent to FDI flows of capital-intensive industries. Along the lines of the above sector estimations, regressions are run for the three sub-sectors listed above, using as controls the same country-level exogenous variables with the exception of sub-sector cash flows and wages. Unit labor costs had to be replaced by real wages as information on sub-sector productivity was not available.[122]

The regression results in Tables 10 and 11 confirm the hypothesis that investors in capital-intensive industries react more decisively to variations in the investment climate than do those in the more labor-intensive information/ communication technology (ICT) sector. In both regions, the regression coefficients on administrative risk confirm the postulated differences between the chemical and the other two sectors, perhaps with the seeming exception of ICT in Latin America for which the coefficient is significant at the 5% level. Still, the hypothesis holds as the standardized beta coefficient for the chemical sector is twice as high as the one for ICT, apart from the slight difference in

[121] Including the sub-sector "Manufacturing of equipment for the production and distribution of electricity".

[122] This certainly represents a limitation, and at first glance this bias seems to enter into the results of the sub-sector regressions for Latin America with *RWAGE* being significantly positive in each case (see Table 8). However, tentative regressions for Latin America (not shown here) incorporating real wages *adjusted for overall growth of value added in manufacturing* (i.e. not differentiated by sub-sector, which also adds a certain bias) did not reveal major differences to the regressions reported in Table 8: the coefficients of *RWAGE* for CHE and MAE kept their positive significance levels, and only the coefficient for ICT, while remaining positive, turned insignificant.

significance levels. The results for MAE consistently conform to the hypothesis with the outcome being insignificant in both cases. No clear pattern emerges for the other control variables which may owe something to the possibility that country-level variables do not pick up characteristics of the sub-sectors.

Table 10: Estimations for Latin America at the Sub-Sector Level

FGLS estimation, with individual country effects, adjusted for heteroskedasticity and cross-sectional correlation
Dependent variable: *FDISUBSEC*; number of observations: 60

	(13) CHE	(14) ICT	(15) MAE[123]
PRSADMIN	3.427	1.686	0.391
	(3.57)***	(2.22)**	(0.94)
GDPCAP	0.573	2.488	-0.122
	(0.27)	(1.50)	(-0.12)
RWAGE(subsec)	6.673	7.712	2.680
	(3.71)***	(2.45)**	(2.53)**
DUTY	-0.152	0.849	1.207
	(0.19)	(0.50)	(2.67)***
DEBT	-0.427	-2.070	0.741
	(-0.73)	(-2.08)**	(1.89)*
AGGLO	-3.155	-2.159	0.009
	(-2.88)***	(-2.79)***	(0.02)
CFLOW(subsec)	0.793	-0.151	-0.452
	(0.87)	(-0.32)	(-1.11)
RERVOL	1.606	0.316	-0.168
	(2.44)**	(0.42)	(-0.54)
PseudoR^2	0.61	0.36	0.31

Note: z-values in parentheses; *** = significant at the 1% level, ** = significant at the 5% level, * = significant at the 10% level

[123] As in regressions (9) and (10), the hypothesis of no autocorrelation in the residuals was rejected (ρ = -0.384). Hence, the estimation for MAE in the Latin American sample countries again includes adjustment for first-order autocorrelation.

Table 11: Estimations for Asia at the Sub-Sector Level

FGLS estimation, with individual country effects, adjusted for heteroskedasticity and cross-sectional correlation
Dependent variable: *FDISUBSEC*; number of observations: 50/60 (see below)

	(16) CHE	(17) ICT	(18) MAE
PRSADMIN	2.181 (3.34)***	0.109 (0.75)	-0.664 (-1.12)
GDPCAP	3.669 (1.49)	-0.322 (-0.39)	-1.680 (-0.56)
RWAGE(subsec)	0.595 (0.20)	2.102 (1.66)	-6.870 (-1.86)*
DUTY	5.473 (2.80)***	0.651 (1.99)*	-1.253 (-1.04)
DEBT	6.091 (4.86)***	0.364 (1.56)	-1.850 (-2.72)***
AGGLO	3.021 (1.69)*	-1.568 (-2.43)**	5.723 (2.98)***
CFLOW(subsec)	0.032 (0.07)	-0.896 (-4.90)***	0.117 (0.25)
RERVOL	-1.245 (-2.01)**	-0.188 (-2.34)**	2.028 (5.85)***
PseudoR^2	0.56	0.68	0.61
Number of observations	50	60	50
Sample countries	India, Korea, Malaysia, Philippines, Thailand	India, Korea, Malaysia, Philippines, Singapore, Thailand	India, Korea, Malaysia, Philippines, Singapore

Note: z-values in parentheses; *** = significant at the 1% level, ** = significant at the 5% level, * = significant at the 10% level

5 Conclusions of Chapter II

The contribution of this chapter to the FDI literature lies in an innovative definition of an investment flow variable and in the affirmation that the issue of country risk, and in particular of political/administrative risk, does matter in the case of German FDI flows to Latin American and Asian emerging markets in the 1990s.

As to the former, the endeavor to virtuously combine fully-consolidated FDI data from the Bundesbank stock statistics with the evident merits of considering flow data yielded a quasi-flow variable embodying first differences of annual direct investment stocks corrected for effective participation rates, previously included balance-sheet depreciation and subsequently repatriated profits. Put plainly, this new variable seeks to emulate overall FDI flows – unavailable from the balance of payments – at near-market prices and pursuant to the IMF's directional principle as well as the comprehensive OECD benchmark definition of foreign direct investment.

Regarding empirical results, the regression outcome for the size-adjusted FDI flow variable confirmed the widely-held hypothesis that a high degree of economic and political risk is detrimental to cross-border equity participation. Aiming to put this verdict on a broader foundation, the study used two professional country risk indices, both of which turned out to be highly significant for the Latin American and Asian sub-samples. This finding thus confirmed the presumption that international investors indeed perceive impending changes in the macroeconomic and regulatory environment.

Subdividing country risk into its components, it was found that economic risk represents the main driving force behind this unequivocal result, whereas the evidence for headline political risk is best described as erratic owing to its disparate individual elements. While, for both regions, the measure of administrative quality alias corruption and malfeasance by the host government was strongly associated with marginal FDI inflows, the variable of host country political stability turned out insignificant or even displayed a negative sign. Investors' dislike of unwarranted government behavior, inter alia excessive payment of bribes, restrictions on intra-company transfers, or outright expropriation, was especially pronounced in the Asian sample countries, with the administrative risk variable being robust against the inclusion of other controls.

With respect to these control variables, the regression results differed markedly between the two regions. In Latin America, FDI inflows throughout the last decade are to be called "market-seeking" in that German firms were apparently impelled to establish a presence abroad by the necessity to overcome critical host country tariff barriers and, in a sense, to react in a timely manner to rising direct investment on the part of foreign competitors. By contrast, German multinationals accessing the Asian markets seemed to have been in search of low labor and financing costs as well as an open trade regime since their direct investment is arguably vertical in nature. These differences caused a test on identity of coefficients between regions to be rejected, implying that factors determining FDI flows differed between Latin America and Asia. Hence, as far as Germany is concerned, there does not seem to be a unique pattern of foreign direct investment across regions of emerging market economies. Incidentally, real exchange rate volatility apparently propelled German FDI in Asia, and, in fact, in none of the country-level regressions did this measure end up being significantly negative. These findings tend to strengthen the hypothesized positive impact of exchange rate fluctuations on the willingness of investors to establish production facilities abroad.

In addition, the availability of firm-level data in the FDI database allowed for sectoral and sub-sectoral analysis. Direct investment flows to manufacturing sectors abroad generally mimicked the characteristics of those at the country level with the main exception of GDP per capita being negatively related to inflows to Latin America and strongly positively related to those to Asia. Moreover, the measure of trade barriers lost its significance in the Latin American sample, while for the Asian countries the agglomeration variable then also passed the robustness test.

Lastly, the compelling hypothesis that capital-intensive industries react more strongly to deteriorating investment conditions was confirmed by German FDI data, as the administrative political risk variable displayed strongly positive coefficients in the regressions for the capital-intensive chemical sector in both regions while those for the more labor-centered information/communication technology industry were found to be insignificant each time.

On the whole, researchers studying foreign direct investment in emerging market economies ought to take increased account of non-traditional variables such as country risk or agglomeration effects. The econometric results of this study affirm that the discernible trend towards factoring in measures of the regulatory environment facing foreign investors is clearly called for. As "soft" locational factors become more material in the eyes of investors, analyses incorporating qualitative assessments of host countries are likely to gain further prominence in FDI research.

Appendix to Chapter II

Table 12: Estimations for *Absolute* FDI Flows at the Country Level

FGLS estimation, with individual country effects, adjusted for heteroskedasticity and cross-sectional correlation
Dependent variable: *FDIFLOW*; number of observations = 60 (Latin America), 80 (Asia)

	LATIN AMERICA	ASIA
GDP	401467.1	804215.1
	(2.32)**	(5.38)***
PRSCRISK	161743.85	622329.8
	(2.46)**	(7.76)***
ULC	128567.9	54335.3
	(1.46)	(0.71)
DUTY	84559.7	203260.0
	(0.95)	(1.49)
DEBT	-46180.9	325552.7
	(0.78)	(2.85)***
AGGLO	100.7	490867.4
	(0.00)	(3.78)***
CFLOW	55865.13	-13074.4
	(1.08)	(0.23)
RERVOL	15233.9	177001.7
	(0.21)	(2.30)**
pseudoR^2	0.28	0.69

Note: z-values in parentheses; *** = significant at the 1% level, ** = significant at the 5% level, * = significant at the 10% level

Table 13: List of Exogenous Variables Employed

Variables	Definition	Dimension/Timing	Further explanations	Source
Market size				
GDP	Real absolute GDP	in constant 1995 US$ (logs)		World Development Indicators (WDI)
GDPCAP	Real GDP per capita (PPP)	in constant 1995 US$ (logs)	Purchasing Power Parity-adjusted	World Bank WDI
Country Risk				
PRSCRISK	Country risk	January of following year	50% Political Risk 25% Economic Risk Current Account Balance (7.5%),GDP/capita (2.5%), GDP growth, Inflation, Budget Balance (each 5%) 25% Financial Risk Current Account/Exports (7.5%), Import Cover of Currency Reserves (2.5%), Foreign Debt/GDP, Debt Service/Exports, Exchange Rate Stability (each 5%)	Political Risk Services (PRS): International Country Risk Guide (ICRG)
→PRSERISK	Economic Risk	Financial/economic risk only		PRS-ICRG
→PRSPRISK	Political Risk	January of following year	PRSADMIN+PRSSTAB	PRS-ICRG
→PRSADMIN	Efficiency of bureaucracy	January of following year	18% Bureaucracy Quality 27% Corruption in Government 55% Investment Profile	PRS-ICRG
→PRSSTAB	Stability of government	January of following year	20% Law & Order 40% Government Stability 40% Internal Conflict	PRS-ICRG
EMCRISK	Country Risk/ Macroeconomic Risk (without Political Risk)	Year-end average: sum of scores for September and March divided by two; values were rebased for the years 1990 and 1991	25% Political Risk 25% Economic Performance (GNP per capita etc.) 10% Debt Indicators 10% Debt in default/rescheduled 10% Credit Ratings 5% Access to Bank Finance 5% Access to short-term finance 5% Access to capital markets 5% Discount on Forfaiting	**Euromoney**, various editions

(Table 13 continued)

Labor costs				
ULC	Unit labor costs	Labor costs p.a. per worker/ gross value added per worker	Labor costs and value added in manufacturing	ILO: Labor costs WDI: Value added
RWAGE (subsec)	Real wages	Real wages p.a.	Real wages in manufacturing sub-sectors	ILO: Wage data
Degree of Openness				
DUTY	Effective taxation of trade	Taxes on international trade (% of current gov't revenue)		World Bank WDI
OPEN	Trade Intensity	Total Trade/GDP, adjusted for Real GDP per capita and Population		World Bank WDI
Foreign Debt				
DEBT	Foreign indebtedness	External Debt/GDP (in current US$)		World Bank WDI
Agglomeration				
AGGLO	Present and past FDI flows	Three-year moving average of total (global) FDI inflows/host country GDP	Uses present year and the two previous years	World Bank WDI
Financing conditions				
CFLOW (sec/subsec)	Cash flow of German parent	Cash flow (t-1)/total corporate assets	Aggregated at country, sector or sub-sector level	Deutsche Bundesbank
Exchange rate (volatility)				
RER	Bilateral real exchange rate	RER (host country vs. Germany)		IMF (International Financial Statistics)
RERVOL	Volatility of bilateral real exchange rate (RER)	Two-year moving average of squared percentage changes in the bilateral RER	Uses the two previous years	IMF (International Financial Statistics) and own calculations
Structural reforms				
STRUCT	Index of structural reforms *only for Latin America*	Average score	Arithmetic average of 5 individual indices (trade, financial, tax, labor market reforms and privatization)	Lora (2001)

Chapter III: Foreign Bank Entry into Emerging Economies – An Empirical Assessment of the Determinants and Risks Predicated on German FDI Data

1 Introduction to Chapter III

Over the past decade, a large number of countries, especially those in emerging markets, opted to open their banking sectors to foreign equity participation. Since the onset of this type of financial liberalization, foreign direct investment of banks domiciled in industrialized countries has grown strongly, attracting the attention of researchers. Studies on the locational choices of multinational banks have gradually proliferated in the empirical literature. There is now an established body of evidence on commonly agreed determinants of banking FDI. These investigations highlight the role of market integration, causing banks to establish foreign subsidiaries when their customers go international (via trade or direct investment), as well as of locational factors abroad such as financial sector development or the lack of competition tantamount to large banking margins.

Several studies, most prominently perhaps the one by Focarelli and Pozzolo (2001), use microeconometric methods to explore which banks expand abroad and have found that the size of banks, their efficiency, and restrictions on banking at home are generally decisive factors.[123] In recent papers, Buch and Lipponer (2004a, 2004b) furnish micro-level, i.e. bank-specific evidence that bank size, profitability and the degree of internationalization are unquestionably positively correlated with the decision to enter foreign banking markets. Even so, most studies analyze FDI by banks between developed economies and, thus, do not consider the distinctive framework concerning various risk factors which is prevalent in emerging markets. Another common limitation is that many studies use relatively dated time series which inhibits analysis of the changed financial market conditions in the aftermath of the Asian crisis.

This study aims at closing this gap in the empirical literature by investigating the factors crucial to the locational decisions of multinational German banks in selected emerging markets between 1994 and 2001. Specifically, emphasis is placed on testing variables of macroeconomic and financial sector risk. The

[123] See Clarke et al. (2001), pp. 10-13, for a survey of the empirical literature.

latter is measured by a crisis variable taken from the literature on "early warning indicators", which, as it turns out, strongly impacts FDI by banks.

As dependent variable, quasi-flows derived from differences in adjusted FDI stocks are used. These are the "quasi-flows" of FDI capital that are used in Chapter II. Aggregate German banking FDI flows to the 20 countries in the sample quintupled during the sample period. This finding also holds for global FDI flows into emerging banking markets. As Galindo et al. (2002) illustrate, foreign control of local banks in Latin America more than quadrupled throughout the sample period, with the most extreme case being Mexico whose foreign control rate went up from almost zero in 1994 to nearly 80% in 2001. By the end of the sample period, eastern European banking markets were also under majority control by foreign institutions (see Table 19, Appendix III). In Asia, even though FDI inflows were among the largest world-wide, foreign control of local banks was virtually non-existent at the time, which suggests that governments in emerging Asia were keen on opening up to foreign investment capital while retaining control over domestic banks by allowing minority stakes only.

This chapter is structured as follows: The next section discusses theoretical approaches to selecting explanatory variables for foreign banking activity, which reflect the risk-return tradeoff an individual bank faces when maximizing its utility within a two-country portfolio choice model. Section three provides a review of the literature on foreign direct investment in the banking sector with special emphasis on the issues of market openness to FDI and financial system instability. At the end of that section the model is presented along with three sets of exogenous variables that correspond to the theoretical considerations in section two. The empirical analysis is carried out in section four. After presenting stylized facts on the time-varying distribution of FDI stocks of German banks across the sample countries and details on the estimation technique applied, panel estimations are carried out for the whole sample and subsequently broken down by region and time period. The study closes with a brief appraisal of the empirical results in section five.

2 Approaches to Modeling Foreign Banking Activity

Within the literature on FDI of financial services companies, models of banking investments are clearly dominant. While it is possible, in principle, to extend such models to the direct investments of insurance firms, it has to be kept in mind that certain determinants, such as the interest rate spread between loans and deposits, only apply to banking institutions. Most studies take an ad-hoc approach to estimating determinants of FDI. However, even the few structural models of banking FDI – see, for example, Sabi (1988), Buch (1999, 2000) – are relatively straightforward, recurring on the optimization of shares of portfolio investments. Combining the aforementioned approaches and tolerably simplifying them, banks' utility is dependent on expected returns (R^e) and the variability of returns (σ_R^2), such that:[124]

$$(9)\quad U_B = U(R^e, \sigma_R^2), \quad where \frac{\partial U}{\partial R^e} > 0 \quad and \quad \frac{\partial U}{\partial \sigma_R^2} < 0.$$

In a two-country setting, expected (net) returns are calculated as the sum of interest earned on domestic and foreign loans net of interest costs on domestic and foreign deposits, whereas foreign positions are also subject to changes in the exchange rate:

$$(10)\quad E[R^e] = r_L L + (r_L^* + \Delta e)L^* + r_F R - r_D D - (r_D^* - \Delta e)D^*,$$

with r_L (r_L^*) and r_D (r_D^*) being the expected interest rates on domestic (foreign) loans L (L^*) and corresponding deposits D (D^*), respectively, Δe the expected change in the bilateral nominal exchange rate and r_F the interest rate to be earned on a risk-free asset R. Variable administrative costs and the bank's initial wealth are dispensed within this context.

The variance of expected returns for portfolio shares x_i is defined as:[125]

$$(11)\quad \sigma_R^2 = \sum_{m=1}^{4} x_m^2 \sigma_m^2 + 2\sum_{m=1}^{4} \sum_{\substack{n=1 \\ m \neq n}}^{4} x_m x_n \sigma_m \sigma_n \rho_{mn}, \quad where\ x = \begin{pmatrix} x_1 \\ x_2 \\ x_3 \\ x_4 \end{pmatrix} = \begin{pmatrix} L \\ D \\ L^* \\ D^* \end{pmatrix} \quad and \sum x_i \overset{!}{=} 1.$$

with σ and ρ denoting the standard deviation of and the correlation coefficient between portfolio shares, respectively.

[124] See Buch (2000), pp. 5-7.

[125] See Buch (1999), p. 15.

Maximizing the bank's utility subject to the restriction that total loans must not exceed available deposits, while noting that the volatility of returns from abroad also hinges on exchange rate fluctuations, the bank's optimal portfolio is determined as follows:[126]

$$(12)\quad \frac{\partial U_i}{\partial x_i} = \frac{\partial U_i}{\partial E(R^e)} * \frac{\partial E(R^e)}{\partial x_i} + \frac{\partial U_i}{\partial \sigma^2(R^e)} * \frac{\partial \sigma^2(R^e)}{\partial x_i} = 0.$$

Solving for x_i, the optimal portfolio shares turn out to be a function of expected excess returns on loans and deposits (e.g. excess return on loans = $r_L - r_F$), both at home and abroad, and on the degree of risk aversion of the individual bank.

This model, however, neglects the specific framework in which foreign direct investment is carried out. It does not account for costs incurred by entering (or potentially exiting) the market, which, as Galindo et al. (2002) show for Latin America, vary substantially across jurisdictions and do influence foreign banking activity.[127] Nor does the analysis involve the real option value of postponing FDI in favor of continuing to lend to the foreign market. As to the latter factor, a stylized partial equilibrium model exploring the inter-linkages between policy uncertainty, real option value and the timing of FDI at the firm level was recently put forth by Chen and Funke (2003). As a caveat, the authors point out that their microeconomic model cannot be mechanically translated to aggregate investment, as it does not capture the strategic interaction among firms in the sense of early movers prompting similar investment by competitors which would otherwise have chosen to wait it out.[128] Blandón (1998) aims at assessing the importance of timing for direct investment. In a study on FDI in Spain, he shows that it is the banks with the strongest comparative advantages (size, international experience) that enter a new banking market first, lending support to the theory of ownership-specific advantages as an explanation for firms' expanding abroad (see section 3.2.1 below).

Returning to the portfolio choice approach, a distinct drawback concerning the empirical testing of the above model is, typically, the scarce availability of information on the expected rate of returns. This holds true even more for emerging markets, where economic conditions tend to vary greatly. Therefore,

[126] See Buch (1999), p. 17.

[127] The authors report that in the empirical analysis differences in the legal setup of host countries reduce bilateral (foreign) participation in the banking system abroad by at least 13%; see Galindo et al. (2002), pp. 13-15.

[128] See Chen and Funke (2003), p. 14.

appropriate proxies for expected returns need to be derived. In general, it is possible to think of a variety of variables influencing the rate of return. Some are more direct than others, such as the prevailing interest rate spread or real interest rates as well as the degree of competition in the banking market determining whether monopoly rents may be reaped by prospective entrants. Among the variables which have an indirect influence on banks' profitability abroad are those relating to specific beneficial characteristics of a certain location or to the ability of a given bank to capitalize on distinct ownership advantages.

Thus, a linear relationship between expected return and an array of proxy variables for such factors is hypothesized:[129]

$$(13)\quad R^e_{i,t} = \alpha_{i,t} + \sum_{j=1}^{J} \beta \mathbf{I}_{j,i,t} + \sum_{k=1}^{K} \gamma \mathbf{P}_{k,i,t} + \varepsilon_{i,t}\ ,$$

with **I** and **P** denoting vectors of proxy variables for the degree of banks' *internalization* of comparative advantages and their *profitability* (in country i and year t), respectively. The vector **I** can be thought of as representing the ability to provide specific services j to home country clients that local banks abroad could not (see section 3.2.1), while **P** is deemed to depict characteristics (i.e. opportunities, challenges) of local banking markets k.

However, the above model addresses the issue of risk only indirectly, hiding it in the assumed variability of the proxy variables. The degree of risk is an important determinant of whether to enter an emerging market at all and if so, which foreign location to choose. In expanding to developing countries banks expose themselves to risks not present in their domestic markets.[130] If a certain bank relies heavily on income from unstable foreign locations, both borrowers, owing to possible non-renewal of loans, and creditors worried about the safety of deposits may reconsider their relationship with the bank.

Even so, it is the question of whether country risk or financial vulnerability matters for German banks that is at the heart of the present study. To isolate country-specific factors that have a more or less immediate influence on variability of banks' foreign earnings, a set of risk variables is explicitly included in the estimations.

---

129 See Sabi (1988), p. 435.

130 See Williams (1997), pp. 85-86.

3 Review of the Literature and Hypothesized Variables

3.1 Endogenous Variable Measuring Foreign Banking Activity

Of the 17 empirical studies on foreign banking activity reviewed here, less than half actually consider outright foreign direct investment by banks (Sagari (1992), Buch and Lapp (1998), Yamori (1998), Buch (2000), Moshirian (2001)[131]) or investigate the incidence of foreign bank entry at the firm level by employing correlation analysis or probit estimation (Cardone-Riportella et al. (2000), Focarelli and Pozzolo (2001)). The remaining studies use as a dependent variable total assets of banks' foreign subsidiaries (Nigh et al. (1986), Sabi (1988), Goldberg and Johnson (1990), Miller and Parkhe (1998), Moshirian and Van der Laan (1998), Galindo et al. (2002)), the number of offices abroad (Goldberg and Johnson (1990), Brealey and Kaplanis (1996), Miller and Parkhe (1998), Papi and Revoltella (2000, variable: number of "FDI initiatives")), foreign banks' share in the host market (Claessens et al. (1998)) or subsidiaries' total lending (Seth et al. (1998)). In a sense, the use of total banking assets is the most comprehensive measure of foreign banking activity, and FDI represents – from a purely accounting perspective – merely a subset of total assets. Still, each concept depicts reasonably well the degree of cross-border funds supplied by parent companies which are predominately located in industrial countries.

The endogenous variable used in this study is the year-on-year difference in FDI stocks (direct and indirect holdings) of the German banking sector adjusted for deviating reporting dates, actual participation rates for indirect participating interests as well as repatriated profits, relative to host-country GDP.[132] This normalized variable has the merit of automatically deflating the time series and accounting for exchange rate effects while at the same time largely eliminating unwarranted non-stationarity in the data.

131 The study by Moshirian (2001) uses merely balance-of-payments data when defining German FDI. This is methodically questionable as doing so fails to account for indirect participating interests (i.e. those via a holding company, possibly located in a country other than the host country to be examined). Then again, other studies do not bother to explain the derivation of FDI stocks or flows at all.

132 The definition used here includes asset management corporations, leasing companies, mutual funds and holding companies making direct investments. For a detailed description of the definition of FDI and of the various adjustment procedures, see Chapter II, section 2.1.1. In the present study, no correction for balance-sheet depreciation was carried out because the share of fixed assets in banks' balance-sheets is traditionally low in comparison to the manufacturing sector.

It would have been desirable to relate the FDI flow to the size of the banking sector in the host country but, as it turns out, the national accounts of several sample countries include in the definition of the banking sector the real estate industry or personal services in the financial sector without detailing the sub-components. While this limitation could, in principle, be tolerated, the fact that the Russian statistics, as provided by the IMF, include unrelated activities, *inter alia* subsoil resources and exploration, in financial services prohibits using the size of the financial sector as a normalization variable.

3.2 Exogenous Variables Considered for Banking FDI

3.2.1 "Follow the Client" Motive

As banking is an information-intensive industry, foreign banks can differentiate themselves from their counterparts in the host country by offering complex and specialized services to their home country corporate customers. The ability to custom-tailor these services – financing, information brokerage and transaction banking – is frequently rooted in a longstanding relationship with the client. Over the years, banks gain proprietary information about their clients' particular financial needs, the knowledge of which is – at least initially – unavailable to host country institutions. The flow of information enables the bank to assess loan renewals at low marginal cost because of earlier assessment work. This lower marginal cost translates into a competitive advantage over incumbent local banks. As informational asymmetries mean that the value of this type of information is difficult to price by potential buyers (i.e. other banks), market failure arises: The internal information cannot be traded on markets and therefore needs to be exploited by the institutions possessing it. In the literature (Grubel (1977)), this rationale has been termed "defensive expansion". To prevent multinational corporations from soliciting these local or other competitors from foreign countries, banks are impelled to *follow the client* by opening an office (branch, subsidiary) abroad themselves in order to defend their unique bank-client relationship.[133]

[133] See Williams (1997), p. 86, and, on the "competitive edge"-argument, also Blandón (1998), p. 8.

Also, foreign banks tend to provide easier access to hard currency or international credit and are frequently perceived as more secure than local banks. This exploitation of ownership-specific advantages[134] in terms of differentiated products, advanced technology or superior human skills constitutes a distinct intangible asset.[135] Once again, these factors are not readily tradable and are more difficult to emulate than relatively standardized, less information-intensive products, thereby endowing foreign banks with a longer term competitive edge over competitors.[136] Note that foreign bank entry occurs despite the possibility to serve the client from the headquarters or via correspondent banks because by having a presence abroad, the bank can react faster and more efficiently to whatever needs the client may have in a given situation abroad.

In the literature, virtually every study incorporates as explanatory variables outward FDI of the non-financial sector and/or the degree of trade linkages between the home and host economies.

3.2.1.1 FDI of the Non-Financial Sector

All but two of the studies reviewed account for FDI outflows of the non-financial sector (in some cases, manufacturing FDI or total outward FDI), either in flows or stocks, depending on the characteristics of the endogenous variable. Most studies indeed find a strongly positive relationship between non-financial FDI and the corresponding stakes of the banking sector. Notably, the studies by Buch and Lapp (1998), Buch (2000), Moshirian (2001) and Brealey and Kaplanis (1996) stand out because they put data on German outflows to the test. While the first three papers find a positive link, the last-named study reports an

[134] There is a controversy in the literature (see overview by Williams (1997), pp. 82-84) between proponents of *Dunning's* (1977) *eclectic theory*, which stresses the necessity for firms to have monopolistic advantages (concerning ownership, location, internalization) in order to imperil local incumbents' position, and adherents of the *Coasian view*, which explains the existence of firms by pointing to transaction costs causing firms to prefer ownership of assets rather than incurring costs of contracting in the market. The former theory is firmly grounded on ownership characteristics (generation of assets) which are subsequently internalized (asset use), while the latter emphasizes cost advantages (or rather, the trade-off between total costs and total benefits) of internalizing operations. In other words, the difference in opinion is rooted in the question of whether market failure is caused by incomplete markets or excessive transaction costs. In reality, the distinctions between both paradigms may be smaller than hypothesized by both camps, especially when markets for information-intensive assets are underdeveloped to begin with as is likely to be the case with emerging markets.

[135] See Sagari (1992), p. 98, and, similarly, Blandón (1998), p. 7.

[136] See Williams (1997), p. 81.

insignificant coefficient for (total) outward German FDI to both industrialized and developing countries. As a caveat, it should be mentioned that Brealey and Kaplanis use as dependent variable simply the number of foreign bank offices, and that the regression is a cross-section for 1992 and can therefore only be considered a snapshot view. Fittingly, Miller and Parkhe (1998) offer panel evidence on the link between foreign banking assets/offices and total U.S. FDI in *developing countries only*: while for total banking assets the coefficient is insignificant, the results for foreign branches and subsidiaries turn out to be highly positively significant.

Most prominently, the study by Seth et al. (1998) is exclusively devoted to investigating the relationship between lending of foreign banks in the U.S. and the financing patterns of fellow non-financial firms operating there. It is hypothesized that if there is to be a "follow the client" behavior, the foreign subsidiaries should mainly be serving their home-country clients' financing needs and not engage in lending to other, presumably American, customers. The authors are able to refute the hypothesis for banking subsidiaries from all G7-countries save German institutions. Showing that bank borrowing by US affiliates of German multinationals exceeded total lending by German banks' subsidiaries in all sample years (1981-1992), the authors are led to conclude that this is "the only group of banks for which we can say it is possible that they exclusively followed home-country customers".[137] Conflicting evidence is presented by Moshirian and Van der Laan (1998): U.S., U.K. and German FDI of the non-banking sector is each shown to be negatively correlated to *foreign assets of banks from the respective country*. However, this finding does not entirely contradict the other results as it may well be that the assets of *foreign subsidiaries* (or other more-than-10% interests), being merely a subset of total (consolidated) assets, move in line with non-financial FDI. Actually, Moshirian, in a later study (2001), now finds a positive sign for German non-banking FDI when relating it to *total FDI in banking* as a dependent variable. Consequently, a positive sign of the non-financial FDI variable, *FDINONBK*, is expected for the present study. The variable is lagged by one period to account for banks' reaction time in following the clients abroad and also to forestall simultaneity bias.

[137] Seth et al. (1998), p. 14. This effect, of course, is shown to apply to a highly developed banking sector and may not be present in emerging markets.

3.2.1.2 Trade Linkages

Analogous to the relationship between banking and non banking FDI, trade links are deemed to propel foreign bank entry.[138] It has been argued that without the physical presence of banks shepherding trade operations of domestic exporters abroad, most trade transactions would appear to become rather difficult or not viable at all.[139]

Empirical evidence generally supports the theoretical notion that strong trade links will foster banking FDI in the destination country. This holds true for banks from Germany (studies by Buch (2000) as well as Moshirian), the U.S. (Goldberg and Johnson, Moshirian), the U.K. (Moshirian), Japan (Yamori), Spain and Finland (Cardone-Riportella et al.), and for all of the OECD countries (Focarelli and Pozzolo) investing abroad. FDI inflows to transition countries are shown by Papi and Revoltella (2000) to be driven by strong trade links as well. Conversely, Miller and Parkhe (1998) find an insignificant or even negative sign for U.S. bilateral trade with developing countries when relating it to banks' total assets or number of offices, respectively. In light of the overall evidence, a positive coefficient is hypothesized for *TRADE*, the variable measuring total bilateral German trade with the sample countries (relative to host country GDP and also lagged).

3.2.2 Market Characteristics

3.2.2.1 Host Country Income

Ideally, the size of the host country's banking market, measured by sectoral GDP or loan volume, should feed into the investing bank's utility function because a larger market offers the potential for exploiting economies of scale and thus for decreasing marginal costs of production.[140] Since, in the present study, FDI flows have already been adjusted for market size by relating them to host country GDP, adding an exogenous size variable would make little sense,

[138] Interestingly enough, an alternative measure for capturing trade relations is geographical distance, as trade tends to be strongest with neighboring countries. In the study of Papi and Revoltella (2000), distance is found to be insignificant for FDI inflows to transition countries, either because of little between-group variation in the sample or because total trade is simultaneously accounted for in their regressions. As an alternative measure Blandón (1998) suggests cultural proximity, notably a dummy variable for countries of FDI origin that belong to the "same cultural group" as the host country, Spain. Blandon's regression shows similarity in culture to foster FDI inflows into the Spanish banking sector.

[139] See Sagari (1992), p. 96, footnote 4.

[140] See Sabi (1988), p. 437.

even less so considering the fact that, as mentioned above, the definition of the financial services sector is far from consistent across countries. In order to still account for the host countries' purchasing power and thus demand for banking services, *real GDP per capita* is included in the regressions. This measure aims at capturing between-group effects in terms of diverging national income levels as well as within-group growth effects by having those levels vary throughout the sample period.

Most studies reviewed here incorporate a certain type of income variable, be it real absolute GDP (Brealey and Kaplanis, Moshirian and Van der Laan) or GDP per capita (Buch and Lapp, Buch (2000), Claessens et al., Papi and Revoltella, Sagari, Yamori) and largely find a strongly positive relation to FDI or foreign banking assets. The only exceptions to this finding are the studies by Nigh et al. (variable: manufacturing production), and Sagari, which report insignificant regression outcomes, and by Goldberg and Johnson, who, remarkably, find negative coefficients for per capita income when measuring the determinants of US banking activity abroad (assets/number of foreign branches, from the early 1970s to the mid-1980s). Given the empirical evidence, in this study a positive sign for the income variable *GDPCAP* (in logs) is expected.

3.2.2.2 International Financial Centers

The aspect of market size may still be captured by trying to determine whether a given banking market sector fulfills certain characteristics of a typical international financial center that would almost automatically attract foreign banks. The issue as to what exactly constitutes a financial center is tackled by authors in quite different ways. Methods range from not detailing the methodology at all (Cardone-Riportella et al.) or simply, yet correctly, stating that certain localities (Hong Kong, Singapore and the like) *are* such centers (Buch and Lapp) to using either an adequate proxy variable (Focarelli and Pozzolo: ratio of stock market capitalization to GDP) or econometric modeling (Brealey and Kaplanis: regressing the "abnormal" number of banks on measures of capital market activity; their results for financial centers are also used by Buch (2000)).[141]

[141] Brealey and Kaplanis (1998, pp. 590-594) go about determining financial centers as follows: Upon gaining residuals from a previous regression of banks' foreign presence on exports to the host country and its GDP, the authors regress these residuals on two measures of capital market activity (syndicated loans, value of eurobonds) and find that these measures alone are able to explain between 37% and 49% of the variation in the "abnormal" number of banks domiciled in foreign countries.

Not surprisingly in light of the diverging approaches, the empirical evidence on financial centers is mixed. Cardone-Riportella et al. (2000) report a strongly positive coefficient for Spanish banks expanding abroad, whereas they fail to find such an effect in the corresponding case of Finnish banks. Focarelli and Pozzolo (2001) argue that the negative signs they report for the market capitalization variable are due to an apparent saturation of financial markets, making it unattractive to expand abroad. Arguably the most relevant are the results presented by Buch and Lapp (1998), and Buch (2000), since the authors analyze data on German banking FDI: Their findings from a pooled time-series regression for FDI outflows to developed countries during 1985-1995 and a similar cross-section regression for 1997, respectively, suggest a strong pull effect exercised by financial centers in the sample.

In the present study, the ratio of market capitalization of listed companies relative to GDP of the host economy, *FINCTR*, is used to capture the incidence of financial centers. This discrete variable was preferred to the dummy variable approach as it exhibits considerable variation over time and is, thus, more appropriate in a panel setting.

3.2.2.3 Banking Margin/Competition

Returning to the considerations in section two, various measures for banking market attractiveness or the level of competition have been suggested in the literature. Among these is an elaborate approach by Moshirian and Van der Laan (1998) to measuring the interest-rate differential of lending rates between markets at home and abroad. Problematically, their calculation is based on both expected inflation and exchange rates, and consequently requires econometric estimation of forward rates as proxies for these future rates. The authors find that a negative differential (i.e. higher rates abroad than at home) is positively correlated with foreign assets of, inter alia, German banks. In a later study, Moshirian (2001) uses a cost of capital differential of German banks vis-à-vis host countries, represented by the "required" after-tax interest rate spread (lending minus deposit rates, adjusted for corporate tax rates). His empirical findings suggest that a lower cost of capital structure at home than abroad contributes to German banking FDI. In a similar vein, Blandón (1998) regards the interest margin not only as a measure of market attractiveness but first and foremost as an indicator of the degree of banking competitiveness (the variable in question is insignificant, however).

Other studies simply focus on the signaling effect of high interest margins in terms of profit opportunities. Papi and Revoltella (2000), in a study of banking

FDI inflows to transition countries, report a positive coefficient for the spread on bank interest rates. Yamori (1998) as well as Claessens et al. (1998) consider the definition of the real-interest-rate variable used in the present study, *REALINT*, namely lending rates adjusted for inflation rates abroad. The intuition behind this choice is that, in the absence of capital controls, banks freely decide whether to fund the operations from home or abroad. They can be expected to choose the minimum of interbank rates at home (e.g. LIBOR) and foreign deposit (interbank) rates (adjusted for *expected* inflation or, if solely calculating in home currency, *expected* exchange rate changes). The outcome of this choice is very difficult to track consistently. It seems therefore justified to concentrate on the deflated lending rates abroad as a measure of both profit opportunities and (lack of) competition in the foreign banking sectors. Nevertheless, to check for validity, an alternative profitability variable, *MARGIN*, is computed:

$$(15) \qquad MARGIN_{i,t} = \left(\frac{(1 + l_{i,t}) - (1 + d_{i,t})}{(1 + \Delta NER_{i,t})} \right)$$

where l and d denote average lending and deposit rates (per cent), respectively, and ΔNER is the change in the year-end exchange rate (with $\Delta NER>0$ representing a depreciation of the host country's currency against the Deutsche Mark). The assumption underlying the additional adjustment for exchange rate movements is that the banking spread may not fully incorporate excessive inflation (as seems to have been the case with Brazil in the late 1990s). To obtain the rate that is relevant to a German bank, the host country's banking spread needs to be adjusted for the loss in value due to depreciation of its currency.

3.2.2.4 Openness of the Foreign Banking Market

Host country banking markets are often oligopolistic in nature, and perfect competition is the exception to the rule. These oligopolies are commonly the outcome of barriers to entry which a foreign multinational bank may be deterred by or, conversely, seek to exploit. In fact, this market characteristic may be called a double-edged sword because the benefit of operating in a competition-restricted environment can only be reaped after clearing specific hurdles imposed by the government to protect the domestic banking system. Even if a foreign bank is granted entry, it may still suffer from cumbersome regulations or uneven government treatment, in which case it will operate at a disadvantage compared to local banks.[142] One may assume that the deterring effect of banking restrictions applying to foreign institutions outweigh the conceivable opportunities presenting themselves upon entry into such over-regulated markets.

Most studies on banking FDI rely on dummy variables in measuring the extent of government interference with market provision of financial services. Surveying the literature, approaches range from simple 0/1 dummies (Nigh et al. (1986), Miller and Parkhe (1998)) or somewhat more elaborate scales (Goldberg and Johnson (1990), Papi and Revoltella (2000), Galindo et al. (2002)) to indices composed of several individual criteria (Sabi (1988)) or even a regulatory matrix with a total of 15 sub-classifications (Sagari (1992)) of which those principal components were tested that might theoretically be relevant to U.S. FDI in banking. Galindo et al. (2002), testing for the impact of various administrative impediments on foreign banks, demonstrate that the assets of their subsidiaries are negatively related to higher regulatory burdens in the host countries and to greater differences in banking regulations between the two countries. Sagari (1992) puts two components to the test: one is aimed at measuring discrimination against foreign banking affiliates, and the other one combines measures of barriers to entry and of operating constraints once inside a country.[143] The overriding result of these empirical studies is that a high degree of such openness is conducive to FDI flows in banking. The only study not finding a positive relationship is by Sabi (1988).

Following Sagari's approach, this study uses two measures of banking freedom, both taken from the Heritage Foundation's Index of Economic Freedom that has been published since 1994.[144] The index's factor #6 ("banking and finance") serves as the chief measure of banking freedom, named *BANKFREE*. It consists of five individual factors: government ownership of banks, restrictions on the ability of foreign banks to open branches and subsidiaries, government influence over the allocation of credit, government regulations and freedom to offer all types of financial services. The original data are transformed so that the high score of 4 applies to countries where government involvement in the financial sector is negligible, very few restrictions on foreign banks exist and banks may engage in all types of financial services (overall: restrictions are "very low"). The most negative score applying to the sample countries is 1, denoting heavy

[142] See Williams (1997), p. 91.

[143] See Sagari (1992), pp. 109-110.

[144] The index is published in last quarter of each year, but in the title appears the following year (e.g. the "2003 index of economic freedom" was published in November 2002).

government involvement and corresponding restrictions. In order to account more explicitly for barriers to entry as they apply to FDI flows, an alternative, more comprehensive openness variable, *OPENNESS*, was formed. It consists of *BANKFREE* and, in addition, incorporates Heritage's factor #5 "capital flows and foreign investment",[145] a composite measure of the government's general attitude to foreign investment. For simplicity and admittedly arbitrarily, equal weights were imposed. Both variables are expected to exhibit a positive coefficient.

3.2.3 Risk Factors

Ultimately, the risk of banks' international operations may be defined as the variability of earnings or, more specifically, the variance of the rate of return on assets or on equity. However, it would be a daunting task to try to compute an average rate of return in the aggregate. Hence, there is a need to devise reasonable proxies for macroeconomic and institutional uncertainty affecting the stability of banking profits. Such an attempt is made by Sabi (1988) who, in the absence of profitability data, uses as a proxy for variability of returns the (lagged) deviation of national income from its longer-term trend. The author fails to find a significant FDI effect of his variable, which at any rate is a relatively crude measure of risk facing foreign investors. More elaborate proxies are in fact devised in the literature, as the following sections show.

3.2.3.1 Country Risk/Political Risk

The issue of country risk and, in particular, political risk is a distinguishing feature of developing countries. Although many of the emerging markets exhibit a remarkably high degree of macroeconomic stability, there is still a higher likelihood of unexpected economic downturns than in advanced economies. Oftentimes, this has to do with political instability or institutional deficiencies, for instance in the domestic banking system (see next sub-section below). The majority of empirical studies neglect country risk indicators as explanatory variables because the samples are usually made up exclusively, or at least predominately, of industrialized economies. Among the few studies to use

[145] Index factor #5 comprises the following criteria: foreign investment code, restrictions on foreign ownership of business, restrictions on the industries and companies open to foreign investors, restrictions and performance requirements on foreign companies, foreign ownership of land, equal treatment under the law for both foreign and domestic companies, restrictions on repatriation of earnings, availability of local financing for foreign companies; see Heritage Foundation (2002), chapter 5.

country risk measures are Papi and Revoltella (2000) who find a positive effect for institutional stability of transition countries (as measured by stability indicator of Institutional Investor) and Yamori (1998) who uses Euromoney's country risk index and likewise reports a significantly positive relationship between high scores (low country risk) and Japanese banking FDI in 44 countries (of which at least 25 are emerging markets).[146]

As this present study is concerned with emerging markets only, the inclusion of a country (political) risk variable appears to be warranted. Earlier research on German FDI in developing/emerging economies (see Jost and Nunnenkamp (2002) and the empirical results contained in Chapter II of this study) shows that the *Euromoney* country risk index selected for the present study performs well in explaining the German case. The index's strong emphasis on debt and access to finance is striking, making a separate debt variable as in some of the studies (Sabi; Moshirian and Van der Laar) unnecessary. The variables are named *CRISK* and *PRISK* for country risk and its sub-component political risk, respectively.[147] Because of very high correlation, only one of the variables will be tested at a given time. A positive sign is expected in each case.

3.2.3.2 Likelihood of Banking Crises

The inclusion of country risk to cover macroeconomic variability may not suffice if other types of risk can be shown to influence sectoral FDI flows as well. Indeed, banks may be deterred by factors specific to their field of business. As an innovation to the banking FDI literature, this study tests a banking fragility variable (broad money (M2) to currency reserves) that has been proven reliable in the literature concerned with "early warning indicators".[148] To be sure, there are other indicators of looming banking crises such as output growth, inflation, real interest rates, all of which have been widely tested to predict such crises accurately. However, in the context of this study, many of these factors are already controlled for by GDP per capita, the banking margin or country risk.

---

[146] Remarkably, the country risk variable loses significance when other risk factors such as real interest rates and changes in exchange rates and GNP are accounted for in the same equation; see Yamori (1998), pp. 116-117.

[147] Annual risk scores are derived by summing index scores Euromoney puts out in September and March of the following year and then averaging the sum. As a result, economic or political developments that have unfolded after the September surveys are also taken into account, albeit with only half the weight of the average score.

[148] For a good overview of the literature see OECD (2002), pp. 49-52.

Box 2: Early Warning Systems for Crisis Detection – Development and Features

The concept of "early warning indicators" or, more comprehensively, "early warning systems", representing a set of weighted indicators, originally applied mostly to the timely detection of currency crises, or, if anything, the interaction of banking and currency crises. In the beginning, the literature on banking crises was largely concerned with assessing the risk of financial institutions based on bank soundness indicators. The emergence of systemic banking crises, however, has spurred the development of systems devoted exclusively to predicting wide-spread distress in the financial sector. This kind of fragility can be the result of liquidity risk, traditional credit risk, inadequate regulation/supervision, often connected with abrupt financial liberation, as well as broad macroeconomic developments. The scope and severity of the predicted crisis/distress and a mechanism for generating such predictions requiring one or more explanatory variables are defining features of an early warning system. Leaving models used to predict individual bank failures aside, there are three broad classes of early warning systems: the first one uses qualitative indicators of distress, another one represents a "signal extraction approach", and a third group relies on limited dependent estimation models.

Indicator approaches, such as the one by Honohan (1997), recognize that different banking crises are associated with different warning signals, which makes the proper identification of the source of a crisis crucial. Thus, crises caused by unrestricted credit booms or sudden changes in macroeconomic conditions will have other attributes than those resulting from the misuse of banking assets or directed lending for quasi-fiscal purposes. Yet another kind of crisis lies in regime changes, be it financial liberalization (or depression), exchange rate arrangements or structural reforms (such as privatization). In choosing the appropriate indicator one has to define also a certain threshold, which, when crossed, defines the onset of a banking crisis.

Proponents of the *signal extraction approach*, the most influential of which are Kaminsky and Reinhart (1999), emphasize the value of observing the abnormal behavior of specific variables before and during crises. As in the first case, the problem is defining "abnormal". One viable approach is to set the threshold according to the (average) magnitude of an indicator during periods of crises in the sample countries. The quality of an indicator is judged by its ability to predict crises correctly and so avoid false alarms. Typical indicators comprise: the M2 multiplier, the ratio of domestic credit to GDP, real interest rates, the ratio of lending to deposit rates, the ratio of M2 to currency reserves, the real exchange rate and the terms of trade as well as output growth and the fiscal deficit. Several of these variables are combined to indices, some of which also, questionably, account for the individual performance of an indicator in terms of its noise-to-signal ratio.

Clearly, the occurrence of banking crises is a binary discrete event, which lends itself to assessing the probability of crises via *limited dependent estimation models* (probit and logit) and, at the same time, determining the contribution of each indicator included in the regression. Again, a threshold probability is required to derive early warning signals. Among the most important papers in the area of predicting banking crises are those by Demirgüç-Kunt and Detragiache (1998), and Eichengreen and Rose (1998). Both studies use multivariate binomial probit models. While the former also employs proxies for institutional development, the latter stresses the importance of changes in global economic conditions like interest rates in the Northern Hemisphere and the business cycle of OECD members.

Source: Gaytán and Johnson (2002), pp. 1-11.

With respect to a more banking-specific factor, Kaminsky and Reinhardt (1999) find the ratio of domestic credit to GDP to be a strong predictor of banking crises, whereas Glick and Hutchinson (1999) report insignificant results for this variable. Apart from being causally related to and thus likely correlated with GDP (growth),[149] strong credit growth might also signal market attractiveness and therefore be regarded as a good thing. Moreover, it is likely to be correlated with GDP. Consequently, it cannot be singled out as detrimental at all times and may not serve as a unambiguous indicator to foreign investors.

One factor not yet accounted for is real overvaluation of the currency. Only few empirical studies account for this effect. Moshirian (2001) finds German banking FDI to react significantly negatively to real appreciation of host countries' currencies,[150] whereas Goldberg and Johnson (1990) and Yamori (1998) report insignificant regression outcomes. Note that this study does not attempt to meticulously measure harmful overvaluation directly but instead resorts to an immediate *symptom* of overvaluation, rapid growth of banking deposits due to high real interest rates coinciding with loss of currency reserves.

Therefore, an alternative measure of banking sector fragility is used: Short-term financial liabilities of the banking system (M2) as a share of gross international reserves of the host country, aptly named *M2/RES*. It is a good crisis predictor – be it a currency or a banking crisis or both – because numerator and denominator tend to move in opposite directions when the crisis nears, causing the ratio to display marked deviations from normal in such a case.

Following financial liberalization there are typically strong capital inflows that trigger a lending boom. In the absence of tight banking regulation and supervision, this market exuberance may not be easily dampened, with real

[149] See Demirgüç-Kunt and Detragiache (1998), p. 89.

[150] As measured by the IMF's Multilateral Exchange Rate Model (MERM) index; see Moshirian (2001), p. 326 (footnote 8).

monetary aggregates being inelastic to negative macroeconomic developments.[151] This could be the result of an active credit expansion policy by the government to offset deposit withdrawals, as was the case in the Mexican "tequila" crisis.[152]

The loss of currency reserves, on the other hand, is typically associated with the government's (often futile) attempt to defend an exchange rate regime that has gradually become unsustainable. Not only does this "leaning against the wind" precipitate a balance-of-payments crisis, it is also likely to jeopardize the viability of the banking system as the foreign currency backing of its short-term (often foreign-currency-indexed) liabilities decreases and the currency is rendered vulnerable to negative and persistent money demand shocks.[153] Demirgüç-Kunt and Detragiache (1998, p. 93) argue that the ratio mainly applies to countries with an exchange rate peg. Nonetheless, intermediate regimes should be considered, too, because they likewise imply market interventions causing reserves losses. In fact, the majority of sample countries featured a non-floating exchange rate regime during much of the sample period in order to retain some discretion in managing the currency's external value.

In the empirical literature, the case for *M2/RES* as a dependable banking crisis predictor may be termed as strong. Kaminsky and Reinhardt (1999), while noting that banking crises are typically triggered by negative developments in the real sector, find the above ratio to be the strongest predictor of banking crises among financial sector variables (75% of crises "called"), second only to the real interest rate whose significance is likewise a product of overvaluation. In fact, the ratio also accurately called balance-of-payments crises (81% of cases) as it did in instances of "twin" crises. The authors show that the ratio begins to exceed normal levels of tranquil times significantly (by 40-80 %) about six to nine months before the onset of either crisis (or both). Demirgüç-Kunt and Detragiache (1998) test the ratio of M2 to currency reserves as the only consistently significant measure among four financial variables in a panel of 66 countries between 1980 and 1994. Glick and Hutchison (1999) arrive at a

[151] See Calvo and Mendoza (1996), p. 172.

[152] See Calvo (1996), p. 210. Contrary to the notion of most money demand equations, the Mexican government succeeded in raising real M2 *directly* via credit expansion: higher transfers to the poor in advance of an election stabilized the money demand as the poor are subject to "cash-in-advance" effects. This segment of the population also tends to consume more out of wealth (perceived or actual), thereby propelling economic activity and in turn demand for money. Because of the higher activity, firms are then led to keep higher deposits at banks. The above effects joined in halting the autonomous fall in M2 (ibid., p. 212).

[153] See Glick and Hutchison (1999), p. 10, and Calvo and Mendoza (1996), p. 171.

similar conclusion, showing in a probit regression involving currency crisis indicators that the ratio is significant at the 1% level specifically for emerging markets.[154] Lastly, Eichengreen and Rose (1998) report high predictive qualities for real sector variables (world interest rates and economic growth, and overvalued exchange rates are strongest). Defying any value for typical banking crisis variables such as growth of domestic credit, the authors yet contend that among the variables of domestic financial fragility the ratio of M2 to reserves comes closest to being significant (it actually is at the 20% level).

3.2.3.3 Exchange Rate Volatility

In addition, it would be interesting to know whether the *volatility* of the exchange rate, not just overvaluation, matters for banking FDI. For the real economy there is an indication that high exchange rate volatility may cause firms to establish production sites abroad. This may not be assumed to be stringent for banks.[155] Generally speaking, a high degree of exchange rate volatility renders forecasting of expected returns subject to greater uncertainty and may lead investors to require a higher rate of return in compensation for taking on higher risk. In sum, there is reason to be agnostic about the sign of a volatility measure. Within the studies of the banking FDI literature reviewed here, only the one by Buch (2000) on German FDI in banking (cross sectional regression for 1997) uses an explicit volatility measure, constructed as the average percentage change of the D-mark exchange rate over five years.[156] The author reports a negative sign which is significant at the 10% level. The present study uses a similar measure, *RERVOL*, which, in Chapter II of this study, was tested meaningful for German FDI in Asia. The variable denotes the variance of the indexed real bilateral exchange rate (RER) over past years, i.e. regardless of the direction of the individual change,[157] and is aimed at measuring the excess

[154] Incomprehensibly, the authors do not include this measure in their regression for banking crises, instead using only real sector variables such as inflation and output growth.

[155] As already illustrated in Chapter II, section 2.2.2.4, in the real sector volatile exchange rates induce the relative value of opening the foreign plant to rise. This notion may not hold for *banking*. Locational decisions can be reversed relatively easily because there are no production facilities abroad that would translate into sizable sunk costs.

[156] The author does not detail whether the volatility of a bilateral or Germany's effective exchange rate is taken.

[157] The volatility variable is defined as in Chapter II:

$$RERVOL_{i,t} = \sqrt{0.5\sum_{k=1}^{2}\log\left(\frac{RER_{i,t-k} - RER_{i,t-k+1}}{RER_{i,t-k+1}}\right)^2}$$

where $RER_{i,t}$ is the real exchange rate between Germany and the ith country in a given year.

volatility of the RER over and above the exchange rate movements that could reasonably be expected when considering inflation differentials.

3.3 The Model

Building on the theoretical discussion in sections two and three, the fundamental regression equation for FDI flows of the banking sector has the following form:

$$(14)\quad FDI_{i,t} = \alpha_{i,t} + \sum_{j=1}^{2} \beta_j \mathrm{FOLLOW}_{j,i,t} + \sum_{k=1}^{2} \gamma_k \mathrm{MARKET}_{k,i,t} + \sum_{l=1}^{2} \delta_l \mathrm{RISK}_{l,i,t} + \varepsilon_{i,t}\ ,$$

with "FOLLOW" comprising a vector of up to two variables (the number depending on whether a full or parsimonious model is to be estimated) that aim at capturing home country banks' linkages to the rest of the economy's international operations as a proxy for the degree of internalization of comparative advantages:

- *FDINONBK* (lagged FDI outflows of the non-financial sectors relative to host country GDP),
- *TRADE* (lagged total trade with a given host country relative to its GDP),

"MARKET" containing up to two measures of banking market attractiveness in the host country. These two are taken from the following set of variables:

- *GDPCAP* (real GDP per capita),
- *FINCTR* (ratio of stock market capitalization to GDP as proxy for financial centers),
- *REALINT, MARGIN* (real interest rate, i.e. lending rate minus inflation; and banking margin, i.e. lending minus deposit rates adjusted for exchange rate changes, respectively; both variables serve as proxies for potential profitability and the degree of competition),
- *BANKFREE, OPENNESS* (freedom from restrictions on banking activity, and on both openness to banking and investment flows, respectively), and the

"RISK" vector pertaining to as much as two variables of macroeconomic and institutional uncertainties facing foreign investors. Again, these are from the following set of variables:

- *CRISK* (country risk) and, as a sub-component, *PRISK* (political risk),
- *M2/RES* (ratio of M2 to gross international reserves as proxy for incipient banking crises),
- *RERVOL* (volatility of the real exchange rate).

The descriptions and sources of the variables employed in this study are detailed in the appendix to this chapter (Table 20).

4 Empirical Analysis

4.1 Sample Properties

As a selection criterion for the sample countries, the study adopts the BIS (Bank for International Settlements) set of 24 systematically important emerging markets – Europe: Czech Republic, Hungary, Poland, Russian Federation, Turkey; Latin America: Argentina, Brazil, Chile, Colombia, Mexico, Peru, Venezuela; Asia: China, Hong Kong SAR, India, Indonesia, Republic of Korea, Malaysia, the Philippines, Saudi-Arabia, Singapore, Thailand; Africa: South Africa. Of these, three Latin American countries (Colombia, Peru, Venezuela) that did not receive FDI by German banks were omitted as was Taiwan owing to a general lack of data from official sources. This brings down the number of sample countries to 20.

To ensure a balanced panel of countries, the sample period was chosen to run from 1994 to 2001 (at the time of writing, the most recent data were for 2001 and still preliminary), taking account of the fact that some of the transition countries received their first banking FDI from Germany only in that starting year.[158] The timeliness of the data is a distinguishing feature of this investigation since all other studies reviewed here use older data series (up until the mid-1990s).

[158] Papi and Revoltella (2000, pp. 445-446) classify German banks as generally having been laggards in entering into the emerging financial markets of the transition countries despite the fact that a few banks were among the frontrunners. As a reason for this late entry the authors cite difficulties arising from German reunification.

Figure 6: Top Ten Emerging Market Destinations of German Banking FDI (% of total stocks)

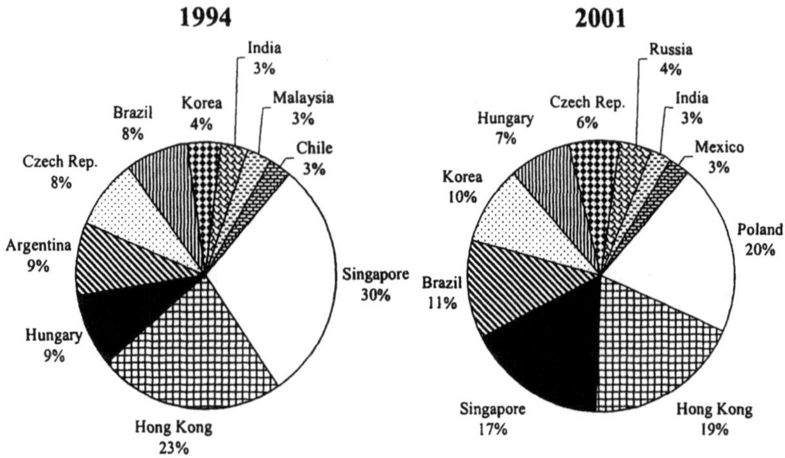

Figure 6 illustrates the development of the largest shares of FDI stocks held by German banking institutions over the sample period. The most astounding change is that Poland, once basically starting from scratch, has now captured the top position from Singapore which has fallen to third place. Remarkably, Argentina has dropped out of the top ten by end-2001 – this, incidentally, is before the "tango" crisis fully evolved in early 2002. This constitutes anecdotal evidence that German banks shunned Argentina in comparison with to other locations even before its financial system collapsed. It is also striking that despite the blow Korea took during the Asian crisis, the country managed to raise its share in German banking FDI from 4% to 10%.

4.2 Estimation Technique

Initially, the familiar panel estimation techniques were applied to the entire sample, i.e. fixed and random effects regressions. However, all specification tests on the existence of individual effects demonstrate that there are indeed none. Both an F-test on fixed effects (testing the null hypothesis that the constant terms are equal) and a Breusch-Pagan Lagrange multiplier test for the random effects model (BP-Test)[159] could not be rejected at the 5% level (Prob>F or Prob>χ^2 were each greater than 0.05 at all times with the exception of regression (17)).

[159] For details on both test specifications see Greene (2003), pp. 289 and 299.

As a consequence, pooled ordinary least squares (OLS) estimation was chosen as the appropriate estimation technique for the sample,[160] with the regression residuals being automatically corrected for possible heteroskedasticity and serial correlation within the groups.[161] This allows correction for very general forms of heteroskedasticity and autocorrelation whereas a feasible generalized least squares (FGLS) estimation procedure would require a more restrictive parametrization of the covariance matrices.[162] Notwithstanding these methodological issues, alternative regressions to the ones contained in Table 15, now using the FGLS procedure, produce broadly similar results (exceptions: the dummy variable is more significant while *FDINONBK* is less so) as the results in Table 21, Appendix III, reveal. The necessity of including time dummies was denied as none of the dummies was significant at conventional levels. Regression results again display "standardized" beta coefficients, allowing for a comparison of the "weights" with which the individual variables enter the equation.[163]

4.3 Discussion of Estimation Results

The following sections present the estimation outcome consisting of different model specifications in order to perform a sensitivity analysis. More specifically, the variables included in each of the three sets derived in section two ("FOLLOW", "MARKET", "RISK") are tested one at a time to isolate the individual variable's effect on the regression outcome. Afterwards, the sample is split up by region and then by time (pre-/post-crisis) to control for individual spatial and temporal effects. Note that for some variables (*GDPCAP*, *FINCTR*, *M2/RES*) the logs were taken to bring their originally skewed distributions closer to normality.

---

160 As there are no individual effects, the subscript i of α is dropped so that the regression equation becomes:

$$(14')\ FDI_{i,t} = \alpha_t + \sum_{j=1}^{2} \beta_j \text{FOLLOW}_{j,i,t} + \sum_{k=1}^{2} \gamma_k \text{MARKET}_{k,i,t} + \sum_{l=1}^{2} \delta_l \text{RISK}_{l,i,t} + \varepsilon_{i,t}$$

161 In STATA, the command for those corrections is "cluster(...)", to be used with conventional OLS estimation.

162 Specifically, a time-constant covariance matrix is assumed for FGLS estimation, and the serial correlation may be represented by a first-order autocorrelated process.

163 Coefficients are corrected as follows: $\beta_j^* = \beta_j\ (s_{xj}/s_y)$ with s_{xj} being the standard deviation of the jth exogenous variable and s_y the standard deviation of the endogenous variable; see Pindyck and Rubinfeld (1981), pp. 90-91.

4.3.1 Full Sample Analysis

The results of the first baseline regression (19) in Table 14, encompassing two variables from each set, are somewhat unsatisfactory since half of the variables turn out to be insignificant. Market integration effects pertaining to FDI flows of the non-financial sector clearly dominate the scenario, considering the weight of the adjusted coefficient and its t-value.

Table 14: Baseline Estimations for Determinants of Banking FDI (Full Sample)

Pooled OLS estimation, heteroskedasticity-consistent standard errors corrected for serial correlation
Dependent variable: *FDIGDP*; number of observations: 160

	(19)	(20)	(21)	(22)
("FOLLOW")				
FDINONBK	0.315	0.291	0.308	0.218
	(9.18)***	(7.70)***	(6.95)***	(3.06)***
TRADE	0.001	-0.265	-0.210	
	(0.01)	(-2.12)**	(-1.52)	
("MARKET")				
GDPCAP	0.130	0.084		
	(2.63)**	(1.88)*		
FINCTR	0.052	0.182	0.268	0.232
	(0.69)	(2.18)**	(2.43)**	(2.41)**
("RISK")				
CRISK	0.039	0.120		
	(0.66)	(1.80)*		
M2/RES	-0.189	-0.150	-0.174	-0.186
	(-3.38)***	(-3.45)***	(-3.65)***	(-3.14)***
DUMMY_CEC		0.405	0.371	0.246
		(2.23)**	(1.73)*	(2.02)*
R-Squared	0.184	0.209	0.206	0.194
F-Test (Prob>F)	0.33	0.81	0.58	0.84
BP-Test (Prob>χ^2)	0.24	0.07	0.32	0.28

Note: t-values in parentheses; *** = significant at the 1% level, ** = significant at the 5% level, * = significant at the 10% level

The picture changes considerably if the diverging motives entertained by German banks entering European transition countries (here: Czech Republic, Hungary, Poland, Russia) are accounted for. When including a transition country dummy, *DUMMY_CEC*, which, as regression (20) shows, is relevant, all variables turn significant (at least at the 10% level) with the expected signs except for the lagged trade variable that exhibits a counterintuitive negative sign.[164] However, the trade variable is far from being robust against varying specifications as can be taken from regression (21) where per capita GDP and country risk, both previously only slightly significant, are left out. Interestingly, the inclusion of trade linkages does not add any meaningful information when already accounting for non-financial FDI or the dissimilarity of the transition countries: in both cases, the trade variable's strong significance (t-value: 3.01, when *FDINONBK* and *DUMMY_CEC* are omitted) completely vanishes.

By dropping *TRADE* as well, the parsimonious regression (22) is reached, which illustrates that exactly one variable of each set is highly significant for German banking FDI in emerging markets: "Follow the client" effects are best depicted by non-banking FDI, within market characteristics the variable for financial centers measured by size-adjusted stock market capitalization stands out, and of the risk variables the backing of short-term deposits by international reserves matters most. In turn, this specification represents the baseline model for the following analyses.[165]

In Table 15, variables from the "MARKET" cluster are added one at a time to the new baseline regression (22).

The insignificant coefficients for either interest rate spread variable (*REALINT, MARGIN)* should not come as a surprise. Conceivably, they are the result of variable misspecification because of failure to incorporate unknown market expectations that could differ greatly from the actual rates.

---

[164] Note that the regressions below do not represent genuine gravity models as a variable of geographic distance is not included. Using distance instead of the CEC dummy yields broadly similar results due to high correlation.

[165] Regarding the relatively low value of R^2, it has to borne in mind that it is composed of "within"- and "between"-group variation. Using a tentative random effects regression, the within-R^2, i.e. the variation across time explained by the model, was constantly rather low (around 0.10), while the between-R^2 hovered at 0.80.

Table 15: Estimations for the Variables Depicting Market Characteristics

Pooled OLS estimation, heteroskedasticity-consistent standard errors corrected for serial correlation
Dependent variable: *FDIGDP*; number of observations equation (23) & (24): 160, (25): 140, (26): 132

	(23)	(24)	(25)	(26)
FDINONBK	0.228 (3.00)***	0.218 (2.79)**	0.207 (3.67)***	0.191 (3.65)***
FINCTR	0.264 (2.41)**	0.263 (2.38)*	0.223 (2.40)**	0.198 (2.60)**
M2/RES	-0.201 (-3.05)***	-0.217 (-3.18)**	-0.182 (-2.86)***	-0.173 (-2.75)**
DUMMY_CEC	0.241 (1.95)*	0.252 (2.00)*	0.238 (1.86)*	0.220 (1.85)*
REALINT	0.021 (0.53)			
MARGIN		-0.023 (-0.56)		
BANKFREE			0.033 (0.57)	
OPENNESS				0.106 (1.98)*
R-Squared	0.189	0.188	0.195	0.203
Test FE (Prob>F)	0.77	0.76	0.84	0.91
Test RE (Prob>χ^2)	0.37	0.36	0.25	0.16

Note: t-values in parentheses; *** = significant at the 1% level, ** = significant at the 5% level, * = significant at the 10% level

More revealing are the results for the measures of host country openness to banking (or both banking and FDI). While the specific banking openness variable, *BANKFREE*, is insignificant, the combined variable, *OPENNESS*, proves to be significant at the 10%-level. Driving this result is the strong significance (at the 1% level) of the freedom-to-FDI component. The results can be interpreted as stipulating that, for German multinationals, banking regulations mattered less than did the absence of general restrictions on capital flows.

Analysis of the third variable cluster comprising risk factors in Table 16 reveals that despite the joint estimation of *M2/RES* and *CRISK* both variables are relevant in regression (27).

Table 16: Estimations for the Variables Depicting Risk Factors

Pooled OLS estimation, heteroskedasticity-consistent standard errors corrected for serial correlation
Dependent variable: *FDIGDP*; number of observations: 160

	(27)	(28)	(29)	(30)
FDINONBK	0.187 (3.67)***	0.165 (3.61)***	0.187 (4.20)***	0.212 (3.23)***
FINCTR	0.187 (2.19)**	0.170 (2.15)**	0.180 (2.34)**	0.213 (2.26)**
M2/RES	-0.169 (-2.82)**		-0.173 (-2.76)**	-0.191 (-3.16)***
DUMMY_CEC	0.263 (2.58)**	0.292 (3.07)***	0.256 (2.64)**	0.241 (2.19)**
CRISK	0.117 (2.03)*	0.150 (2.40)**		
PRISK			0.113 (1.60)	
RERVOL				-0.050 (-1.05)
R-Squared	0.204	0.176	0.203	0.196
Test FE (Prob>F)	0.90	0.94	0.87	0.85
Test RE (Prob>χ^2)	0.09	0.07	0.09	0.20

Note: t-values in parentheses; *** = significant at the 1% level, ** = significant at the 5% level, * = significant at the 10% level

The two risk variables seem to depict different aspects of host country instability, given that the bi-variate correlation is surprisingly low (-0.119). Even if *M2/RES* is lagged by one period reflecting the possibility that the country risk rating reacts belatedly to changes in the deposits-reserves ratio, the correlation rises only moderately to -0.292. Nevertheless, *CRISK* gains significance (now reaching the 5% level) when *M2/RES* is dropped in regression (28).

By contrast, political risk appears to play a less meaningful role as the standard error of its coefficient fails to reach conventional significance levels. The same holds true for volatility of the real exchange rate (*RERVOL*), which is clearly insignificant. The bottom line of the analysis of risk factors is that the early warning indicator *M2/RES* is able to explain the pattern of German banking FDI better than a professional country-risk rating, this being true at least for the sample's country composition and time frame.

4.3.2 Spatial Disaggregation

Having established robust estimators of German FDI activity in banking for the set of emerging markets as a whole, the question as to possible dissimilarities within the three regions arises. Note that, by omitting Turkey, the European sample is restricted to the transition countries in order not to mingle banking sectors at very different levels of development. This, of course, comes at the cost of losing eight observations. Both the European and the Latin American sample thus comprise merely 32 observations. This fact should be borne in mind when interpreting the regression results presented below. The estimation outcome in Table 17 offers a number of valuable insights. Each region exhibits its very own determinants for German banking FDI.

Table 17: Estimations for Determinants by Region

Pooled OLS estimation, heteroskedasticity-consistent standard errors corrected for serial correlation
Dependent variable: *FDIGDP*; number of observations: Europe: 32, Latin America: 32, Asia: 80

	(31) EUROPE	(32) LAT. AM.	(33) ASIA	(34) ASIA
FDINONBK	0.086 (1.12)	-0.064 (-0.42)	0.566 (2.93)**	0.539 (2.90)**
GDPCAP	1.116 (2.59)*	0.043 (0.51)	0.056 (1.20)	0.074 (1.56)
FINCTR	0.006 (0.06)	0.151 (5.92)***	0.293 (2.04)*	
M2/RES	-0.637 (-4.20)**	-0.050 (-0.81)	-0.116 (-2.01)*	-0.108 (-1.76)
OPENNESS				0.154 (4.96)***
R-Squared	0.467	0.077	0.127	0.111
Test FE (Prob>F)	0.22	0.86	0.78	0.96
Test RE (Prob>χ^2)	0.82	0.20	0.11	0.06

Note: t-values in parentheses; *** = significant at the 1% level, ** = significant at the 5% level, * = significant at the 10% level

It is economic growth that matters to banks entering the *European transition countries*. In regression (31) the respective variable, *GDPCAP*, carries by far the greatest weight in the regression and jumps in significance (to a t-value of 5.05) when the highly correlated non-financial FDI variable is dropped. Furthermore, the crisis variable *M2/RES* turns out to be significant at the 5% level and, above all, contributes to the relatively high R-squared by explaining a large fraction of the variation across time. This is most likely the outcome of the variable's signaling the Czech and Russian banking crises of 1997 and 1998, respectively. Follow the client effects do not seem to play a role in the transition countries, thus confirming the hypothesis that this effect mainly applies to more advanced economies (see below). The insignificant result for *FINCTR* is quite logical because stock markets were virtually non-existent in the early stages of the transition process. German banks seem to have gone abroad *despite* the lack of well-established financial markets, seeking to be firmly established when business would take off in the process.

The results for the *Latin American sample* in regression (32) are by and large immaterial (R-squared below 0.10), probably due to small sample size and/or model misspecification in that case. Neither integration effects nor consequences of country risks can be attested. Notwithstanding methodological issues, the latter finding is a bit surprising, considering the multiplicity of financial crises in Latin American emerging markets during the sample period. If anything, German banks were attracted by highly developed financial markets as the strong results for *FINCTR* show. However, the variable is not robust to changes in specification. This is the case if, for example, *M2/RES* is dropped in favor of the country risk variable that is insignificant itself.

In the *Asian banking markets* – regression (33) –, "follow the client" effects play a dominant role as *FDINONBK* is equipped with the largest weight and the highest significance. As alluded to above, this integration effect appears to be a characteristic of more advanced economies where multinationals from the home country are already flocking in large numbers. The marginally significant result for *FINCTR* is caused by two countervailing effects. If a dummy variable is set for the dominant international financial centers of Singapore and Hong Kong, *FINCTR* turns insignificant (t-value = 1.52) while the dummy itself is significant at the 5% level. Hence, as could be expected, banks are also subject to agglomeration effects. The clustering of international banks in those two locations is incidentally the product of these countries' very liberal attitude to foreign bank entry and capital flows in general. The comprehensive banking/ FDI openness variable is not different from zero when added to the equation containing the Singapore/Hong Kong dummy. However, when the dummy is left out, *OPENNESS* gains significance, narrowly missing the 10% level (t-value = 1.76). The notion that open borders to FDI flows are instrumental in becoming a financial center is further substantiated if *FINCTR* is replaced by the openness variable. As regression (34) illustrates, *OPENNESS* becomes significant at the 1% level in that case. The measures of banking margins or exchange rate volatility are insignificant for Asia as they are for the other two regions.

4.3.3 Temporal Disaggregation

After dissecting the sample by region, the other dimension of the panel, namely time, merits attention. The sample was divided into two equally-spaced sub-samples. The first one comprises the years 1994-97, which can be considered the "pre-crisis" period since the impact of the Asian crisis was felt only in late 1997. Accordingly, the other sub-sample is made up of the "post-crisis" years 1998-2001. This qualification is warranted because it is possible to presume the devastating impact of ignoring early warning indicators already publicly known in early 1998.

The following table lists the outcome of re-running regression (20), omitting the insignificant trade variable, separately for both sub-samples.

Table 18: Estimations for Determinants by Time Period (all Countries)

Pooled OLS estimation, heteroskedasticity-consistent standard errors corrected for serial correlation
Dependent variable: *FDIGDP*; number of observations: 80 each

	(35) Years 1994-1997 (Rand. Eff.)	(36) Years 1998-2001 (Pooled OLS)
FDINONBK	0.238 (1.99)**	-0.011 (-0.07)
GDPCAP	-0.040 (-0.34)	0.074 (1.07)
FINCTR	0.075 (0.61)	0.268 (1.89)*
CRISK	0.123 (0.75)	0.329 (1.68)
M2/RES	-0.094 (-0.25)	-0.221 (-3.10)***
DUMMY_CEC	0.322 (2.07)**	0.271 (1.51)
R-Squared	0.255	0.313
Test FE (Prob>F)	0.99	0.32
Test RE (Prob>χ^2)	0.004	0.50
Hausman-Test (Prob>χ^2)	0.48	---

Note: t-values in parentheses; *** = significant at the 1% level, ** = significant at the 5% level, * = significant at the 10% level

The regression (35) for the pre-crisis sample was not estimated by pooled OLS because the Breusch-Pagan test of no random effects was rejected at the 5% level. Taking into account the high value of the F-test (0.99), it is unsurprising that a Hausman-test failed to reject the hypothesis that the difference in coefficients between the fixed and the random effects model is not systematic. Accordingly, random effects estimation is appropriate in this case.

The main difference between the two periods is that, *before the Asian crisis*, variables of country riskiness did not significantly influence the rationale of German banks. Their FDI in emerging markets was largely driven by market integration aspects as the coefficient for the non-financial FDI illustrates. Also, the dummy variable for the European transition countries is also significant at the 5% level, denoting the exceptional role of these economies during their opening-up to capital flows.

By contrast, both variables lose their significance when the *post-crisis* sample is considered. Now, risk aspects rule the picture with the early warning variable, *M2/RES*, reaching very strong significance (at the 1% level) and the additional country risk variable missing the 10% level only narrowly. This is clear indication that German banks learned from the Asian debacle, adjusting their holdings more quickly if the soundness of the financial system deteriorates or proportionally disregarding high risk banking environments altogether. In the later years, there is also a greater tendency towards targeting financial centers as locations for banking activity abroad. Lastly, per capita income cannot be shown to exert a meaningful influence on those locational decisions.

5 Conclusions of Chapter III

This chapter investigated whether the significance of determinants commonly found in the literature on foreign direct investment in the banking sector holds for German banks entering emerging markets via equity participation. Traditional variables depicting market integration effects, represented by FDI of non-banks and as well as financial market development in terms of stock market capitalization, did exert the hypothesized influence on German banking FDI flows. However, in contrast to the evidence presented elsewhere, the investigation failed to find a statistically robust impact of bilateral trade linkages on banks' locational choices. Also, per capita income (or growth effects if considering annual differences) did not matter except in a sub-sample comprising European transition countries.

The strongest case regarding FDI flows can be made for the necessity of including indicators of financial vulnerability. A typical crisis variable measuring the backing of short-term banking deposits by international reserves that was adopted from the literature on "early warning indicators" displayed very high levels of significance throughout the empirical analysis. In other words, when a host country's reserves faded as a result of defending an unsustainable exchange rate regime, German banks tended to reconsider their direct investment position, shifting funds out of high-risk countries into more stable environments. Interestingly, the traditional measure of country risk (*Euromoney* index) was also moderately significant if regressed simultaneously with the crisis variable, indicating that the two measures depict different aspects of instability. Other non-traditional factors such as the destination market's openness to foreign bank entry, also coupled with a liberal attitude to capital inflows in general, or the volatility of the real bilateral exchange rate did not turn out to be meaningful in the German case. The same goes for measures of interest rate margin. Openness to capital flows did matter, though, for banking FDI going into Asia, since the combined openness variable was moderately significant.

The dissimilarity of the four European transition countries was explicitly incorporated by including a dummy variable in the full sample regressions. This dummy was moderately significant throughout, pointing to distinct pull factors such as geographic proximity. Furthermore, regressions were run for each regional sub-sample. Since financial markets were clearly underdeveloped in central and eastern Europe at the start of the sample period, the financial center variable, logically, turned out to be irrelevant, while economic growth was the focal point of German banking expansion in that region. Regarding "follow the client" effects depicted by the influence of non-financial FDI flows, it is noteworthy that this factor did not matter greatly in the CEC countries, while it was the main driving force in the Asian case. This supports the hypothesis that market integration effects matter more for developed banking markets.

Finally, when splitting the sample into two four-year periods, roughly before and after the Asian crisis, learning effects among German investors become evident. While in the outer years both risk variables, country risk and currency-reserve backing of deposits, were virtually meaningless, they gained significance considerably in the more recent sub-sample, with the financial vulnerability variable even reaching the 1% level. This finding suggests that the experience of the emerging market shake-up in late 1997 drastically changed the risk perception of German banks active in emerging markets.

Further empirical evidence on the importance of risk elements in the decision-making process of multinational banks from source countries other than Germany is clearly warranted to verify this conjecture.

Appendix to Chapter III

Table 19: Foreign Bank Ownership in Selected Emerging Markets in 2001

Host Country	Total Assets (US$ bill.)	Number of Foreign Banks	Foreign control in %
Europe			
Czech Republic	50.3	21	93.0
Hungary	28.2	29	68.8
Poland	85.4	39	63.6
Turkey	156.0	45	6.7
Latin America			
Argentina	166.0	97	54.5
Brazil	397.0	138	30.6
Chile	77.1	28	43.7
Mexico	156.0	38	76.5
Asia			
China	1090.0	37	0.2
Korea (South)	496.0	27	8.7
India	273.0	75	0.8
Indonesia	87.4	67	4.9
Malaysia	180.0	51	16.8
Thailand	155.0	23	6.4

Note: Foreign control refers to cases where foreigners own more than 50 % of total equity.

Source: Inter-American Development Bank (2002), p. 108. Numbers shown are estimates based on data from Fitch IBCA's Bankscope database.

Table 20: Descriptions and Sources of Exogenous Variables

FDINONBK	FDI outflows of the non-financial sector relative to host country GDP (both in current DM)	Deutsche Bundesbank (FDI), World Bank (GDP)
TRADE	Total trade (sum of exports and imports) with the host country relative to its GDP (in current DM)	Deutsche Bundesbank (Trade), World Bank (GDP)
GDPCAP	GDP per capita is gross domestic product divided by midyear population (in constant U.S. dollars)	World Bank (World Development Indicators)
FINCTR	Market capitalization is the share price times the number of shares outstanding in relation to GDP. Listed domestic companies are the domestically incorporated companies listed on the country's stock exchange at the end of the year.	Standard & Poor's (Emerging Stock Markets Factbook and supplemental S&P data), variable taken from World Development Indicators
REALINT; MARGIN	*REALINT* denotes the real interest rate, i.e. the lending interest rate (charged by banks on loans to prime customers) adjusted for inflation as measured by the consumer price index. *MARGIN* is the difference between lending minus deposit rates in the host country, adjusted for changes in the bilateral nominal exchange rate.	International Monetary Fund (International Financial Statistics (IFS))
BANKFREE; OPENNESS	*BANKFREE* is the Index of Economic Freedom's factor #6 ("banking and finance"). *OPEN* is the equally-weighted sum of factors #6 and #5 ("capital flows and foreign investment")	Heritage Foundation (annual Index of Economic Freedom)
CRISK; PRISK	*CRISK* is country risk composed of factors of economic (75 %) and political risk (25%). *PRISK* is political risk alone.	Euromoney, various issues
M2/RES	*M2* is money and quasi money (sum of currency outside banks, demand deposits other than those of the central government, and the time, savings, and foreign currency deposits of resident sectors other than the central government). *RES* denotes gross international reserves (holdings of monetary gold, special drawing rights, reserves of IMF members held by the IMF, and holdings of foreign exchange under the control of monetary authorities.	International Monetary Fund (IFS)
RERVOL	RERVOL measures the variance of the indexed real bilateral exchange rate (RER) over the past two years	International Monetary Fund (IFS), own calculations

Table 21: Alternative Estimations Using an FGLS Procedure

FGLS estimation, heteroskedasticity-consistent standard errors corrected for serial correlation
Dependent variable: *FDIGDP*; number of observations: 160

	(19)	(20)	(21)	(22)
FDINONBK	0.132 (1.84)*	0.133 (2.07)**	0.137 (2.05)**	0.115 (2.04)**
TRADE	0.099 (1.18)	-0.041 (-0.50)	-0.054 (-0.64)	
GDPCAP	0.032 (0.90)	0.024 (0.82)		
FINCTR	0.044 (1.18)	0.074 (1.92)*	0.095 (2.28)**	0.083 (2.17)**
CRISK	0.011 (0.03)	0.038 (1.05)		
M2/RES	-0.070 (-2.58)***	-0.062 (-2.30)**	-0.064 (-2.49)**	-0.066 (-2.66)***
DUMMY_CEC		0.269 (3.31)***	0.288 (3.34)***	0.225 (3.49)***
Pseudo R-Squared	0.097	0.207	0.194	0.170
Diff. LogLikelihood	2.66	1.40	1.23	1.00
Serial Correlation?	yes	no	no	no

Note: t-values in parentheses; *** = significant at the 1% level, ** = significant at the 5% level, * = significant at the 10% level

Pseudo R-Squared has to be used instead of standard R-Squared in FGLS estimation. This measure of goodness-of-fit is derived from the likelihood ratio statistic (LR) which is asymptotically equivalent to the Wald test statistic (W). The Wald (or F-) statistic is related to Pseudo R-Squared as follows:

$$F \approx \frac{n}{K-1} * \frac{R^2}{1-R^2} \text{ and } (K-1) * F \approx W \approx LR. \text{ Therefore, } PseudoR^2 \approx \frac{W}{n+W}.$$

Diff. LogLikelihood denotes difference of the likelihood ratios observed in FGLS regressions with and without correcting for serial correlation. As in Chapter II the likelihood ratio statistic is defined as

$$\lambda = -2(\log L_r - \log L_u) = T(\log|\hat{\mathbf{W}}_r| - \log|\hat{\mathbf{W}}_u|),$$

If the ratio for a common AR(1) coefficient is $\chi^2(1) > 3.84$, serial correlation in the residuals is present and needs to be corrected for. This was the case only in regression (19) as (2 * 2.66) > 3.84. In the other regressions, the threshold was not crossed and no correction performed.

Chapter IV: Does Co-Financing by Multilateral Development Banks Increase "Risky" Direct Investment in Emerging Markets? – Evidence for German Banking FDI

1 Introduction to Chapter IV

Multilateral development banks (MDBs) such as the *International Finance Corporation* (IFC), the main private sector arm of the World Bank, or the *European Bank for Reconstruction and Development* (EBRD), operating analogously in the central and eastern European transition countries, have for years been taking stakes (equity or debt) in FDI projects in emerging market economies that were initiated by investors located in industrialized countries. Founded already in 1956, IFC shares commercial risks with foreign investors when they are not yet prepared to invest on their own account (for details on IFC's operations banking sector projects see Box 6, Appendix IV). Similarly, EBRD has helped mobilize private investment and improve the investment climate by loans and equity participations since its establishment in 1991. At times, even large financial conglomerates that undoubtedly have accumulated the needed expertise and experience for venturing independently into emerging markets request and indeed attain support by these institutions in apparently difficult projects, which may raise questions about the rationale of the decision to co-finance such an investment project.

It is often alleged that having such international financial institutions participate in foreign business ventures helps mitigate project risks. For example, the International Finance Corporation (2002) perceives itself as a catalyst that helps clients implement investment plans and mitigate risk, thereby enabling investors to proceed with plans that they otherwise would not implement in light of perceived risks.

This study does not attempt to verify that statement with respect to ordinary commercial risks but concentrates on the issue of sovereign risk, investigating whether German banks that obtain project-related co-financing from the IFC or the EBRD invest more "risk-adjusted" equity capital in emerging banking markets[166] than do ordinary investors. As events during the recent Argentinean

[166] The financial sector represents one of IFC's so-called high-impact sectors, where spillover effects to other parts of the economy are significant. Financial sector projects accounted for about 40% of IFC commitments on average during the 1999-2001 period; see Mavrotas (2002), pp. 2, 4.

crisis have shown – banks were virtually disowned by the forced "pesification" of assets against deposits –, host country governments may perceive the banking sector to be a "strategic" industry for economic development. What followed were discussions at the international level[167] about the safety of FDI in the financial sector and whether instruments or institutions can be devised for protecting foreign investors against political risks.

Analyzing this question with respect to the role of multilateral development banks in foreign direct investment projects is the motivation of this chapter. It is restricted to banking FDI because the inclusion of other sectors would have implied arduous accounting for various industry-specific factors which multilateral development banks consider when deciding which projects to co-finance. The obvious question of whether officially supported projects display a higher profitability[168] cannot be answered in this paper because the data series on earnings are not yet long enough.

The investigation is organized as follows: Section two presents a clear-cut model that outlines the incentives underlying the host country's decision to possibly expropriate the foreign investment position and explains the existence of different investment levels given varying country risk profiles across locations. An innovative variable measuring the amount of investment capital adjusted for the probability of sovereign default and, accordingly, expropriation is presented in section three. After surveying the literature on program evaluation techniques, section four illustrates the propensity score matching approach used for measuring the treatment effect associated with official co-financing, shows how the exogenous variables needed for estimating the individual probability of receiving the treatment are derived and gives an understanding of how the sample of countries and projects was arrived at. Finally, estimation results and significance checks are presented in section five, followed by a brief conclusion in the last section.

---

[167] For example the Working Group of the Committee on the Global Financial System on "FDI in the financial sector of emerging market economies" at the Bank for International Settlements.

[168] There is, however, some evidence that IFC-sponsored projects have, on average, been less successful than other foreign investment projects undertaken independently; see Mavrotas (2002), p. 9, footnote 9.

2 The Model

2.1 Basic Model

The theoretical underpinning to this study is a model propagated by Asiedu and Villamil (2000, 2002) which, in turn, builds directly on work by Eaton and Gersovitz (1983, 1984) as well as to a lesser extent on that by Thomas and Worrall (1994). A comparable model by Schnitzer (1999) is described in a nutshell further below. Central to all of these papers is the notion that a country's decision to default on its external debt obligations is influenced by economic incentives which lend themselves to modeling.

In a two-country setting, the host (or recipient) country has a capital stock which is less than the optimal stock, i.e. the marginal product of the domestic capital stock $f'(k^d)$ is still higher than the required rate of return r. The investor from the foreign country can either receive a return σ from utilizing a safe storage facility or expect to receive r by investing in the host country. Note that Asiedu and Villamil refer to capital injection by lending rather than equity participation, but the results remain valid if r is interpreted as a constant required rate of return instead of a fixed interest rate. In general, $r > \sigma > 0$, actuating foreign firms to invest as much as possible in a given project.

However, the host country government is subject to countervailing incentives. It can choose to be "good" and achieve the utility G, i.e. honor the contractual agreements and receive each period a return from the overall capital stock $f(k_s)$ less the return promised to foreign capital owners $r(k_s - k^d)$, where $k_s - k^d$ is the residual of the entire capital stock and the domestically supplied one. This payoff is converted to net present value terms by applying a discount factor β^{s-t} and is then summed up from now on to infinity.

$$(16) \quad G(k_t) = \sum_{s=t}^{\infty} \beta^{s-t} [f(k_s) - r(k_s - k^d)]$$

This expression can be simplified to:

$$(16') \quad G(k_t) = \frac{1}{1-\beta} [f(k) - r(k - k^d)]$$

$$\textit{where } k = k^f + k^d \textit{ and } \beta = \frac{\theta}{r} \ .$$

Note that the factor β is not simply a discount factor as in Eaton and Gersovitz (1983) but includes a country-specific risk parameter θ denoting "the probability of survival, an idiosyncratic factor that reflects the 'patience' of decision makers in the poor country".[169] High-risk locations where the government, trying to remain in office, is myopic, will have a low θ and thus a large discount on expected returns. Eaton and Gersovitz (1983) account for part of the country risk by discounting income from foreign capital $f'(k_t) * k_t^f$ by multiplying the term with $(1-\tau_t)$, where τ_t is a "tax" rate on foreign capital and $\tau = 1$ means full expropriation.[170]

Alternatively, the government can choose to be "bad", i.e. expropriate the foreign investor's holdings. Hence, it enjoys the entire return on capital $f(k)$ at time $s = 0$ and loses access to foreign capital henceforth – $f(k^d)$ rather than $f(k)$ –, thus being left with the (discounted) national income (in autarky)

$$(17)\quad B(k_t) = f(k_t) + \sum_{s=t+1}^{\infty} \beta^{s-t} f(k^d) = f(k) + \frac{\beta}{1-\beta} f(k^d).$$

Clearly, the host country government will honor its obligations as long as the repayment incentive constraint $G(k) \geq B(k)$ holds in every state. This constraint ensures that the contract is "self-enforcing" which means that the long-term benefits of fulfilling the contract exceed short-term gains to be had by repudiating claims (see also below). It is effectively the threat of halting investment flows altogether that works to forestall expropriation.[171]

In solving the optimization problem, the capital stock k maximizing the host country's present discounted utility of income W is then chosen, subject to the repayment incentive constraint[172]

$$(18)\quad \max W(k) = \frac{1}{1-\beta}[f(k) - r(k - k^d)], \text{ s.t. } G(k) \geq B(k), \quad \forall k.$$

By taking the Lagrangian, the first-order conditions turn out to be (Appendix IV has the proof):

[169] Asiedu and Villamil (2002), p. 479.

[170] See Eaton and Gersovitz (1983), pp. 100-101.

[171] See Thomas and Worrall (1994), pp. 82-83.

[172] Asiedu and Villamil (2002, p. 479) subject the maximization problem to the additional constraint that the foreign investor must receive at least the return available from the storage facility, which is fulfilled here by assumption.

(19) $f'(k) - r = \dfrac{r\lambda(1-\beta)}{1+\lambda\beta}$ *and* $G(k) = B(k)$.

Investment is at its efficient level when marginal revenue $f'(k)$ equals marginal cost r. Accordingly, any "wedge" between the two expressions represents an efficiency loss due to sub-optimal enforcement of the investment contract that leads to under-investment.[173] The right-hand side of (19) and thus the degree of inefficiency depend on the discount factor β, the rate of return r and the extent to which incentive constraint λ binds (if it does, $\lambda > 0$). Obviously, it is desirable for the right-hand side to approach zero. This is the case when $\lambda \to 0$, i.e. the constraint becomes weak, $\beta \to 1$, i.e. political risk decreases, or $r \to 0$, i.e. a lower rate return is to be paid to the investor which is bounded from below by the interest rate σ on the risk-free storage facility. Since r cannot be zero under normal circumstances, it is not a variable to be altered with a view to bringing about the optimal solution. This task is effectively left to the risk measure β as that also has a bearing on whether the constraint will bind or not. Accordingly, the host country's characteristics determine its discount factor, which in turn influences the flow of FDI. In their earlier paper, Asiedu and Villamil (2000) show that the variation in β yields three ranges of foreign investment, of which only case 3 is truly efficient.

Case 1: $B(k) > G(k)$ (constraint set is empty),

Case 2: $\lambda > 0$ (constraint binds): $f'(k) > r$,

Case 3: $\lambda = 0$ (constraint does not bind): $f'(k) = r$.

In case 1, rational investors anticipate expropriation by the host country government and will therefore avoid direct investment. Case 2 describes an intermediate solution: as the constraint binds, the remaining inefficiency owing to a non-zero numerator in (19) renders the investment level sub-optimal, i.e. there is under-investment since no commitment technology exists with which to induce both parties to adhere to the first-best solution after the initial investment has taken place.[174] Case 3 represents the optimal state: the constraint does not bind – there is no risk of expropriation at any time – and foreign investors inject capital until marginal revenue equals marginal cost.

---

173 See also Eaton and Gersovitz (1984), p. 22.

174 See Asiedu and Villamil (2000), pp. 4-5.

A numerical example illustrates why these different zones exist. Suppose that β is near zero, i.e. host country officials are extremely short-sighted. Then $B(k) > G(k)$ (see also Figure 7), i.e.:

$$f(k)+\frac{\beta}{1-\beta}f(k^d) > \frac{1}{1-\beta}[f(k)-r(k-k^d)] \text{ because if } \beta \approx 0, \frac{\beta}{1-\beta} \approx 0 \text{ and } \frac{1}{1-\beta} \approx 1.$$

Therefore, $f(k) > f(k)-r(k-k^d)$.

Figure 7: Case 1 – Autarky Equilibrium

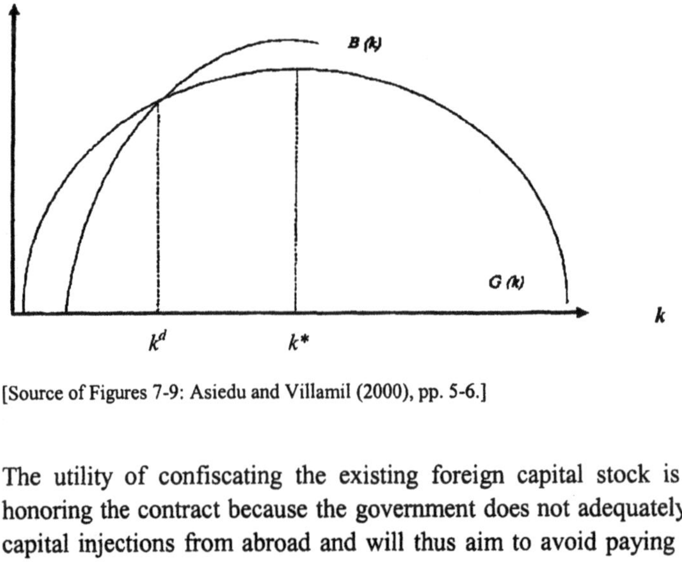

[Source of Figures 7-9: Asiedu and Villamil (2000), pp. 5-6.]

The utility of confiscating the existing foreign capital stock is greater than honoring the contract because the government does not adequately value future capital injections from abroad and will thus aim to avoid paying the return on the modest foreign capital it is still likely to receive.

At the other extreme – when β approaches one – the repayment incentive constraint will tend to be satisfied, i.e. $B(k) \approx G(k)$. This is because both of the above expressions involving β go to infinity as the series cease to converge. However, for very large magnitudes of $r(k\text{-}k^d)$, the country's incentive to rid itself of the external payment burden turns strong, and $B(k)$ will once again exceed $G(k)$. The upper (feasible) bound of k_{max} is where $B(k)$ intersects with the downward-sloping curve of $G(k)$, i.e. with $B'(k) > 0$ and $G'(k) < 0$ (see Figure 9). By contrast, the lower bound k_{min} is determined by the minimal threshold of β in order for the constraint to bind which is the case at the intersection of both functions, with both $B'(k)$ and $G'(k) > 0$.

Algebraically, the threshold β_{min} is reached when

$$B(k) = f(k) + \frac{\beta}{1-\beta} f(k^d) = \frac{1}{1-\beta}[f(k) - r(k-k^d)] = G(k)$$

$$\Rightarrow \beta_{min} = \frac{-r(k-k^d)}{f(k^d)-f(k)};\ given\{[f(k^d)-f(k)] \mid \beta > 0\} < 0 \Rightarrow \beta_{min} = \frac{r(k-k^d)}{f(k)-f(k^d)}.$$

The contract is deemed self-enforcing[175] for values of $\beta \geq \beta_{min}$. Note that k_{max} does not necessarily coincide with the optimal capital stock k^* if at that point the utility of income $W(k)$, being a function of $G(k)$, is not maximized, which is the case if $G'(k_{max}) < 0$. The optimum is determined by $G'(k^*) = 0$ and $G''(k) < 0$. On the other hand, under-investment takes place if k^* cannot be attained because the incentive constraint would not be fulfilled at point k^* (see Figure 8).

Figure 8: Case 2 – Constrained Optimal Equilibrium

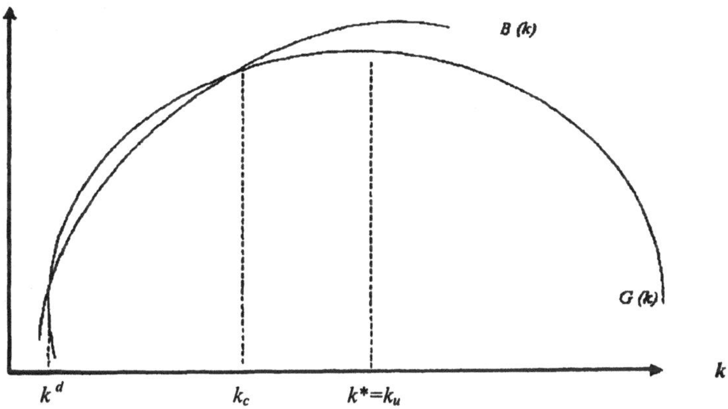

Hence, there will only be the constrained capital stock k_c which is lower than k^* if $B(k) > G(k)$, even though $G'(k) > 0$. Unconstrained investment k_u will be possible if and only if $G(k^*) \geq B(k^*)$ and $\beta^* \geq \beta_{min}$, with β^* being the discount factor corresponding to k^* (see Figure 9).

---

[175] Schnitzer (1999, p. 1119) characterizes „self-enforcing" contracts as involving a certain optimal behavior which represents a subgame perfect equilibrium of the (repeated) game between the parties involved.

Figure 9: Case 3 – Unconstrained Optimal Equilibrium

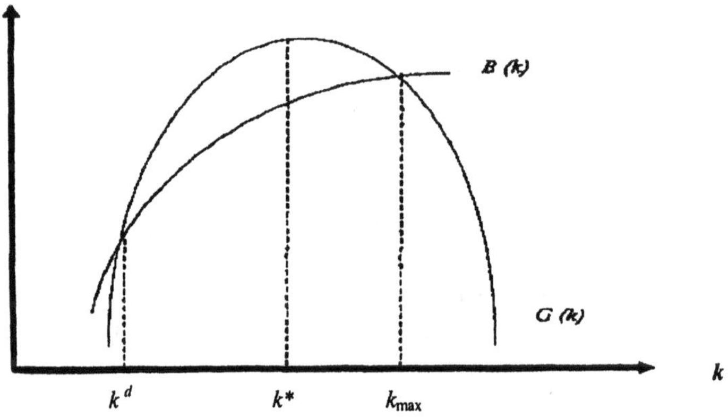

Thus, the three cases can be characterized in more detail as follows:

Case 1: $\beta \in (0, \beta_{min}) \Rightarrow B(k) > G(k)$; no foreign investment, i.e. financial autarky,

Case 2: $\beta \in (\beta_{min}, \beta^*) \Rightarrow G(k) \geq B(k)$ *but* $k_c < k^*$; constrained foreign investment,

Case 3: $\beta \in (\beta^*, 1) \Rightarrow G(k) \geq B(k)$ *and* $\beta^* \geq \beta_{min}$; unconstrained foreign investment.

Clearly, it is desirable for both parties to the contract to widen the area where case 3 applies, or, for high-risk environments, case 2 instead of case 1. The problem is that the perceived β is virtually exogenous, i.e. the host country has hardly any mechanisms at its disposal to *credibly* increase its discount factor in the short-term. Over time, assessments of country risk, for instance by credit rating agencies, may change thanks to improved macroeconomic and political stability, but usually this tends to be a protracted process.

Extending this type of framework, Schnitzer (1999) introduces a dynamic model where each period a certain constant level of both foreign capital investment and "taxation" by the host government are required for the contract to be self-enforcing. As written contracts usually cannot account for all contingencies, there needs to be an implicit agreement prescribing good conduct of both parties. The problem is that they are unable to *commit* to using a specific method of splitting returns. Once investment costs are sunk, the host country is tempted to reap additional rents by imposing taxes or asking for side payments (bribes). Schnitzer's model includes the possibility of investors' threatening to leave the host country in favor of a different production location if such taxation – which can easily amount to creeping expropriation (see Box 3) – becomes too heavy. This explicit modeling of investor behavior is appealing, because the incentives facing the investor to relocate production are accounted for. The easier (i.e. less costly) it is for investors to leave the host country from one period to another ("strong outside option"), the more capital they have to inject for the host government not to expropriate. Indeed, investing too much may be the only possibility to commit to giving a sufficiently large share of the return stream to the host country, thereby forestalling expropriation.[176] Unfortunately, it is not possible to integrate Schnitzer's theoretical framework into this investigation since banking investors typically aim to service a particular market for its characteristics and growth potential, the rational being that services are typically non-tradable. Nevertheless, many of the individual concepts in the two approaches are similar (e.g. upper and lower bound of FDI, participation and incentive constraints facing the parties).

Asiedu and Villamil (2002) discuss policy options available to the host country to tackle this perceived commitment problem. All of these options involve external assistance supplied by either industrialized countries or, more appropriately, by multilateral development agencies. The recipient country can either (a) request a loan subsidy from a bilateral lender, (b) ask for technical assistance or (c) solicit a multilateral development bank's financial support.

In case (a), the subsidized interest rate ρ is lower than the required rate of return r, with the external repayment obligation $r(k\text{-}k^d)$ being lowered to $r(1\text{-}\gamma)\,(k\text{-}k^d) + \rho\gamma(k\text{-}k^d)$, γ being the share of subsidized external financing. By calibration the authors show that for any level of subsidized loans both thresholds β_{min} and β^* are lower than before. It is not hard to see that the effect of subsidization is twofold: in the short run, the incentive constraint is fulfilled for lower values of β, and over the medium term, the country has more low-cost funds at its disposal which act to release budgetary resources for implementing structural reforms. Case (b), technical assistance, works in a different way: by updating production processes, the host country's productivity is strengthened and $f(k)$ rises by the factor $[1+\delta(\alpha)]$, with α denoting the amount of resources spent on technical assistance. In turn, this also lowers the threshold β_{min}.

The final case (c) is the one on which this study centers. It is hypothesized that, by having a multilateral agency participate in an FDI project, β_{min} is lowered to the point at which investment, if constrained, takes place. Asiedu and Villamil (2002, p. 486) argue that at times a single lender – here by means of

---

176 See Schnitzer (1999), pp. 1118-1119, 1123, 1131.

"uncoordinated" bilateral aid – may not be able to reduce $\beta_{\min}$ sufficiently. Therefore, if the individual discount factor is very low, several investors may be needed to overcome the autarky scenario because the required funding may exceed a single donor country's allotted resources. This is where the usefulness of charging a multilateral development bank (MDB) with coordinating the lending effort comes into play. Absent centralized lending, the recipient country might lean towards selective default on some creditors. If instead lenders form a coalition under the roof of the MDB, the host country government will weigh its options more carefully because the future stream of subsidized lending that would be lost when defaulting on multilateral loans might be substantial, even prohibitive.

Box 3: What Exactly is Expropriation?

The taking of investor property by host country governments, commonly called expropriation, is generally in conflict with customary international law unless proven to serve a clearly identifiable public purpose, be non-discriminatory in nature *and* trigger payments of compensation to the investor. These three criteria are now universally accepted and serve as the legal basis in many countries as well as in international investment agreements. While it is generally difficult for investors to prove that there is no public purpose whatsoever to an expropriation and that the act was indeed discriminatory, these days the main controversies surround judging cases of creeping expropriations and regulatory takings, and the question of fair compensation ("at what point" and "how much").

It has been argued (Mistry and Olesen (2003)) that the risk of expropriation, while not disappearing entirely, will be superseded by the more general concept of "contract frustration". For example, host country governments can delay completion or obstruct operation of FDI projects, putting investors under great financial pressure to accept re-negotiation of terms or make side-payments to safeguard their interests. Unlike outright expropriations it is difficult to detect such *creeping* expropriations where incremental but cumulative infringements on recognized ownership rights lead to the effective negation of the investor's interest in the property, or *regulatory* takings, in which the exercise of governmental regulatory power diminishes the economic value of the affiliates' assets without actually denying formal ownership. In such cases, it is difficult to identify the exact point at which the removal of rights gives rise to the duty to compensate. The latter category is especially troublesome because a wide interpretation of such takings collides with the right of an otherwise liberally minded government to penalize improper investor behavior under limited and transparent circumstances in order to protect consumers, the environment or public health. So there is a regulatory trade-off between securing the interests of needed foreign investors and aiming to achieve public policy objectives even at the cost of diminishing property values. It is clear that in cases of entirely justifiable regulatory takings confiscation without compensation is called for.

This raises the following question: when is an action lawful and when does it amount to expropriation? Increasingly, dispute settlement bodies (such as the one under the *North American Free Trade Agreement* – NAFTA), in determining the case for compensation, tend to consider the effects of a regulatory taking rather than *merely* the public purpose underlying the action. In some cases, NAFTA governments, convinced they had properly exercised their regulatory rights, found themselves convicted of unlawful expropriation and forced to make compensation payments. Mindful of the ambiguity associated with this narrow legal boundary between adequate regulatory action and the violation of owners' rights in cases of regulatory takings, governments might choose to refrain from undertaking legitimate regulatory action (for example, in complying with international environmental agreements) for fear of being taken to court. Some international investment agreements contain so-called carve-outs as potential remedies, which safeguard legitimate exercise of regulatory power.

While the issue of compensation is almost always addressed in such agreements, the method of calculating it is usually imprecise. Terms like "appropriate", "just", or "prompt, adequate and effective" abound. Under national law arriving at an amount of compensation is within the discretion of the state concerned. Not surprisingly, this legal void causes disputes at the international level over the fair level of compensation (see Box 4).

Sources: UNCTAD (2003), pp. 110-113, 115, and Mistry and Olesen (2003), pp. 27-28

Structuring project finance such that international financial institutions are introduced as financial partners can act as a strategic risk mitigation mechanism.[177] Put differently, the additional payoffs arising from multilateral financing that would be lost after a possible default in the autarky situation matter strongly when the country, as can be expected in the case of emerging markets, is a frequent customer with the multilateral agency. Thus, if a large share of a country's current *and* future external financing comes from the World Bank or one of the regional development banks, default against these institutions is really not an option, as doing so may result in the cessation of all lending operations already scheduled.

Applied to the question under study, participation of a multilateral agency in an FDI project acts as a deterrent to the conceivable expropriation of the foreign subsidiary as there is much more at stake for the host country than just the expected payments from a particular project. Losing all of one's multilateral subsidized credit may seem a harsh penalty for a possibly minor selective

[177] See Mistry and Olesen (2003), p. 28.

default, but it is certainly something to be reckoned with when taking hold of a project in which a multilateral agency is invested.[178]

2.2 Discussion of Model Extensions

2.2.1 Forbearance by the Multilateral Agency

In extending the model, we may ease the strong restriction of an automatic freezing of future official credit somewhat by introducing a *leniency* factor μ (with $0 \leq \mu \leq 1$) denoting the probability that the multilateral development bank, keen on minimizing its losses, and thus all other private creditors, assured by the implicit guarantee of MDB forbearance, will decide[179] *not* to stop lending to the host country even though the rights of the agency are infringed upon.[180] This variable is deemed to depend on the country's track record with its external creditors that is partially reflected in its current β, and on the amount of total debt and equity capital "owed" to the MDB ("too big to fail" doctrine). Therefore, the host country will violate its external obligations only if $B(k) - G(k) > 0$, i.e.:

$$(20)\, f(k)+\frac{\beta}{1-\beta}\{f(k^d)+\mu(\beta,k^{MDB})[f(k^f)]\}-\frac{1}{1-\beta}[f(k)-r(k-k^d)]>0.$$

Note that the leniency factor provides the host country also with a *countervailing* incentive with respect to its discount factor. As its reputation as a decent borrower rises in line with prudent macroeconomic management and investor relations, it will have greater leeway to tamper with its external obligations. On the other hand, the country is given the incentive to become a substantial borrower, and in turn this status will materialize only if the country

---

[178] A theory of the relationship between the multilateral agency and the host country under asymmetrical information and diverging interests is elaborated by Pallage and Robe (2003) who show that the agency can supplement its inferior state of information about the success of the projects at hand by requiring that the country invest its own funds in the project that the agency wants undertaken.

[179] It is assumed that this decision is made in the same period as the initial investment and expropriation in order to integrate this event into the static model.

[180] As the recent past has shown, this less restrictive assumption is supported by empirical evidence. The MDB has a politically motivated self interest in preventing the debtor from defaulting against the MDB and has options at its disposal to avert such an event. For instance, after the Argentinean default towards its private creditors, the IMF and the World Bank essentially deferred Argentina's debt service by floating exactly the funds needed to prevent the country's multilateral debt from becoming past due.

initially plays by the rules. Thus, at least in the short run the leniency factor will be quite low (near zero) for the bulk of emerging markets, and they must fear getting cut off from official finance in the case of default. Applied to the wide spectrum of emerging market economies, this also means that the benefit of involving an MDB tends to diminish as the state of development advances.

2.2.2 Threat of Judicial Enforcement

One can further alter the model by incorporating the likelihood that the investor is able to recoup all or part of the initial investment with the help of an *enforcement technology* such as the one provided by courts. Indeed, Krasa and Villamil (2000) account for imperfect judicial enforcement that both parties will want to avoid because using it causes a deadweight loss.

The foreign government, in deciding to disown the investor, must make allowances for the possibility of getting sued in court after an expropriation. To forestall this outcome, the government may determine to voluntarily pay the investor a certain sum of money that would be sufficient to avert judicial enforcement. This payment will have to at least equal the expected legal costs of a lawsuit to be borne initially by the plaintiff plus the amount of investment the investor could reasonably expect to recoup by legal action multiplied by the subjective probability of a ruling in the investor's favor. Thus, the utility from non-cooperation is further expanded to

$$(20') \quad B(k) = f(k) + \frac{\beta}{1-\beta}\{f(k^d) + \mu(\beta, k^{MDB})[f(k^f)]\} - c - \eta(x * k^f),$$

where c = the supposedly fixed legal costs, η = the probability of the investor's legal success and x = the share of the investment likely to still be recouped ($0 \leq x \leq 1$).

Alternatively, should the government decide to take its chances and wait for the lawsuit to evolve, the set-up would have to become intertemporal and thus unnecessarily complex.[181] Such a setting would mean taking the model too far considering its rather straightforward purpose.

[181] The model would then have to be a dynamic non-cooperative game with several decision knots. Put simply, first the MDB makes the decision whether or not to suspend payments to the recipient country. In case of forbearance, the investor then decides whether or not to take legal action. If the investor sues, the court then rules whether or not the claim is valid. If the ruling is in favor of the plaintiff, the investor must then try to enforce its claim, which may or may not be feasible. In effect, a series of contingent probabilities would have to be accounted for, all of which are hardly quantifiable.

Box 4: Dispute Settlement Procedures

Procedures to settle disagreements between countries concerning cases of malevolence in FDI projects are typically included in international investment agreements, such as the provisions of the WTO pertaining to FDI. This is seldom the case regarding the rights of investors in investment disputes with states (they are not included, for example, in the EU-Mexico Partnership Agreement, the Framework Agreement on the ASEAN Investment Area or a number of association/cooperation agreements recently concluded by the EU). In some cases host countries have included in their FDI laws the investor's right to choose freely between national and international dispute settlement. If no such provisions are laid down, the investor will have to exhaust internal legal remedies under host country law before turning to international arbitration tribunals, unless otherwise prescribed by the host country's international treaty obligations. Normally, the parties will, however, seek to solve the dispute amicably and informally. Only when all such off-the-record efforts fail will parties consider third-party involvement: first, mediation and only then – in case of failure – arbitration. Often, this gradation of measures is prescribed by investment agreements, and the explicit inclusion of international dispute settlement, or the ad-hoc willingness to allow this, is likely to be motivated by the government's desire to create a favorable investment climate, thereby securing capital inflows. Even so, in difficult disputes an institutional system represents a more promising means of reaching mutually agreeable rulings. This is because parties are constrained from attempting to undermine the proceedings, and awards made will more likely considered "fair" and thus more easily enforceable.

The *International Centre for Settlement of Investment Disputes* (ICSID), created in 1965 under the auspices of the World Bank, provides such a forum accessible to investors from around the globe. Of the 80 cases that, at the time of writing, the *International Centre for Settlement of Investment Disputes* (ICSID) had concluded since 1972 (see www.worldbank.org/icsid/cases/conclude.htm) 34 ended with the ICSID rendering an award to the claimant, 28 were discontinued upon arriving at a settlement, and the remaining cases were either discontinued at the claimant's request or outright rejected as the ICSID declined jurisdiction over the dispute. Most bilateral investment agreements now refer to the ICSID system or other international arbitration systems of investor-state dispute settlement – prominently, the rules of the *United Nations Commission for International Trade Law* (UNCITRAL) – in case amicable means fail to resolve the disagreement. The main advantage of the ICSID is that it provides a structured procedure for resolving investment disputes encompassing jurisdiction, initiation of proceedings, selection of panels, choice of applicable law, rules of procedure as well as recognition and enforcement of awards. ICSID arbitration is especially significant in that the awards bind the parties. Contracting states must recognize and enforce the obligations imposed by the award as if they were a final judgment of a court of the state involved. There are also certain prerequisites for submitting a case to the ICSID: A dispute must be between a state and a national of another state, the parties must agree to ICSID conciliation or arbitration through a clause in an investment agreement or by agreeing ad-hoc to submit an existing dispute to the Centre, and agreement to settle the dispute cannot be unilaterally withdrawn.

A case in point is the *Dispute Settlement Provisions of the North American Free Trade Agreement.* Claimants may choose between the ICSID or the UNCITRAL rules if they decline to pursue remedies in the host country's courts (NAFTA Chapter 11). However, there is a gradation of means in that a party may call for the establishment of an arbitral panel only after state-to-state consultations and a meeting of the NAFTA Free Trade Commission have been futile. Regulations concerning panel selection, rules of procedure and panel decisions are meticulously laid down in Chapter 20 of NAFTA.

Sources: UNCTAD (2003), pp. 114-116; World Bank (2003), p. 22, and NAFTA (www.nafta.sec.alena.org)

Hence, the construct of a lump-sum payment appears to be an elegant way to model the financial pressures associated with possible judicial enforcement mechanisms. Nevertheless, calculating this compensatory payment appears to be a daring task as none of the parameters are readily available. Most problematically, there is no clearly established legal practice in such cases that would help determine the likelihood of a lawsuit's success.[182]

Given the lack of dependable evidence, that would suggest that the allowance for contingent reimbursements should be substantial, the probability weighting factor η and thus the chances of judicial enforcement will be close to zero. Even so, the foreign government may want to display its (possibly feigned) willingness to cooperate by making some voluntary payment in line with the one modeled above. In the end, having an independent MDB stand ready to help enforce the contract by threatening to withhold development credit causes the constraint λ to bind. Regarding the "loss" of investment capital this parallels the "court scenario" where the government must expect an outflow of capital by way of the investor's entering an action.[183]

---

[182] In isolated cases, German investors have been able to obtain a warrant that in principle would enable them to seize the debtor country's physical foreign assets, of which there are almost none to be had in reality. Nicaragua provides a good related case in that the country has so far been successful in proving to judges involved in lawsuits by American investors for repayment of defaulted government debt that under the U.S. Sovereign Immunity Act assets (everything from landing rights owed to the Nicaraguan government by an American airline to a portion of the privatized state telephony company) cannot be seized; see Barham (2003), p. 26.

[183] The second event is not always entirely contingent on the first because an impatient investor may preemptively sue the country in court regardless of what the MDB will do. However, in most cases the investor will await the outcome of the MDB's attempt to enforce its claims.

If, indeed, the involvement of multilateral institutions helps mitigate ad-hoc the risk of default in high-risk environments, commercial investors in such projects should be willing to commit larger amounts of risky capital compared to regular investment projects without official backing. The next section describes the derivation of an appropriate dependent variable.

3 Endogenous Variable Measuring Risk-Adjusted Capital

Analogous to the VaR-concept applied in the finance literature, this study proposes a variable measuring the *capital-at-risk* (*CAR*), which, unpretentiously, is defined as the absolute amount of FDI capital invested in a given foreign bank multiplied by the probability of an individual host country's defaulting on any of its sovereign debt issues over the medium term.[184] In other words, abstaining from complementary legal enforcement technology, the *CAR* represents the expected ex-ante (at least temporary) loss of capital or "exposure", given the likelihood that a particular host country will violate contractual agreements by imposing (additional) capital account restrictions which inhibit the *immediate* access of foreign nationals to their investment and its payoffs.[185] Admittedly, that risk may sometimes be less severe than a country's sovereign risk because the government may decide to leave the investment project untouched regardless of possible multilateral participation. On the other hand, the government may decide to disown private investors before defaulting on its sovereign debt issues. Absent compelling evidence in favor of either position, it appears fair to assume that a country under financial distress is going to obstruct foreign investment projects after a sovereign default.

It is fair to mention that the institutional alternative to involving an MDB financially is to obtain political risk insurance from official or private sources. However, this route is typically quite costly and only compensates for the negative event that co-financing by multilateral agencies seeks to avoid (see Box 5 for details).

[184] As the sample comprises four years (see section 4.4), the absolute amount of equity capital was adjusted in each case for minor inflationary effects using the German GDP deflator.

[185] This harmful action need not necessarily be outright expropriation as discussed in the model.

Box 5: Political Risk Insurance

Historically, official and private insurers have offered protection against various hostile acts by host country governments, the most severe of which is outright expropriation. As explained earlier, this type of risk is lessening in favor of the more comprehensive risk of "contract frustration". Here the problem is that a creeping expropriation, where operations of foreign affiliates are constantly obstructed by the host government, is certainly also categorized as political risk but one against which "event-triggered" risk insurance does not give protection. Furthermore, political risk insurance does not cover risks which cannot be anticipated in advance. While natural disasters ("acts of God") can be insured against, there is typically no risk cover for cumulative policy failures, global acts of terrorism or events triggered by civil society. Nor do they cover action by sub-sovereign levels of government. All in all, non-commercial risk insurance covers less than 5% of FDI stocks in developing countries. After all, this type of insurance cover is costly and does not eradicate the underlying causes of these political risks. Investors would rather that the events that harbor the risk of political risk insurance payment not materialize in the first place. Therefore, any institutional arrangement that will alter the behavior of the host country government such that the incidence of contract frustration becomes highly unlikely appears superior to insurance.

Obtaining risk insurance from multilateral agencies is frequently viewed by investors as too time-consuming or bureaucratically burdensome. Conversely, private insurers, while being more flexible and responsive to investors' needs, cannot rely on governmental guarantees and have to lay it off costly across other insurers and re-insurers. Official bilateral insurers, in spite of large losses over the past two decades, remain the main source of risk insurance against standard political risks. These institutions have paid out more than $150 billion in insurance claims since 1989, with the risk insurance exposure to developing countries rising strongly. German investors needing to cope with high-risk environments can obtain *political risk insurance* offered by the World Bank entity *MIGA* or in Germany by *PriceWaterhouseCoopers* on behalf of the German government. Commenting on the U.S. equivalent *OPIC*, Eaton and Gersovitz (1983, pp. 98-99) argue that this type of insurance does not provide an incentive to carefully weigh the opportunities and risks in a given destination country. Even worse, probably knowing that investors' concern about default is less severe in that case, host governments are less compelled to compare the utilities of honoring contracts and non-cooperation. In such a case one could, therefore, argue that there is no such thing as *capital-at-risk* but solely the "loss" of up-front insurance fees should the insurance eventually prove to be unnecessary. Therefore, direct investors are in less of a truly risky situation. Problematically, some host countries that are prone to commit hostile acts against investors are barred ex-ante from insurance.

A great obstacle to empirically testing the impact of political risk insurance in this study is the fact that *MIGA* does not have very many banking projects in its portfolio. In general, according to a *MIGA* official, political risk insurance is far less likely to be obtained for banking FDI than it is for manufacturing FDI. For these reasons, this study refrains from measuring the effects of political risk insurance on FDI flows.

Source (in part): Mistry and Olesen (2003), pp. 27-32.

The idea of relating invested capital to the probability of default is employed by Razin et al. (2001) who in a lending scenario determine the risk-free required rate of return by adding the residual value of the firm weighted by the default probability to the contracted principal and interest payments weighted by the no-default probability. The probability-weighting approach is also implicit in the discussion instigated by Eaton and Gersovitz (1983, p. 87) who contend that "risk neutral lenders will set the interest rate so that the probability of repayment times the amount to be repaid just equals the gross return that can be made on a safe loan".

The probability of default of sample countries is derived from medium-term default rates of sovereign debt as supplied by leading rating agencies.[186] The first two columns of Table 22 below show Moody's and Standard & Poor's historical default rates for sovereign (and corporate) bonds five years upon issuance, i.e. typically the transition rates for issues downgraded from a speculative investment rating to selective default (SD)[187] over that time span.

Table 22: Credit Ratings and Default Rates

Rating	S&P Sov 5yr (1975-2002)	Moody's Sov 5yr (1985-2002)	Average Sov 5yr	S&P Corp 5yr (1981-2002)	Moody's Corp 5yr (1985-2002)
AAA	0.00	0.00	**0.00**	0.10	0.00
AA	0.00	0.00	**0.00**	0.14	0.20
A	0.00	0.00	**0.00**	0.51	0.56
BBB	5.08	0.00	**2.54**	2.24	2.16
BB	7.46	12.62	**10.54**	10.86	12.99
B	20.00	22.22	**21.11**	31.68	33.18
CCC	n/a	n/a	**n/a**	50.46	59.44*

Source: Standard & Poor's (2003) and Moody's (2003); * also includes ratings "Ca" and "C".

186 A concept similar to the *CAR* is used in practice by, inter alia, the African Development Bank that links the expected loss of a given credit facility over the tenor of the facility (in % of the loan) to an internal risk score.

187 Standard & Poor's generally defines default as the failure of an obligor to meet a principal or interest payment on the due date (or within the specified grace period) contained in the original terms of the debt issue. For that matter, Moody's definition differs somewhat as the borrower is considered in default even if the delayed payment is made within the grace period. Apart from missing repayments, both agencies' definition of default also comprises a country's offer to reschedule its obligations on less favorable terms (lower coupon or par value) in order to avoid a more severe event of default; see Moody's (2003), p. 4, and Standard & Poor's (2003), p. 17.

The ratings of the two most prominent rating agencies do not differ substantially, as the table illustrates.[188] Sub-letter grades (e.g. BBB-) were estimated by regressing the average sovereign default rates (third column above) on the sub-values of Euromoney's credit rating (scores 0-10; original order reversed) using a third-order polynomial.[189] Note that there is no default rate for sovereign issues CCC and lower. This does not mean there have not been any defaults on such highly speculative instruments. On the contrary, according to S&P the CCC/CC default rates were 83% and 100% after one and three years, respectively. However, S&P also advises that with the number of defaults still being very low, the statistical base is subject to small sample bias. It remains yet to be seen how the default rates will evolve as more and more high-risk issuers tap the market for sovereign debt.[190]

It might have been reasonable to set the default rate for such issues uniformly at 50%, as this number takes account of the historical five-year default rates for CCC/CC-rated corporate issues – the lower of the two ratings is 50.7% (see column four) – to which the sovereign default rates are expected to converge over time.[191] Up until recently, the so-called sovereign ceiling set the upper limit for corporate issues. In other words, the rating of a domestic corporation effectively never exceeded the one for its country.[192]

---

[188] The striking difference in the BBB ratings is probably due to a diverging rating for Indonesia, which was initially rated investment grade by S&P while, presumably, being included by Moody's in the speculative investment cohort from the outset; see Standard & Poor's (2003), p. 5.

[189] The resulting equation was $y=-0.6151x+1.1876x^2-0.0731x^3$ ($R^2=1.0000$; the small negative constant term was omitted to render the fit virtually perfect).

[190] The number of emerging market issuers placing sovereign bonds for the first time has picked up sharply since the mid-1990s. After a temporary slump due to the Asian and tech-related stock market crises, the number appears to have leveled off at around three new issuers per year; see Grigorian (2003), pp. 14, 19.

[191] Standard & Poor's (2003) review of historical default rate stresses that the difference in default probability between sovereign and corporate issuers as shown in the right hand-side columns of Table 22 should not be viewed as significant because of the small number of rated sovereigns ever having defaulted on their bonds. As that number rises over time, the sovereign default rate should broadly parallel the default rates for similarly rated corporate issuers. For reference, columns four and five display Moody's and S&P's five-year default rates for corporate issues. As can be seen, the differences between the average sovereign default rates and those for the corporate side are relatively small already now that the base of speculative grade sovereign issuers is just beginning to take shape.

[192] See Kräussl (2003), p. 32. This longstanding notion was recently annulled in the Argentinean case when sovereign bond spreads rose above corporate ones; see Schobert (2003), p. 175. Even so, the sovereign ceiling is by and large substantiated by the incidents of default observed across the letter grades displayed in Table 22.

However, to still make a distinction between relatively "viable" countries with a CCC rating and those in or close to default, the empty continuum, i.e. the range between credit ratings lower than BBB- and highly risky countries in default or without rating, is filled by linking the default probability to Euromoney's comprehensive country risk score, which, in the event, ranged between 34.93 and 16.71. An exponential trend of default rates as has been shown to be the case with better-rated issues shall not be assumed. Instead, for simplicity, a linear relationship is implied: Bangladesh, having the highest country risk score of the sub-sample, is given the estimated default rate immediately below the one of a B- rating, while lowest-rated Yugoslavia is assigned a 65% probability of default (for a full list of country rates see Table 28, Appendix IV).[193]

4 Estimation Techniques, Exogenous Variables and Sample Selection

As mentioned before, the purpose of this investigation is to determine whether there is indeed a causal effect of a certain "treatment" – in this case a multilateral development bank's participation in an FDI project – on said outcome variable, *CAR*, experienced by units in the population of interest which is the group of projects with MDB participation. Before turning to the matching estimator approach and describing the exogenous variables used in this study as well as the selection of the sample, the following sections review the literature on the application of program evaluation methods.

4.1 The Problem of Self-Selection in Program Evaluation

It is only in purely experimental settings, i.e. the random drawing of program participants from a pool of eligible individuals, that there can be certainty about the absence of differences in unobserved characteristics related to participation in the program. Accordingly, self-selection of participants can be ruled out in this case. It is then possible to estimate the treatment effect for the group as a whole (at the "population level") because, irrespective of actual participation, any individual or project could have been chosen. The same applies if sampling is non-random but units react uniformly to the treatment (homogeneous treatment effects). However, if projects are assigned to the treatment using a certain decision rule (or self-select into the program) *and* the treatment causes units to perform differently (heterogeneous treatment effects), only the effect of

[193] The two projects in the *West Bank and the Gaza Strip* (Palestine authorities) were assigned a country risk score of 10, while the one on the *British Virgin Islands* received a score of 40, which in 1999 was about the average of the small island economies in the Caribbean.

the treatment on the treated units can be evaluated. The following two sections will elaborate further on this distinction and its implications for measuring the treatment effect.

4.1.1 Homogeneous Treatment Effects

Assuming homogeneous treatment effects of a uniform treatment effect α for all participants (which is more likely to occur in an experimental setting), it is sufficient to simply compare the average outcome of the "treated" units given their participation in the program $(Y_1 \mid D = 1)$ and "non-treated" ones given their staying aloof $(Y_0 \mid D = 0)$.[194] Hence, the observed outcome for the treated unit i is

(21) $Y_i = Y_{0i} + D_i(Y_{1i} - Y_{0i})$ or : $\hat{\alpha} = \bar{Y}_1 - \bar{Y}_0$, denoting differences in mean outcomes.[195]

This simple comparison is possible because the control group of non-participants is statistically equivalent to the treated group. Formally, the expected outcomes for both groups in case of non-participation – hypothetically so with respect to the participants – are equal. The "ideal" case of homogeneous effects is, however, rarely observed in practice. Even in an experimental setting the behavior of participants when administered the treatment might change. Thus, the case of heterogeneous treatment effects may be considered to be the standard.

4.1.2 Heterogeneous Treatment Effects

The treatment is likely to have divergent (heterogeneous) effects on the group of program participants – individuals react to the program in different ways and consequently achieve different outcomes. Blundell and Costa Dias (2000, pp. 432-434) show that if the homogeneity assumption is lifted in favor of an individual effect α_i, only the impact of the program on the group of participating ("treated") projects can be identified. This introduces another error term ε_i denoting the deviation of unit i from the population mean, whereas the term $E(\varepsilon_i \mid D_i = 1)$ signifies the mean deviation of the treatment effect among participants. Thus, the outcome regression equation, ignoring other regressors and time subscripts, now has the following form:

---

194 Given that the selection criteria are applied to both groups, $D = 0$ indicates that the project at hand either did not meet the eligibility criteria or, more likely, was not submitted for consideration in the co-financing program.

195 See Sianesi (2001), p. 2, and Blundell and Costa Dias (2000), p. 434.

(22) $Y_i = \beta + D_i\bar{\alpha} + [U_i + D_i\varepsilon_i] = \beta + D_i\bar{\alpha} + [U_i + D_i(\alpha_i - \bar{\alpha})]$

as $\alpha_i = \bar{\alpha} + \varepsilon_i$ and $\alpha_{treated} = \bar{\alpha} + E(\varepsilon_i \mid D_i = 1)$,

where $\bar{\alpha}$ is the mean impact at the population level.

Assuming heterogeneous effects, ε_i will be non-zero for one or more units. Consequently, the expected individual error term $E(D_i\varepsilon_i)$ should also be different from zero, as should the mean deviation of the impact $E(\varepsilon_i \mid D_i = 1)$. The OLS estimator, by construction, attempts to measure the average treatment effect for all units:

(23) $E(\hat{\alpha}) = E(Y_i \mid D=1) - E(Y_i \mid D=0)$

$= \{\beta + 1 * [\bar{\alpha} + E(\varepsilon_i \mid D=1)] + E(U_i \mid D=1)\} - \{\beta + 0 * [\bar{\alpha} + E(\varepsilon_i \mid D=0)] + E(U_i \mid D=0)\}$

$= \bar{\alpha} + E(\varepsilon_i \mid D=1) + E(U_i \mid D=1) - E(U_i \mid D=0).$

However, even if the two latter terms are zero because of non-correlation of the U_i with the participation status D_i, the estimator has trouble keeping apart the genuine treatment effect α and the apparent effect which incorporates $E(\varepsilon_i \mid D_i = 1)$. The estimates will therefore be biased if the latter term is different from zero.[196] Put another way, even if the control group turns out to be comparable to the treatment group based on observable information, it is not possible to be sure about the absence of differences in unobservables which are related to individual program participation. It might well be the case that superior (inferior) firms predominately self-select into the sponsorship program. As each unit may be assumed to take individual performance characteristics into account in applying to a program, its specific component of the treatment effect will then be correlated with the decision process. If treated banks are more (less) capable than their non-treated counterparts, there is reason to expect that they should perform better (worse) even if they were not chosen for the program. As this situation cannot be observed, the OLS estimator would therefore overstate (or understate) the treatment impact. In other words, we have no information about the performance in the hypothetical counterfactual situation – a typical missing-data problem. Constructing the suitable counterfactual or, alternatively, correcting for selection bias are to be considered the central issues that evaluation techniques seek to address.

[196] For a detailed description of the problem of non-random selection and the associated bias see also Goldstein and Montiel (1986), pp. 316-319.

4.2 Overview of Evaluation Techniques

4.2.1 Evaluation Techniques Correcting for Unobservable Factors

Given that most project evaluations take place in a non-experimental setting, evaluation techniques must handle the central problem of the non-random selection of program participants and the identification of the suitable counterfactual outcome. This is typically done by constructing an optimal control group of non-participants whose outcomes closely emulate the unobserved results program participants would have displayed in the hypothetical case of non-participation.[197] In other words, a proper measure of program effectiveness would isolate the impact of the program on the outcome and compare it with what would have resulted in the absence of the program.[198] By contrast, some methods – the *Heckman Selection Model* and the *Generalized Evaluation Estimator* – seek to correct for the influence of unobservable characteristics on program outcome.

In the literature several measures have been proposed to construct appropriate counterfactuals. Beyond the simplistic "*before-after*" approach (which compares outcomes in the pre-program period with those upon completion of the program under the unrealistic assumption of all other exogenous factors remaining the same) and the only marginally more sophisticated "*with-without*" method (which contrasts participation and non-participation outcomes under the false, bias-prone prior that program participants do not ex ante differ systematically from the rest of units),[199] there are four noteworthy approaches to program evaluation that try to deal with the selection bias problem (see for reference Barro and Lee (2002), pp. 23-27, Blundell and Costa Dias (2000), pp. 427-441, Bulíř and Moon (2003), pp. 14-20, and Haque and Khan (1998), pp. 10-11, 23-24).

4.2.1.1 Instrumental Variables Technique

It is possible to circumvent the problem of the self-selection problem if at least one instrument is available that is related to the selection decision but exogenous to the dependent variable in the outcome equation. This regressor must fulfill three requirements. First, it must to able to determine program participation, i.e. the coefficient must be significantly different from zero. Second, there is a

---

[197] See Blundell and Costa Dias (2000), pp. 428, 437.

[198] See Haque and Khan (1998), p. 7.

[199] See also the critical remarks about both approaches by Barro and Lee (2002), p. 24.

transformation for the instrument that is found to be uncorrelated with the error term. Finally, the instrument is not (almost) completely determined by the exogenous variables. In other words, the instrument represents a source of independent variation that is correlated with the selection decision but does not influence the outcomes from program participation directly.[200]

Unsurprisingly, the main difficulty with this approach is the lack of good instruments that would meet all three conditions. A solution can be to use lagged values of the independent variables as instruments, but only under the rather bold assumption that these are not strongly correlated with future values. In the presence of heterogeneous treatment effects, the instrument variable approach cannot be applied because the estimator will be biased given that the error term includes the participation status which itself is directly determined by the instrument. In the empirical evaluation literature the instrument variables technique has been applied in cross-country regressions by Przeworski and Vreeland (2000), Barro (2001) and Barro and Lee (2002).

4.2.1.2 Heckman Selection Model[201]

This technique, which was developed by James Heckman (1979), corrects for possible selection bias arising from units' self-selecting into the program. In other words, the selection is truncated when some projects in the pool of possible program participants are less likely than others to enter into the program or are even barred from participation given certain characteristics. To correct for the bias, the participation decision has to be estimated via probit simultaneously with the outcome equation containing performance and policy parameters, thereby allowing for the endogenous determination of the participation variable. If the error terms of the participation equation $z_i^* = w_i'\gamma + u_i$ and the outcome equation $y_i = x_i'\beta + \varepsilon_i$ are correlated ($\rho_{ui,\, \epsilon i} \neq 0$) the coefficient of the policy variables cannot be estimated consistently. Accordingly, to correct for the bias there has to be at least one regressor among the w_i in the participation equation with a non-zero coefficient that is independent of the error term u_i. To achieve joint normality of error terms, the Heckman correction for selectivity bias has to be performed. The idea of this estimator is to control directly for the part of the error term in the outcome equation that is correlated with the participation status, thus rendering an error term that is no longer

[200] See Blundell and Costa Dias (2000), p. 438.

[201] For a detailed critique of the Heckman correction see Puhani (2000).

correlated with the participation decision.[202] The expected outcome given program participation now is[203]

$$(24)\quad E(Y_i \mid d_i = 1, x_i, z_i) = x_i'\beta + \delta^{prog} + \rho\sigma_\varepsilon \frac{\phi(w_i'\gamma)}{\Phi(w_i'\gamma)},$$

$$\left[\begin{array}{l} \text{since } E(Y_i \mid z_i^* > 0) = E(Y_i \mid u_i > -w_i'\gamma_i) = x_i'\beta + E(\varepsilon_i \mid u_i > -w_i'\gamma_i) = x_i'\beta + \rho\sigma_\varepsilon\lambda_u, \\ \text{with } \lambda_u \text{ equivalent to } \dfrac{\phi(w_i'\gamma/\sigma_u)}{\Phi(w_i'\gamma/\sigma_u)} \end{array}\right],$$

where x_i is the vector of all predetermined policy and other exogenous variables, β is the vector of parameters to be estimated and δ measures the effect of program participation. The additional correction term is the *inverse Mills ratio* $\Phi(\bullet)/\Phi(\bullet)$, i.e. the quotient of the standard normal probability density function and the standard normal cumulative density function for the exogenous variables in the participation equation, multiplied by ρ being the correlation between the equations' error terms and σ_ε the standard deviation of the outcome equation's error term. The inverse Mills ratio needs to be estimated by means of probit estimation. Correspondingly, the expected outcome for the non-participants results to be

$$(24')\quad E(Y_i \mid d_i = 0, x_i, z_i) = x_i'\beta + \rho\sigma_\varepsilon \frac{-\phi(w_i'\gamma)}{1-\Phi(w_i'\gamma)},$$

where $1-\Phi$ is the truncated normal distribution. The difference in expectations of the participants and non-participants then depends only on the effect of program participation, corrected for selection bias:

$$(25)\quad E(Y_i \mid d_i = 1, x_i, z_i) - E(Y_i \mid d_i = 0, x_i, z_i) = \delta^{prog} + \rho\sigma_\varepsilon \frac{\phi(w_i'\gamma)}{1-\Phi(w_i'\gamma)}$$

$$\left[\text{since } \frac{\phi}{\Phi} - \frac{-\phi}{1-\Phi} = \frac{\phi(1-\Phi)-(-\phi\Phi)}{\Phi(1-\Phi)} = \frac{\phi}{\Phi(1-\Phi)}\right].$$

As a result, after appropriately accounting for selection bias, the genuine impact of the treatment can effectively be separated from the influence of the selection process.

---

[202] See Blundell and Costa Dias (2000), p. 439.

[203] See Greene (2003), pp. 782-783 and 787-788.

4.2.1.3 Generalized Evaluation Estimator (GEE)

Developed by Goldstein and Montiel (1986) originally to assess the effectiveness of IMF country stabilization programs, the Generalized Evaluation Estimator attempts to capture the effects of policy variables on the outcome variables. The model is set up to incorporate non-program determinants of outcomes so that the outcomes that would have resulted in the absence of program participation can be identified. In effect, the model tries to render endogenous not only the outcomes but also the behavioral reactions of all units at the population level. In contrast to other evaluation techniques, the GEE is not based on the distinction between program and non-program units since program participants are not separately identified as such.[204]

The GEE works as follows: first, a regression for participation in a program is run which accounts for pre-program differences in characteristics between units that determine a country's decision to participate in a program. This procedure, which is also used by the matching approach (see section 4.2.2), is deemed capable of describing systematic selection of program participation based on observable information. Participation status is thus determined empirically. Next, the GEE aims to capture the impact of policy and other variables on the outcomes in that it expressly considers the formulation of policies that would have materialized in the absence of the program. In the context of IMF programs the change of a country's macroeconomic policy instruments between periods will depend on the gap between the desired value of the target variable and its actual value one period ago. It suffices to say that the government will want to bring a target variable that has been off-course back to its normal level. Technically speaking, the below reaction function (26) has to be fitted to observable data for the non-participants, replacing for participants the desired outcomes by a set of country-specific constants. By using data on actual policy reactions of non-participants to assess those for participants, the fitted values then constitute the correct counterfactual for program countries. Specifically, the policy reaction function regresses the change in policy variables Δx_i on the required adjustment to an imbalance, represented by a prespecified (desired) improvement y_i^d in the outcome variable over its lagged value $(y_i)_{-1}$, so that

$$(26) \quad \Delta x_i = \gamma'[y_i^d - (y_i)_{-1}] + \varepsilon_i .$$

The left-hand variable is defined as the autonomous policy reaction that provides the basis for estimating the counterfactual outcome for program

[204] See Goldstein and Montiel (1986), pp. 306, 308-309.

participants.[205] The coefficient of the target variable γ can be thought of as the speed of adjustment to exogenous shocks, assuming that all projects, both program and non-program units, are potentially hit by the same shocks. Lastly, the unobserved hypothetical policy changes are replaced by the estimated policy reaction parameters above. The independent effect of program participation ("treatment") on the outcome variable in first differences can then be estimated using OLS. The GEE can be combined with the Heckman correction if there is reason to assume that non-random selection based on unobservable characteristics is present.[206]

Some critics have questioned whether the change in the policy reaction function really constitutes the near-perfect counterfactual. Specifically, knowledge of the elements of the policy reaction function is required which also puts some demands on data availability.[207] Nevertheless, the GEE approach has emerged as a widely-used evaluation technique, having been applied but also criticized at the same time by, for example, Conway (1994)[208] and Dicks-Mireaux et al. (2000).[209]

---

[205] See Goldstein and Montiel (1986), p. 311, 324-325.

[206] Ibid., pp. 325-326.

[207] See Haque and Khan (1998), p. 11. On a different note, Barro and Lee (2002) challenge Haque and Khan's (1998) method of correction for selection bias in their GEE application on grounds of unreasonable assumptions associated with the selection equation – variables that are excluded from the performance equation do not appear in the former.

[208] Among other things, Conway decomposes the beneficial treatment effect of an IMF program into a "credentialling" and an "adjustment" effect. The former is associated with the pure announcement benefit that a country reaps by attaining access to IMF credit and is technically isolated by considering countries that did not draw down any of the allocated IMF funds. The adjustment effect, in turn, is analyzed for countries that implemented IMF conditions and consequently were capacitated to use up IMF funding over the program period. The author was able to give empirical support to the adjustment effect while finding no such evidence for the credentialling effect; see Conway (1994), pp. 384-385.

[209] Dicks-Mireaux and his co-authors question the assumptions underlying the GEE's policy reaction function. In a multi-country setting individual countries are likely to formulate policies with respect to different or changing objective functions and constraints. Also, according to the authors it is doubtful that all countries, both participants and non-participants, should have identical reaction functions. The functions themselves, using simple lagged values related to desired contemporaneous ones, also express the assumption that all shocks are transitory, meaning that one-period changes in target variables are fully reversed in the following period. Moreover, the commonly used additive constant term δ^{prog} may not be sufficient to capture the multitude of channels through which program (here: IMF) support could affect target variables. The authors also point to the necessity to conduct standard specification tests for both the GEE and the policy reaction function before deriving hard conclusions from the estimations. For their sample of countries they show the estimates of the reaction function to be poor and thus only a weak basis for deriving estimates of the unobservable counterfactual policies for program periods; see Dicks-Mireaux et al. (2000), pp. 499-500, 508.

4.2.1.4 Comparison of Simulations (SIM)

As the name implies, the SIM technique does not evaluate actual programs but examines the general effects of changeable policy packages by simulating what the program outcome would be, given a specific set of policy measures. The main advantages of the SIM approach proposed by Khan and Knight (1981, 1985) are a larger set of information as all units – not just those in a program – can be analyzed, the avoidance of incorrect conclusions about program success for insufficiently implemented programs since in the simulation all programs are completed, and the focus on the direct relationship between the policy mix and policy targets.

As is the case with all experiments, the drawback of the SIM is, of course, that real-world problems such as time-varying parameters are assumed away in favor of fixed relationships in the model. Logically, the actual effect of experimental policy packages may differ considerably from the simulated outcome, and the cause of this discrepancy is difficult to foresee. Another practical problem is determining the impact of policies on crucial macroeconomic variables to be included in a comprehensive model. Even if such a model existed, the Lucas critique of the inappropriateness of ex ante econometric policy evaluation would still apply. Perhaps for these reasons, the SIM approach has not caught on in the empirical evaluation literature.

4.2.2 Selection on Observables: Propensity Score Matching

The non-parametric propensity score matching approach deals with the problem of selection bias by instructing to select observable project characteristics so that units with the same "values" of these factors will not exhibit systematic differences in their reactions to reform. This approach can be described as "selection on observables" and thus differs markedly from the Heckman model that aims to correct for selection on unobservables.[210] It overcomes the common failure to "weight comparably" by creating a *control group* and then re-weighting its data to equate the distribution of observable characteristics in the participant and non-participant samples:[211] Every treated unit is matched to a non-treated unit which at the time before the treatment is as similar as possible, if not virtually identical, in its characteristics. Outcome differences between the

[210] See Blundell and Costa Dias, pp. 429-430.

[211] See Heckman et al. (1997), p. 626. The authors give an example of the "classical" application for the matching estimator which is the evaluation of the effectiveness of job training programs.

groups can then be attributed to the treatment.[212] Therefore, it is possible under some assumptions to estimate the *average treatment effect* (ATT) at the population level – a concept that goes back to the work of Rubin (1974). Algebraically, the causal effect that results from co-financing by the MDB is

(27) $E[Y_1 - Y_0 \mid D=1] = E[Y_1 \mid D=1] - E[Y_0 \mid D=1]$.

While the first term can be estimated as the mean value of the outcome variable of treated units, the second term denotes the "correct yardstick",[213] which is the unobservable counterfactual result – the outcome the participants would have experienced, on average, had they not participated.[214] This method is termed "observational" (or "non-experimental") because it uses data of non-participants to infer counterfactual outcomes for program participants.[215] Note that the matching approach only delivers unbiased results if the *conditional independence assumption* (CIA) postulated by Rubin (1977)

(28) $(Y_0, Y_1) \perp D \mid X = x \; (CIA)$ is fulfilled.

The condition describes the situation where participation in the program and potential outcome are independent for units with the same set of conditioning variables ($X = x$). Put differently, under the CIA the outcomes of country group units are independent of the participation status, once observable characteristics are controlled for. Assuming this non-correlation, the selection occurs only on observables. Importantly, the set of conditioning variables completely determines the participation decision: all units, if offered the treatment, would choose to participate. This means that knowledge of the relevant variables suffices to construct a control group with the desired similarities to the participants.[216] The independence assumption is a necessary condition because a Heckman correction is not performed in non-parametric treatment models. If the CIA is valid – there are on average no systematic differences between firms with and without "official support" and therefore no selection bias – then $E(Y_0 \mid D=0, X=x)$ can reasonably be used as a measure of potential outcome for the program participants:

(29) $E[Y_0 \mid D=1, X=x] = E[Y_0 \mid D=0, X=x]$.

---

[212] See Wagner (2002), pp. 288-289.

[213] Haque and Khan (1998), p. 7.

[214] See Sianesi (2001), p. 3, and Almus and Czarnitzki (2003), pp. 229-230.

[215] See Heckman et al. (1997), p. 610.

[216] See Blundell and Costa Dias (2000), pp. 445, 447.

The *average effect of treatment on the treated* then is

$$(30) \quad ATT = E[Y_1 \mid D=1, X=x] - E[Y_0 \mid D=0, X=x].$$

However, the CIA is entirely fulfilled only if *all* variables that influence the participation status[217] are known as well as quantifiable. This stipulation may not hold for non-experimental data if the treatment decision D depends on additional variables which are not independent of Y_0 given X.[218] It is, therefore, crucial to emulate the actual decision-making process of the sponsoring agency as accurately as possible so that after-the-fact deviations from the agency's postulated measurable selection criteria are virtually non-systematic. This set of criteria used in matching can be considered a "filter" for re-establishing the conditions of an experimental setting. Under the assumptions associated with the matching approach, the only remaining difference between treated units and members of the control group is program participation.[219] However, there may also be non-measurable factors – for example, information asymmetries among investors – that influence the resultant volume of investment. In the absence of such firm-level information, it is therefore necessary to assume that, on average, the two groups do not differ in this respect.

To characterize similar firms, a large number of their exogenous properties is required in larger samples to ensure validity of the CIA (high "dimensionality" of X). This necessity represents an obstacle to estimating the causal effect because there are hardly any firms that are virtually identical in all of their characteristics.[220] To overcome this "curse of dimensionality", the study matches the *propensity scores* between groups which is the probability that a given project has received treatment, given a set of individual characteristics that are depicted by the conditioning variables[221]

$$(31) \quad \Pr[D_1 \mid X=x] \textit{ with } 0 < \Pr < 1 \textit{ for } x \in \widetilde{X};\ \widetilde{X} = \text{common support region}.$$[222]

---

[217] It is important to keep in mind that the participation decision cannot be observed among non-participants. These units may have abstained either because they were not invited to participate or because they were rejected by the decision-making body after filing an application; see Blundell and Costa Dias (2000), p. 447.

[218] See Heckman et al. (1997), p. 611.

[219] See Blundell and Costa Dias (2000), pp. 444-445.

[220] See Almus and Czarnitzki (2003), p. 230.

[221] See Sianesi (2001), p. 4.

[222] Common support signifies the ability to find comparable control group units for program participants. There will be a bias if not all projects are on common support; see Heckman et al. (1997), p. 611.

As Rosenbaum and Rubin (1983) show, it is sufficient to condition on the one-dimensional propensity score to ensure statistical independence between potential outcome and acceptance into the program if the CIA is indeed fulfilled. In this study the propensity scores are obtained by a probit estimation of a dummy variable indicating whether or not a given bank is a participant on all the relevant firm characteristics at the time of the MDB's co-financing decision.[223]

Having estimated the propensity scores, each treated unit i is "paired" to some group of "comparable" non-treated units using a certain measure of proximity with respect to the scores. There are a number of matching estimators that can be grouped into "individual neighborhood" ("one-to-one" procedure, such as "nearest neighbor" or, in case of substantial gaps between units, "caliper" matching) estimators and those using "weights". In the present study, an estimator from the second group is used since, given the relatively small sample size, there may not be a close-by nearest neighbor, or a "near-perfect twin", within the control group. For this reason, *kernel-based matching* is applied which represents a weighted average over the outcomes of multiple non-treated units in the control group where the weight given to non-treated unit j is proportional to the proximity of the observables of units i and j.[224] The associated matched outcome is[225]

$$(32)\quad \hat{y}_i = \frac{\sum_{j\in\{D=0\}} K\left(\frac{p_i - p_j}{h}\right) y_j}{\sum_{j\in\{D=0\}} K\left(\frac{p_i - p_j}{h}\right)},$$

with the control group's outcome y_j weighted by

$$w_{ij} = \frac{K\left(\frac{p_i - p_j}{h}\right)}{\sum_{j\in\{D=0\}} K\left(\frac{p_i - p_j}{h}\right)},$$

[223] See Wagner (2002), p. 291.

[224] In other words, if the weights are derived from a symmetric, non-negative and unimodal kernel, the average places a higher weight on units close in terms of their characteristics and a lower weight on those with more distant propensity scores; see Heckman et al. (1997), p. 630, where one also finds a good overview of alternative matching estimators (pp. 631-632).

[225] See Sianesi (2001), pp. 10-11.

where p is the propensity score, h is the bandwidth and K(•) denotes the Kernel function. In the empirical application the Gaussian Kernel is used.[226] Consequently, the difference between the observed outcome and the matched outcome is the treatment effect – here, the hoped-for impact of involving a multilateral development bank in a banking FDI project.

Propensity score matching is being increasingly applied in the literature on the firm-level effects of foreign takeovers. For example, Pfaffermayr and Bellak (2003) use both nearest neighbor and caliper matching to determine the difference in growth of firm size and productivity upon the takeover for Austria, while Ilmakunnas and Maliranta (2004) as well as Martins (2003) use – in addition to applying the regular propensity score matching – the related "difference-in-differences" estimator to determine the post-takeover productivity and wage differentials in the Finnish and Portuguese economies, respectively.

4.3 Exogenous Variables

As mentioned before, to obtain the propensity scores a probit regression of the participation likelihood on the units' characteristics, represented by certain exogenous variables, needs to be run. The exogenous variables required to depict the sample projects' characteristics were derived by interviewing IFC officials[227] (for a more detailed description of IFC's selection process and the choice of variables; see Box 6, Appendix IV).

As it turns out, there are five central selection criteria that are regularly applied by IFC's decision-making bodies (name, definition and source of corresponding exogenous variables in parentheses):

[226] On the intricacies of kernel-based matching see Greene (2003), pp. 452-456 and 704-708.

[227] Interviews conducted with banking projects officers at the IFC in Washington D.C. on April 17 and 22, 2003. No such interview was solicited from the other multilateral agency included, the EBRD in London, as the number of German banking FDI projects sponsored exclusively by this multilateral agency only amounted to five (i.e. 25 % of the sub-sample of treated investors). It is to be assumed that EBRD's selection criteria do not differ substantially from those applied by IFC.

- A lack of development of the financial market abroad (*CREDGDP*, specified as 100 minus *claims on the private sector*[228] divided by GDP; taken from the World Bank's World Development Indicators),
- the quality/stringency of banking regulation and supervision in the host country (*BANKREG*; taken from the database compiled by Barth et al. (2001)[229]),
- the prior experience of the individual German investor in emerging market FDI projects (*EXPERIENCE*, a binary choice variable set to equal one if there were at least five previous projects at the time the MDB made its decision; derived from the database of the Deutsche Bundesbank containing the German FDI stock statistics),
- the investment target's return on assets in % (*RETURN*; derived from the FDI database),
- the investment target's equity capitalization in % (*CAPRATIO*; paid-in equity capital[230] divided by total assets; derived from the FDI database).

Note that the first two criteria can be termed macroeconomic as they describe the banking environment in the host countries while the other variables depict characteristics at the firm level. It cannot be ruled out that in particular cases IFC applies other, not objectively measurable standards. These subliminal factors are then non-systematic, however.

The following table gives an overview of the means, standard deviations and extreme values of the variables employed:

---

[228] Includes gross credit from the financial system to individuals, enterprises, non-financial public entities not included under net domestic credit, and financial institutions not included elsewhere.

[229] The scores of *BANKREG* range from 0 to 20 points and were derived by summing up the individual scores assigned to responses to a survey questionnaire distributed among national banking supervisory agencies. The supervisors responded to 16 questions relating to the *official supervisory power* (sub-classified into prompt corrective action, restructuring power, declaring insolvency power) and 4 questions on *supervisory forbearance discretion*. A single point was assigned when the answer was favorable with respect to actual supervisory power; see Barth et al. (2001), pp. 19-20, 62, 66 (not all countries appear in Figures 13 and 17 of that paper – in the case of missing data scores were re-calculated using the information contained in the corresponding database). As the two survey areas of banking supervision are closely intertwined, the two scores were combined into a single one, called *BANKREG* here. The non-evaluated Palestine territories were assigned a rating of zero by default.

[230] Note that, due to lack of information, the equity capital could not be risk-adjusted.

Table 23: Statistical Properties of Exogenous as well as Endogenous Variables

Variable	Observations	Mean	Std. Deviation	Minimum	Maximum
CREDGDP	77	65.580	27.452	0.000	100.000
BANKREG	77	13.701	3.947	0.000	20.000
EXPERIENCE	77	0.766	0.426	0.000	1.000
RETURN	77	-1.683	11.575	-74.845	9.089
CAPRATIO	77	33.061	34.897	0.209	100.000
CAR	77	857.841	1363.609	0.160	9805.114
CAR_TA	77	0.001416	0.022358	0.000010	0.108293

The negative mean for the return variable may come as a surprise but it should be borne in mind that almost all of the projects are at an infant stage and that set-up costs dominate the picture. This supposition is substantiated by the wide distribution of capital ratios. Some of the banks were initially financed by equity only (see the maximum of 100%). Tables 29 and 30 in Appendix IV show the descriptive statistics for the treatment and control group, respectively.

4.4 Sample Selection

To bring about relative homogeneity of investment projects and thus to fulfill the central independence assumption to the greatest possible extent, the sample of host countries was carefully restricted to comparable cases. In doing so, apart from G7, EU and EFTA countries as well as Australia and New Zealand, some advanced financial centers such as Hong Kong, Taiwan, and Singapore were omitted. Other relatively developed emerging market economies, such as some of the countries which will accede to the EU, remained in the sample, as did a number of developing countries in Africa whose financial markets, given private equity flows into the banking sector at least from Germany, are to be called *emerging*.

The sample's time period was set to run from 1998 to 2001 (FDI data for 2001 were still preliminary at the time of writing). Usable firm-level data are available in the Bundesbank's FDI stock statistics only from 1996 onward. The late starting year was chosen, for one thing, to account for changed investor behavior in the aftermath of the Asian crisis. For another, by leaving out FDI projects initiated before 1998, it is ensured that in-sample projects in more advanced countries serve rather specialized purposes since the large commercial banks surely entered several periods beforehand. Next, all majority-owned subsidiaries were eliminated from the sample because the MDBs would not co-finance such projects that are dominated by one investor. Two projects that were unambiguous outliers (their capital-at-risk was greater than full-sample average *CAR* multiplied by five times the variable's standard deviation) had to be excluded as well.

Overall, the restricted sample comprises 77 FDI projects undertaken by 21 German investors[231] in 47 emerging financial markets. Of these projects, 20 were identified to have been co-financed[232] by IFC and/or EBRD.[233] Usually, firms solicit the participation of IFC or EBRD shortly after making the initial investment. Only in rare instances is there a consortium of private and official investors seeking to establish a jointly-owned bank abroad.

5 Empirical Results

Both principal program evaluation methods – the Heckman selection model, sometimes also referred to as the treatment effects model,[234] and the propensity score matching approach – could be used in the empirical investigation. However, applying the former is actually not feasible in this study, as none of the exogenous variables that are necessary for estimating the outcome equation are known. In principle, it would be possible to apply the common determinants of banking FDI – for example, the size of the financial market, GDP per capita or trade linkages. However, it would be daring to make inferences for this sample's exclusive group of banking projects. There may be different forces at work for these rather specialized projects than for large "mainstream" ones.

If the Heckman correction technique is applied nonetheless it becomes obvious that the model is misspecified because the outcome equation lacks exogenous variables. Table 31, Appendix IV, illustrates that, while the treatment effect

---

[231] While investment targets were restricted to those operating in the financial sector, no such limitation was imposed on investors. Nonetheless, only 3 firms investing in 4 different projects abroad were classified as belonging to non-financial sectors.

[232] Eight projects were co-financed by lending, four projects by providing equity capital, and another four projects received hybrid financing. For the remaining four projects no exact information was available on the type of capital invested.

[233] To the best of the author's knowledge, none of the other major MDBs (e.g. the African Development Bank, the Asian Development Bank and the Inter-American Development Bank) co-financed German banking FDI projects over the sample period.

[234] For details and instructions for empirical application see StataCorp. (2003), References S-Z, pp. 273-283.

(coefficient of *SPONSOR*) is positive for the dependent variable *CAR*, it is also insignificant at conventional levels. Moreover, the Heckman correction does not work because the inverse Mills ratio turns out to be insignificant as well. The correlation between the error terms (*rho*) is negative, but, as the error term of the outcome equation has to absorb the remaining variation, the result is not meaningful. The results do not change much if *CREDGDP* is included in the outcome equation (and eliminated from the participation equation), reasonably assuming that foreign banks seek to enter financial markets that are not fully developed yet. While *CREDGDP* turns out to be significant at the 10% level for absolute capital-at-risk, both treatment parameters do remain insignificant (δ = 0.57, λ = -0.36). Consequently, as long as there is no insight into the motivation underlying this type of banking FDI, the Heckman selection model cannot be put into practice here.

5.1 Absolute Capital-at-Risk

Propensity score matching is more appropriate for testing the hypothesis of this paper because it does not require an outcome equation to be estimated. Put simply, the matching method ignores the question of why a certain bank carried out an FDI project in a given location. Rather, it simply measures the relevant (i.e. counterfactual-based) difference in the dependent variable given that a certain project was supported by a multilateral development bank. Applying the matching approach yields the probit estimation and matching outcome contained in Table 24.

Note that both exogenous macro variables turn out to be highly significant for the decision whether a project given its characteristics is to be supported. The variable depicting lack of financial market development, *CREDGDP*, is significant even at the 1% level. This finding is fully in line with the primary task of IFC/EBRD in this area which is fostering the establishment of private banks in underdeveloped financial markets. Prior exposure of investors in emerging markets also matters for the selection, as the high z-value of *EXPERIENCE* illustrates. The unexpected lack of significance of the other two firm-level variables may owe something to either variable misspecification or the mere fact that the MDBs selected a number of projects despite lackluster performance of these banks. It may well be that these variables do not matter as much in the decision-making process after all.

Table 24: Propensity Score Matching and Treatment Effects (Absolute CAR)

Probit estimation, matching method: kernel, metric: propensity score, observations: 77, pseudo R^2: 0.2265

Variable	Coefficient	z-score	P>|z|
CREDGDP	0.0299	2.68	0.007
BANKREG	0.1114	2.02	0.043
EXPERIENCE	1.2260	2.06	0.039
RETURN	0.0108	0.26	0.797
CAPRATIO	0.0040	0.68	0.499
Sample (Procedure)	***CAR*** **(DM 1000s) Treated Group**	***CAR*** **(DM 1000s) Control Group**	**Difference**
Unmatched *(simple average)*	1213.06	733.20	479.86
ATT *(Average Treatment on the Treated)*	1213.06	793.68	419.38

The lower part of the table displays the treatment and matching effects.[235] Average capital-at-risk of the treated group of banks after matching was roughly 420,000 Deutsche Mark (DM) or 52.8% higher than the control group's risk-adjusted investment. This shows that banks are indeed willing to invest more risky funds if the venture is backed by MDB co-financing. Notice that by applying the matching routine the hypothetical outcome of the treated banks had they not participated exceeds the simple mean of the non-participating banks by almost 60,000 DM (or 8.2% of the initial value), which illustrates that applying matching procedures can make a difference in project evaluation.

Nevertheless, these treatment results still need to be checked for statistical significance. Fortunately, *bootstrapping* can be used to give some idea of the sampling variability of the estimators.[236] The procedure is performed to determine confidence intervals and is based on the empirical distribution in place of the true population distribution, assuming that the former is a good estimate of the latter. The sampling distribution of an estimate is its probability distribution under independent repetitions of the sampling process. Knowledge of this distribution enables measurement of the precision and bias of the estimate as well as development of confidence intervals. Essentially, from the sample *N*

[235] All 77 projects were on common support (results not shown in table). On the notion of common support, i.e. all treated units have a counterpart in the non-treated group, see Blundell and Costa Dias (2000), pp. 445-446.

[236] See Greene (2003), p. 702.

observations are drawn (with replacement), with *N* equal to total sample size. Next, the resampling procedure is repeated by drawing on total *k* times from the actual sample. The number of replications was set at $k = 1000$, which is thought to produce generally very good estimates.[237] This procedure produces *k* realizations of the estimated treatment effect. For the 90% level of significance, the confidence interval is obtained as the distance between the 50th and 950th realizations in the set of ordered estimates. From the resulting data set of estimated statistics, the standard deviation can be calculated.[238]

Note that the estimated statistic is not necessarily a better estimate than the one observed in the original sample. In fact, a bias can be calculated as the difference between those two values.[239] The resulting bootstrap distribution may involve a bias which can be adjusted by the procedure suggested by Efron (1982) – the inventor of the bootstrap –, who also recommends applying a bias correction if the relation of the bias to the standard deviation is greater than 0.25.

As Table 25 shows, the fraction found in the sample (397.51/683.09=0.58) is actually greater than this threshold, which means that the bias-corrected bootstrap estimate[240] is used. The bootstrap outcome demonstrates that the capital-at-risk variable is significant at the 10% level (*CAR* is different from zero at that significance level as the confidence interval is greater than zero).

---

[237] See StataCorp. (2003), pp. 115-116.

[238] The following standard formula is used for calculating the standard deviation:

$$\left[\frac{\sum(\theta_i^* - \bar{\theta}^*)^2}{(k-1)}\right]^{0.5}, \textit{ where}$$

θ_i^* = statistic calculated using the ith sample,

$\bar{\theta}^*$ = average of the bootstrapped estimates,

k = number of replications.

[239] See Efron (1982), p. 33.

[240] For biased statistics, i.e. where the distribution is non-symmetrical, the *bias-corrected* method is thought to produce confidence intervals with better coverage probability than the alternative *percentile* method (the results of which are consequently suppressed in table 27); see StataCorp. (2003), p. 118. The bias-corrected intervals can be shown to be second-order accurate, i.e. the errors in matching go to zero faster than when using the normal and percentile methods; see Efron and Tibshirani (1993), p. 184-186 on the application of the bias-corrected method, and p. 187 on its superiority to the other two methods.

Table 25: Bootstrap Statistics for Absolute Capital-at-Risk

Number of observations: 77, Replications: 1000

Variable	Observed	Bias	Std. Error	[90% Confidence	Interval]	Method
BS_90	765.18	-397.51	683.09	-359.44	1889.80	Normal
				132.97	**2213.75**	Bias-corrected
Variable	**Observed**	**Bias**	**Std. Error**	**[95% Confidence**	**Interval]**	**Method**
BS_95	765.18	-385.70	713.85	-635.46	2166.01	Normal
				-104.67	**2421.09**	Bias-corrected

Another bootstrap at the 5% level did not produce a significant outcome (see lower panel).

5.2 Size-Adjusted Capital-at-Risk

One could object that the significant result presented above is due to differences in project size, i.e. equity capital invested abroad. While there is no indication that either multilateral agency has a preference for co-financing relatively large FDI projects – a disposition which could be driving the estimation outcome – a conceivable size effect is now removed by relating the absolute values of *capital-at-risk* to *total assets* of the investment target.

Table 26 shows that the treatment effect is still present for this normalized endogenous variable, *CAR_TA* (the unchanged probit estimates were omitted to save space):

Table 26: Treatment Effect (Size-Adjusted Capital-at-Risk)

Sample (Procedure)	*CAR_TA* Treated Group	*CAR_TA* Control Group	Difference
Unmatched *(simple average)*	0.016952	0.013179	0.003773
ATT *(Average Treatment on the Treated)*	0.016952	0.009374	0.007578

By removing the influence of project size, the outcome for the treatment effect now amounts to 80.8%. Notice the strong impact of applying the matching technique. The difference between the observed and the matched hypothetical outcome rises from 8.2% to 29%, now even increasing the treatment effect.

As Table 27 illustrates, the outcome becomes significant even at the 5% level (again, the bias-corrected estimator needed to be chosen):

Table 27: Bootstrap Statistics for Size-Adjusted Capital-at-Risk

Number of observations: 77, Replications: 1000

Variable	Observed	Bias	Std. Error	[90% Confidence	Interval]	Method
BS_90	0.011119	-0.005056	0.009020	-0.003731	0.025970	Normal
				0.003381	**0.027810**	Bias-corrected
Variable	**Observed**	**Bias**	**Std. Error**	**[95% Confidence**	**Interval]**	**Method**
BS_95	0.011119	-0.004747	0.009041	-0.006628	0.028861	Normal
				0.001565	**0.032920**	Bias-corrected

6 Conclusions of Chapter IV

For the given set of German banking FDI projects in emerging banking markets the estimation outcome verified the hypothesized positive impact of having a multilateral development bank (MDB) acquire a stake in the foreign business venture. Compared to their non-sponsored counterparts, German firms benefiting from co-financing on part of a multilateral agency invested on average a significantly higher amount of equity capital (in absolute terms or relative to project size) subject to the risk of expropriation or similarly harmful measures instigated by the foreign government. It is the exposure to these specific political risks that the novel endogenous variable of a sovereign-risk-adjusted capital position seeks to capture. Moreover, the matching approach was shown to provide meaningfully different results than a simple comparison over across-group averages.

A word of caution is in order, though. It would be presumptuous to derive general conclusions from the estimation outcome presented in this study. Instead, the results should be taken with a "grain of salt" because the number of observations in the sample is undoubtedly quite small. Naturally, the treatment effect may be weaker when other data sets – countries as well as sectors – are put to the test. Moreover, the study is based on some arguably strong assumptions such as the non-systematic influence of unobserved firm characteristics on program participation and outcome or the supposed willingness of non-participants to stand ready for "treatment" by the multilateral development banks. Lastly, it remains an open question whether the observed treatment effect is indeed more widely beneficial at the global level. While it may well be that the induced rise in FDI increases the utility of the host country, the risk-mitigating effect of involving MDBs may also lead to moral hazard on the part of investors and thus to possible misallocation of capital.

Further research will certainly have to be carried out to validate the theoretical considerations about the risk-mitigating impact of supranational third-party lending or equity participation. Nevertheless, the results should be understood as an initial indication of the constructive role multilateral development institutions may play in private foreign investment projects.

Appendix to Chapter IV

Table 28: List of Host Countries in the Sample of Individual FDI Projects

Europe	No. of Units	Initial Year	Avg. Probability of Default (in %)	Asia and Middle East	No. of Units	Initial Year	Avg. Probability of Default (in %)
Albania	1	2001	45.53	Bangladesh	1	1999	28.15
Bosnia & Herzeg.	3	1999	53.53	Cambodia	1	2001	44.77
Bulgaria	1	2001	18.66	China	1	1998	0.36
Croatia	3	1998	4.75	India	2	2001	9.49
Georgia	3	1999	44.02	Israel	1	1999	0.06
Hungary	1	1999	1.90	Rep. of Korea	4	1999	1.76
Lithuania	1	1999	6.49	Kyrgyz Rep.	1	2001	48.39
Macedonia	1	2000	34.14	Lebanon	1	1999	15.10
Poland	5	1998	1.91	Oman	1	2000	2.54
Romania	2	2000	22.32	Pakistan	1	1999	37.92
Russia	3	1999	24.66	Philippines	5	1998	7.02
Slovak Republic	1	1999	7.44	Saudi Arabia	1	1999	4.72
Slovenia	1	1999	1.00	Thailand	3	1999	4.51
Ukraine	2	2000	25.53	West Bk./Gaza	2	1999	79.43
FR Yugoslavia	4	2000	65.03				

Latin America/ the Caribbean	No. of Units	Initial Year	Avg. Probability of Default (in %)	Africa	No. of Units	Initial Year	Avg. Probability of Default (in %)
Argentina	1	1999	11.62	Burundi	1	1999	57.05
Bolivia	1	2001	15.67	Cameroon	1	1999	42.14
Brazil	1	2000	15.10	Egypt	1	1999	5.58
El Salvador	1	2001	6.49	Lesotho	1	1999	33.74
Jamaica	1	1999	13.92	Malawi	1	1999	37.74
Mexico	1	2001	6.49	Mali	1	1999	34.44
Nicaragua	1	2001	21.11	Morocco	1	1999	8.94
Virgin Islands (UK)	1	1999	17.72	South Africa	3	1999	6.04
				Swaziland	1	2001	29.20
				Togo	1	1999	38.89

Table 29: Statistical Properties of Variables – *Treatment* Group

Variable	Observations	Mean	Std. Deviation	Minimum	Maximum
CREDGDP	20	81.083	17.217	22.542	96.171
BANKREG	20	14.450	2.800	10.000	20.000
EXPERIENCE	20	0.950	0.224	0.000	1.000
RETURN	20	0.751	2.965	-4.571	6.361
CAPRATIO	20	28.260	29.100	0.956	97.130
CAR	20	857.841	1363.609	0.160	9805.114
CAR_TA	20	0.016952	0.025853	0.000281	0.094004

Table 30: Statistical Properties of Variables – *Control* Group

Variable	Observations	Mean	Std. Deviation	Minimum	Maximum
CREDGDP	57	60.144	28.394	0.000	100.000
BANKREG	57	13.439	4.268	0.000	20.000
EXPERIENCE	57	0.702	0.462	0.000	1.000
RETURN	57	-2.538	13.267	-74.845	9.089
CAPRATIO	57	34.745	36.801	0.209	100.000
CAR	57	733.202	997.289	0.159	3918.031
CAR_TA	57	0.013179	0.021163	0.000010	0.108293

Table 31: Heckman Selection Model (Absolute Capital-at-Risk)

Variable	Coefficient	z-score	P>|z|
Outcome equation:			
SPONSOR (δ^{prog})	953.89	1.33	0.185
Participation equation:			
CREDGDP	0.0299	2.68	0.007
BANKREG	0.1114	2.02	0.043
EXPERIENCE	1.2260	2.06	0.039
RETURN	0.0108	0.26	0.797
CAPRATIO	0.0040	0.68	0.499
Lambda (inverse Mills ratio: Φ/Φ)	-364.92	-0.76	0.448
Rho (ρ)	-0.2695		
Sigma (σ)	1354.33		

Box 6: IFC Selection Procedure for Co-Financing of Banking Projects in Emerging Markets. Condensed Protocol of the Interviews Conducted at IFC in April, 2003

In making a decision on whether to co-finance direct investment projects in the banking sector of developing countries carried out by commercial banks or parastatal development banks, IFC takes into account determinants at the country and sector level as well as data pertaining to the investment target. Despite applying a number of generally-agreed determinants, the final decision still involves a certain degree of discretion since it is also based on the findings of a thorough on-site examination conducted by IFC staff.

IFC's internal decision process works as follows. First, an investment proposal is made based on basic investment information which is then refined to a so-called "project data sheet" to be submitted for early review to the corporate investment committee. If the tentative verdict on a particular project is favorable, a team of specialists is then sent abroad to examine the actual financial situation of the investment target and, based on the findings, put together an appraisal report. This document represents the factual input to an ensuing high-level decision meeting which precedes formal approval by IFC's Board of Directors.

Apparently, IFC is of the opinion that a good deal of skepticism is required when interpreting banks' balance sheet and profitability data. Taking information on non-performing loans at "face value" may be misleading as the standard of "90 days past due status" is not consistently enforced across countries. In fact, some countries exhibit great leniency towards such loan classification, granting banks as much as two years time upon suspension of credit servicing to finally grade such loans as non-performing. Eyeballing collateral is potentially deceptive as well since it may not be marketable after all and thus worth less than recorded. Regarding banks' provisioning, the loan loss reserves listed in the balance sheets may not be consistent in a cross-country comparison because of internationally differing accounting treatments.

In sum, while data on asset quality (non-performing loans or loan loss provisions) and capital adequacy (*risk-adjusted* equity to total assets) may be indicative of trouble ahead, they in turn cannot ensure viability of a given project. Foreign equity participation in an emerging market bank is likely to guarantee that the direct investment target is not blatantly undercapitalized. However, a well-capitalized target bank is supposed to be more likely to get selected. Other supposedly reliable measures of bank performance or efficiency of capital invested, if measured consistently, are *return on equity* (RoE) or *return on (total) assets* (RoA). Focussing on single efficiency measures and taking into account country and sector information, the set of factors influencing the investment decision is limited to the following, consistently measurable variables:

- *Banking sector abroad*: As a general rule, IFC financially supports FDI projects in underdeveloped financial sectors. This means that an investment by a large German commercial bank in such a market is as likely to be co-financed as one originated by a parastatal development organization such as *Deutsche Investitions- und Entwicklungsgesellschaft* (DEG). Insufficient development may take various forms pertaining to the degree of competition or market insufficiencies: dominance by state-owned banks (tantamount to a low share of private sector banks), lack of medium or long-term financing, or a low rate of credit to the private sector relative to GDP. Given availability of data, the last criterion was chosen for the empirical analysis. Furthermore, markets in which the quality of banking regulation and supervision is rather poor generally run the risk of being neglected by IFC. The investigation uses a corresponding data set compiled by Barth et al. (2001).

- *German investors*: The German company making the initial investment in a foreign bank is called the sponsor or, at times, "technical partner", whereas the latter term may also apply to consulting firms not making financial contributions. As the reliability and the expertise of the sponsor by virtue of imposing better corporate governance do matter a great deal for the project outcome, IFC also takes into account the characteristics of the sponsors. Theoretically, ratings could be used to distinguish between the quality of investors. However, most of the German financial institutions are rated investment grade, which means this selection criterion does not apply. Rather, IFC looks at either the success of heretofore joint projects with the Corporation or, in the case of new sponsors, previous experience in doing business in emerging markets. A proxy for such experience is the number of equity investments (subsidiaries) in emerging markets at the time of IFC's selection decision.

- *Foreign target banks*: Arguably the most important determinant of project success is the soundness and profitability of the foreign bank to be invested in. As has been argued above, one should predominantly try to measure the efficiency of banking operations in terms of level and efficient use of capital. Indicators are, therefore, the ratio of paid-in equity capital to total assets and the return on total assets.

Lastly, why are there equity *and* debt investments? As a general rule, IFC floats equity only if the project is deemed adequately profitable ex-ante (discounted cash flow analysis yielding an internal rate of return of approximately 15%) and if an *exit option* can be secured. This option may consist in a put-back to the sponsor at book value (or a multiple of earnings) or in the requirement for the mature investment target to go public and achieve a certain trading volume, in which case the put option would be eliminated. Should neither method be viable, IFC would consider debt financing, by either senior debt or quasi-equity, i.e. subordinated or convertible debt as well as preference shares.

Proof of Equation (19), given the Optimization Problem in Equation (18):

$$(18)\quad \max \mathrm{W(k)} = \frac{1}{1-\beta}[f(k) - r(k - k^d)], \quad \text{s.t.} \quad G(k) \geq B(k), \quad \forall k.$$

using the Kuhn - Tucker condition : $f(x_1,...,x_n) \leq c$ with the constant c set to equal 0.

$$\Rightarrow B(k) - G(k) \leq 0$$

$$\Rightarrow L = W(k) - \lambda[0 - (B(k) - G(k))] = W(k) - \lambda[G(k) - B(k)].$$

To solve, take the first - order condition of the Lagrange function :

$$L_k = \frac{\partial L}{\partial k} = W'(k) - \lambda[G'(k) - B'(k)] \stackrel{!}{=} 0$$

$$L_k = \frac{1}{1-\beta}(f'(k) - r) + \lambda\left[\frac{1}{1-\beta}(f' - r) - f'(k)\right] \stackrel{!}{=} 0$$

$$\Rightarrow \frac{1}{1-\beta}(f'(k) - r) + \frac{\lambda}{1-\beta}[(f'(k) - r) - ((1-\beta)f'(k))] = 0 \quad | \quad \textit{multiply by } (1-\beta)$$

$$\Rightarrow (f'(k) - r) + \lambda[(f'(k) - r) - ((1-\beta)f'(k))] = 0$$

$$\Rightarrow (f'(k) - r) + \lambda(f'(k) - r) - \lambda((1-\beta)f'(k)) = 0$$

$$\Rightarrow (f'(k) - r) + \lambda f'(k) - \lambda r - \lambda f'(k) + \lambda\beta f'(k) = 0 \quad | \quad \textit{add } [\lambda\beta r - \lambda\beta r] = 0$$

$$\Rightarrow (f'(k) - r) + \lambda\beta f'(k) + [\lambda\beta r - \lambda\beta r] - \lambda r = 0$$

$$\Rightarrow (f'(k) - r) + \lambda\beta[(f'(k) - r)] + \lambda\beta r - \lambda r = 0$$

$$\Rightarrow (f'(k) - r)\,(1 + \lambda\beta) = \lambda r - \lambda\beta r$$

$$\Rightarrow (19)\quad f'(k) - r = \frac{r\lambda(1-\beta)}{1+\lambda\beta}$$

Chapter V: Concluding Remarks

1 Summary of Results

The empirical parts of this study analyzed the impact of a number of risks and other FDI-specific determinants on German FDI. More specifically, Chapter II dealt with country and political risk, scrutinizing in particular the detrimental consequences of administrative insufficiencies and domestic political instability. Chapter III drew attention in particular to the question of how strongly FDI inflows are affected by looming crises in emerging financial markets, as measured by an early warning indicator, and their differential openness to foreign bank entry. Chapter IV measured indirectly the probability of expropriation by the host government with a linkage to the risk-taking of banking investors in unsafe foreign markets. The quantitative results can be summarized as follows.

Chapter II focused on estimating the effects of so-called non-traditional factors such as country risk and agglomeration effects, which are widely regarded as influential for FDI in emerging market economies, and found that country risk, and partially political risk, has indeed been detrimental to investments of German enterprises. Of these political risk factors, a combined variable measuring the degree of corruption, the quality of the local administration, and the risk of expropriation and payment restrictions was tested highly significant. Furthermore, German FDI in Latin America was found to have been market-seeking while that in emerging Asia tended to exploit low factor costs. Making empirical use of German firm-level data, additional estimations were performed for direct investment of the manufacturing sector, with the results staying largely the same as before, and three of its sub-sectors. Regarding the latter, the hypothesis that capital-intensive industries react particularly strongly to changes in the regulatory environment of the host country was confirmed by the data.

The estimation results in Chapter III make a strong case for the devastating impact of financial market instability on German banking FDI. In almost all regressions, the early warning indicator chosen as a variable for banking crises showed a highly significantly negative correlation with FDI flows. Other exogenous variables tested to have a strong pull effect are, as expected, agglomeration effects measured by flows of German non-banking FDI and financial market development abroad in terms of the ratio of stock market capitalization to GDP. By contrast, neither country risk nor the openness of the financial sector could be shown to affect FDI. Interestingly, it is instead the general attitude of the host country towards FDI that was found to be linked to German investment flows; this finding applies specifically to the Asian region. Surprisingly, the variable of trade linkages, otherwise typically described as most meaningful for banking FDI, lost its significance in isolation when a dummy variable for host countries in central and eastern Europe was included. This suggests it is geographic proximity to Germany that explains much of German banking FDI. Disaggregation of the sample by region illustrated that the main factors at work differ between the continents (Europe – financial stability; Latin America – development of financial markets; Asia – agglomeration effects). Comparing pre- and post-Asian-crisis time periods, it was found that both variables of country riskiness gain significance in the later sub-sample, with the result being especially pronounced for the measure of financial vulnerability. This finding indicates that German banks learned from the Asian debacle, adjusting their holdings when the viability of the foreign financial system was increasingly deemed at risk or proportionally shunning risky banking environments altogether.

Chapter IV investigated the effect of co-financing by certain multilateral development banks on the willingness of German banks with such institutional backing to commit more "risky" equity capital in emerging market banks relative to self-sufficient investors. Notwithstanding some limitations as to the assumptions made and small sample size, the econometric outcome demonstrated that the probability of an FDI project being selected for co-financing by a multilateral development bank hinges primarily on the lack of development of the host country's financial market and the quality/stringency of the banking supervision regime abroad. Using an innovative matching approach, the study found that, as postulated, there is indeed a meaningful positive treatment effect of a multilateral agency's participation in an FDI project: both the average value of the *capital-at-risk* of the treated group and the one adjusted for target firm size exceeded the average exposure measures of the control group by more than 50% and 80%, respectively. That is, in the German case co-financing by multilateral development banks had a positive impact on the extent of risk-adjusted FDI, indeed. These results were shown to be statistically significant at conventional levels. Moreover, applying the matching procedure changed the relevant outcome of control group banks by up to nearly 30% of the initial simple average, thereby exemplifying the importance of choosing the correct counterfactual outcome.

2 Dismantling Barriers to FDI – Policy Responses and Further Suggestions

In concluding the investigation, the following sections review the steps taken by countries, regional associations and multilateral institutions to tackle investment barriers, corrupt practices, financial system instability and expropriation risk. In addition, recommendations for further policy action are put forth.

2.1 Investment Barriers

There are generally two ways of handling investment barriers as well as administrative and political risks. Investors can utilize existing financial methods (avoidance or transfer of risks), possibly with the assistance of international financial institutions; or, if these impediments persist, they can start negotiations on containing them.[241] Historically, apart from countries' unilaterally opening up there have been bilateral, plurilateral and multilateral approaches to lowering investment barriers, which will be reviewed and evaluated briefly below. In general, there is a tradeoff between diversity in contractual arrangements and the international community's need to agree on a set of basic rules governing FDI. Much can be said in favor of bilateral treaties that give countries free rein to design and negotiate the parties' rights and responsibilities, thus retaining their freedom to accommodate differences in national preferences and conditions. Excessive activity of international institutions could violate the subsidiarity principle and sovereign rights.[242] On the other hand, it is only such institutions as the *World Trade Organization* (WTO, formerly the GATT) and the *Organisation for Economic Co-operation and Development* (OECD) that can advance effectively the FDI agenda by providing a forum for discussing and balancing the interests of the individual countries that might otherwise find themselves locked in a sub-optimal scenario of antagonistically mimicking each other's FDI policies (for example, the widespread use of costly investment incentives draws a rising number of countries into a "subsidy game"[243]). These organizations alone can bring the parties back on a universally beneficial path by supplying them with a public good, such as internationally accepted investment rules, or core principles, that would seek to guarantee investors a basic level of protection everywhere they may go.[244] Thus the question becomes: are countries able to tackle FDI issues

[241] See Moosa (2002), p. 155.
[242] See Hoekman and Saggi (1999), p. 16.
[243] See Blomström and Kokko (2003), p. 38.
[244] See Stark and Hartenstein (2002), pp. 20-21, 25.

bilaterally or within a region, or is there a specific role for international financial institutions in fostering FDI? And, in case good arguments in favor of multilateral action can be found, who exactly should take the lead? The different approaches are reviewed and their success evaluated in the following sections.

2.1.1 Investment Incentives as Unilateral Measures

These days, there is no shortage of ingenious attempts on the part of developing countries to attract investors by offering them financial benefits. There is a wide array of *investment incentives* ranging from tax holidays/subsidies and grants to provision of infrastructure and even monopoly rights. In fact, there is hardly a country anymore that does not compete for FDI without resorting to offering some kind of investment subsidy. This proliferation was brought about largely by the loss of traditional policy options – increasing integration of capital markets has limited the scope for exchange rate policy, and the same goes for trade policy.[245]

Anecdotal evidence points to the ineffectiveness of fiscal incentives. A survey by Farrell et al. (2004) of executives at multinational companies entering the Indian market revealed that these fiscally costly incentives were in fact the least important factor in their locational decision, with the top motivations being a developed supplier base, availability of skilled labor and the quality of the infrastructure. Sometimes, as in the Brazilian automobile industry, overly generous subsidies can actually prompt overinvestment, eventually leading to overcapacity, i.e. misallocation of capital. Then again, once the incentive has expired or been terminated, investors may opt to relocate into a country with better "fundamentals". In the end, the costs of promoting FDI via financial and other incentives,[246] particularly when arising from "bidding wars", are likely to exceed the benefits for many emerging market economies. This is true especially in cases where foreign firms would have invested regardless of the availability of subsidies, which means that the incentive turns into a mere transfer from the host government to the investor. While one should not disregard the possibility that international competition for FDI is actually welfare-improving on a global scale, one also must not confuse this efficiency issue with that of the transfer of rents: competition may lead to an efficient outcome and yet fail to be in the

[245] See Blomström and Kokko (2003), pp. 37-38.

[246] For example, "export processing zones" are established to shield the foreign investor from the regulatory rules and practices prevailing elsewhere in the host country; see UNCTAD (2003), p. 124.

interest of the developing world as a whole.[247] Absent international cooperation on restricting these incentives, host countries may find themselves stuck in a "prisoner's dilemma" setting. Coordinating policy action then becomes the only means with which to limit the use of inefficient incentives on a broad scale (see section 2.1.3 below).[248] That, however, is difficult given the wide range of conceivable incentives, which would likely leave loopholes to circumvent prohibitions.

2.1.2 Bilateral Investment Treaties

As emerging market economies typically have difficulties guaranteeing property rights, *bilateral investment treaties* (BITs) can be used as explicit commitment devices to overcome dynamic inconsistency problems associated with host country negligence once the investment is sunk. BITs usually include dispute resolution mechanisms (e.g. submitting to binding arbitration through the ICSID) and provisions for compensation in the event of expropriation or measures tantamount to expropriation, thereby guarding against unwarranted governmental action. While the host government can usually assert its sovereign immunity, leaving little scope for recourse to the domestic legal system, under a BIT it is obliged to consent to the arbitration of disputes that are covered by the treaty. Recently, the cases pending in the ICSID have surged, partly because of the sharp rise in the number of BITs concluded, partly due to widened publicity generated by NAFTA arbitration cases favoring investors' claims. The danger of the proliferation of BITs – the number has risen to around 2,000 by now[249] – is that investors may enter countries offering BIT protection for the wrong reasons, i.e. moral hazard and adverse selection problems are bound to emerge as a consequence of the de-facto insurance BITs provide. Also, BITs are often viewed as giving foreign investors greater property protection than is enjoyed by domestic firms.[250] Even so, despite their undisputed merits, BITs do not offer a reliable enforcement technology in the sense that uncooperative host governments would be forced to fulfill claims awarded by arbitration. Another shortcoming of BITs – with the exception of those the U.S. has entered into – is that they do not generally address the issue of liberalization of market entry.[251]

[247] See Hoekman and Saggi (1999), p. 22.
[248] See also Moran (2002), p. 29.
[249] Ibid., p. 30.
[250] See Hallward-Driemeier (2003), pp. 2-9.
[251] See Hoekman and Saggi (1999), p. 16.

A recent study by Hallward-Driemeier (2003) finds very limited evidence that BITs have, over a twenty-year period, indeed stimulated additional FDI flowing from OECD member states to developing countries. The dummy variable depicting BITs or appropriate instruments chosen to avoid endogeneity turned out to be insignificant or even negative, with the exception of a specification regressing the share of home country FDI on the BIT dummy. One particular finding is especially important with respect to institutional barriers. Verifying the hypotheses that BITs could make up for weak institutions in the host country (substitution effect) or that a certain level of institutional development has to be attained for a BIT to be credible, an interaction term composed of the BIT dummy and the ICRG measures of law and order as well as corruption is reported to be strongly positive and significant. Incidentally, this result ties in with the evidence reported by Morisset (2003) that the better the investment climate, the more effective domestic investment promotion agencies are. Hallward-Driemeier concludes that "BITs are more, rather than less, effective in settings of higher institutional quality and where institutions are already being strengthened. This undermines a central rational [sic] for some of the less developed countries that enter into these agreements hoping to bypass the need to strengthen property rights and institutions more generally. Put differently, if host countries are committed to trying to attract more FDI, BITs have not provided a short-cut from the need to implement broader reforms of domestic institutions."[252]

Therefore, the focus of policy-makers should rest on first removing the specific administrative and political obstacles deterring foreign investors; only then should they seek to attract more FDI by clarifying additional terms in investment treaties.

2.1.3 Multilateral and Regional Investment Agreements

With the demise of the *OECD Multilateral Agreement on Investment* (MAI), the first-ever global initiative to negotiate on a comprehensive framework for FDI (see also Box 7, p. 160), the WTO has been the main conduit for liberalizing investment at the *multilateral level.* Particularly the issue of *performance requirements* has received much attention. Covering FDI in the real sector, the *WTO Trade Related Investment Measures (TRIMs) Agreement* negotiated in 1994 as part of the Uruguay Round has phased out local content requirements, trade-balancing requirements, restrictions on corporate foreign currency inflows,

[252] Hallward-Driemeier (2003), pp. 21-22.

and export controls. The agreement does not regulate other TRIMs, most prominently export performance requirements and mandatory technology transfers.[253] Meanwhile, the transition periods for all member states, even the one applying to the least developed countries (seven years), have expired.

Regarding FDI in the services sectors, the other main WTO agreement, the *General Agreement on Trade in Services* (GATS) of 1994, stipulates that host countries must allow capital inflows related to foreign establishment and free movement of capital related to cross-border financial transactions when they constitute a crucial part of the service provided. This is an important point because, in contrast to goods, services are non-tradable and typically need to be rendered directly on the market abroad. If a member state voluntarily liberalizes a sector in accord with the GATS, it must also allow related capital flows. Nevertheless, members may impose restrictions on services and capital transfers in case of balance of payments difficulties – *in consultation with the IMF or at its request*. This particular "carve-out" ensures the ability of member states to use capital account restrictions which have not yet been abolished or are introduced temporarily to alleviate a crisis. This avoids a potential inconsistency in the joint WTO-IMF-framework, as GATS members, having promised to refrain from imposing capital account restrictions (in the context of services), can still exercise such restrictions under Article VI of the IMF's *Articles of Agreement*. Furthermore, as laid down in Articles XI and XIII of the GATS, the WTO defers to the IMF on matters in the Fund's jurisdiction – capital controls and other restrictions on payments and transfers – and is bound to base its conclusions concerning restrictions made for balance of payments reasons on the IMF's assessment of a country's current external viability.[254]

[253] For detailed lists of prohibited trade-related investment measures and respective notifications to the WTO see UNCTAD (2003), pp. 12, 18-19, 21-23.

[254] See Lehmann et al. (2003), pp. 8-9, 18-19. There may be extreme balance of payments difficulties that justify imposing temporary restrictions. For example, Indonesia, experiencing a severe crisis in the late 1990s, was convicted of breach of commercial contract in the widely publicized MidAmerica case. Notwithstanding the poor public governance that existed in the country at the time, Indonesia was in dire need of foreign exchange with which to import the vital necessities for the suffering population; see Moran (2002), p. 29. On this basis, one may wonder whether prompt commercial arbitration is always the appropriate mode for settling investment disputes or whether *force majeure* could be declared or the case be postponed until external balance is restored, the latter likewise at the IMF's judgment.

Box 7: Plurilateral/Multilateral Agreements on FDI Liberalization

International financial institutions such as the *World Bank Group*, the *Organisation for Economic Co-operation and Development* (OECD) and the *World Trade Organisation* (WTO) have been instrumental in combating investment barriers and political risk throughout. As illustrated above, the *World Bank* has several entities – IFC, MIGA, and ICSID – that foster private sector development and mitigate risks both in financial and technical terms.

The *OECD*, in 1995, set up the negotiation round on the *Multilateral Agreement on Investment* (MAI), which represents the most important proposal on establishing a binding comprehensive multilateral framework for FDI that has been advanced so far. It was deemed a free standing international treaty, open to all OECD members and the European Communities, and to accession by non-OECD member countries. Essentially, the MAI was aimed at reducing investment barriers and providing legal security for foreign investors. The negotiations were begun in the heyday of FDI, with investment flows to the developing world growing by leaps and bounds – but only to a rather limited number of destinations. An important objective of the MAI was, therefore, to foster FDI in less attractive countries displaying a high level of political uncertainty. Three years into the discussion of the initiative, the MAI failed, with France withdrawing from the negotiation table. Critics of the MAI – largely from developing countries as well as non-governmental organizations – contend that the agreement

- ignored public concerns about effects on capital mobility, labor rights and financial stability,
- failed to involve developing countries in drafting the MAI,
- would have given international investors new rights while not holding them accountable for any social and environmental damage their investment might cause.

In addition, investors would have been given excessive power to challenge host country regulatory policies allegedly having a negative impact on FDI. Certain provisions on investor-state dispute resolution, actually drawing on those used by *NAFTA*, would have enabled investors to sue governments for damages caused by MAI violations in an attempt to recoup costs associated with environmental/health regulations. The prospect of legal battles might lead host governments to abstain from pursuing fully-justified regulatory action against investors. Whether or not this criticism is founded, foreign investors would have clearly enjoyed greater rights to claim compensation than domestic firms. Another major problem with the MAI was the inclusion of other capital flows (intangible capital and portfolio investment), prompting opposition from host governments fearing loss of their ability to regulate such flows. On the other hand, the issue of investment incentives was not included in the discussions.

The other main set of regulations governing FDI at the multilateral level is contained in the *WTO General Agreement on Trade in Services* (GATS) of 1994. Apart from the principal obligation to apply "most-favored-nation" (MFN) treatment – GATS members must treat services providers in the same way as those from their most favored trade partners – the agreement requires countries to allow capital inflows related to FDI and guarantee free movement of capital related to cross-border financial transactions, when they are an essential part of the provision of a service. The GATS represents a "hybrid approach" in that it combines a "negative list" of exceptions to the MFN obligation with a "positive list" with respect to the member states' granting to investors sector-specific market access.

Sources: Moosa (2002), pp. 157-158, Hoekman and Saggi (1999), pp. 19-20, and Lehmann et al. (2003), p. 9.

Traditionally not themes at the *regional level*, performance requirements are increasingly addressed in some regional treaties: while Mercosur prohibits export requirements, NAFTA on top of that bans domestic equity participation rules and the transfer of technology requirements. The empirical evidence on the effectiveness of performance requirements is inconclusive. Only in cases of both strong locational advantages and inelastic investor demand for equity participation have such requirements proven to be effective and efficient. Paralleling the trend in industrialized countries in earlier years, mandatory requirements are, however, being more and more substituted by a policy of providing subsidies to investors.[255] One potential disadvantage of regional investment agreements compared to a multilateral approach is that they could discriminate between member and outside countries, possibly leading to unwarranted diversion of investment. Also, investors may choose to enter a certain country not for its economic characteristics but simply because it serves as a "hub" giving access to a number of "spoke" countries under a regional investment agreement. Therefore, these agreements should be judged by the degree to which they go beyond the GATS in eliminating discriminatory practices – the more these agreements liberalize in addition, the greater the potential negative spillovers. It appears, however, that the GATS commitments of regionally committed countries do not differ significantly from those made under the regional agreements.[256]

As alluded to above, the GATS is based on a "positive-list" approach, where countries open up particular sectors in services voluntarily, while reserving all other sectors for possible restrictions. Interestingly, in regulating *foreign entry via FDI*, NAFTA and some BITs involving Japan use the opposite concept, a "negative list" approach, where member countries make commitments across the board and only make reservations for single sectors. While developing countries tend to prefer positive lists because of the greater regulatory flexibility they provide (this having been voiced by Korea, India, Malaysia and Brazil, but, interestingly, also by Japan and the EU), many investing countries headed by the U.S. and Canada, unsurprisingly, favor the latter approach because it is thought to lead to narrower exceptions. Paragraph 22 of the Declaration of the Doha Ministerial Conference declares that further work in the *WTO Working Group on the Relationship between Trade and Investment* should, inter alia, essentially consider a positive-list approach. In fact, many representatives in that working group have been reported to view the positive list as a realistic way of approaching the issue of multilateral rules on investment because it provides a

[255] See UNCTAD (2003), pp. 119-121.

[256] See Hoekman and Saggi (1999), pp. 13-14, 20.

balance between safeguarding policy discipline and giving flexibility to developing countries.[257]

While *investment incentives* have traditionally been covered less in international investment agreements, the *WTO Agreement on Subsidies and Countervailing Measures* does prohibit a relatively broad range of subsidies if relating to foreign investors' activities in trade in goods. That, of course, affects incentives for attracting FDI indirectly at best, and some WTO members are exempted or not yet included to begin with. At the bilateral and regional level, some investment treaties (e.g. NAFTA) prevent countries from using regulatory incentives ("no lowering of standards" clauses), but these rules cover only the post-establishment treatment of foreign investors. Meanwhile, in 2003, the *OECD Committee on International Investment and Multinational Enterprise*, in guiding host countries' management of incentives by a consultation mechanism, agreed on a "checklist" for assessing costs and benefits of incentives, broken down into six categories and a total of 20 questions designed essentially to investigate whether a proper framework is in place for the incentives to succeed. A good starting point for arriving at an international accord on outright wasteful investment incentives lies in Article XV of the *GATS*, which notes that incentives may have distortionary effects in that area and that WTO members will negotiate ways to avoid such trade diversion. Restricting the volume of investment subsidies – by necessity via regional or multilateral negotiations – would foster development by freeing up resources to be used for improving infrastructure and other factors that determine a country's competitiveness.[258] Regrettably, the momentum to initiate such broad-based negotiations is arguably quite weak, and further research on the sensibility of investment incentives will have to be carried out to possibly make a stronger case for taking coordinated policy action to remove them.

A *multilateral approach to regulating FDI*, whether within the WTO or a new initiative, could be an important complement to bilateral and regional investment agreements in that it could establish a common legal basis or a "floor of standards". The ultimate outcome would depend on the extent to which countries view a multilateral approach as attractive, but even then it would certainly be challenging to negotiate such a universally agreeable set of

---

[257] This flexibility in controlling foreign investors' entry and activities was elaborated in a list of objectives, or development provisions, presented to the Working Group, which encompasses, for example, technological development including putting greater emphasis on value added activities, expansion of small and medium scale enterprises, and the avoidance of crowding out of domestic firms; see Moran (2002), pp. 18, 23-25.

[258] See UNCTAD (2003), pp. 124-128.

standards. As opposed to trade, FDI is highly unbalanced between industrial and developing economies in terms of the direction of FDI flows, and a wide range of FDI policies exists. The developing world might fear that these rules could be restricting the scope for national policy too much and also expose them unduly to legal battles under the WTO dispute settlement mechanism. By contrast, industrial countries might find a negotiated outcome too lax, undercutting the level of protection other agreements already provide. Therefore, multilateral negotiations could lead to a "lowest-common-denominator" compromise, unless both camps brought to the bargaining table other related "hot-button" issues such as free movement of labor, good corporate citizenship, competition regimes and policies for more development-friendly outcomes. In this case the WTO, designed to liberalize trade, would cease to be the appropriate institution, and a new framework would have to be devised. Hoekman and Saggi (1999, p. 23), skeptically, ask against the backdrop of the MAI failure: "If OECD countries with their much more uniform policy environment and similar goals fail to reach an accord, how can one expect developing countries that differ more substantially from one another to agree on a common set of principles regarding investment?"

Most important for emerging markets is the notion that multilateral negotiations would allow them to pool resources and thus give them greater bargaining leverage than regional or bilateral settings, assuming they can find common positions on the issues of greatest importance to them. Even if a multilateral approach did produce only meager results, this would still be a good starting point for more comprehensive negotiations at the regional level or, upon establishment of the Free Trade Area of the Americas, even between regions.[259]

2.2 The Global Drive Against Corruption

International financial institutions have increasingly taken the lead in the worldwide fight against corrupt practices. Notably, the IMF and the World Bank have built governance issues into the ongoing dealings with their constituency and have defined international standards as a basis for more transparent policy formulation and implementation. Having previously largely avoided the terms "governance" and "corruption" in its programs with emerging market economies, the IMF has moved from eliminating rigidities giving rise to corruption to directly urging its members to address instances of poor governance and corruption. In 1997, the IMF's Executive Board approved guidelines on "The Role of the IMF in Governance Issues", mandating a more

[259] See UNCTAD (2003), pp. 94-95. On expanding the scope of negotiation issues see also Hoekman and Saggi (1999), pp. 7, 21-22.

comprehensive treatment of governance issues in its surveillance function and IMF-supported programs as well as a more proactive approach in advocating policies and the development of institutions that eliminate the opportunity for corruption and related practices.[260] This resolution also led the IMF to design "standards and codes" incorporating good international practice in economic management and propagated the timely dissemination of statistical information on fiscal, monetary and financial developments. Participation in these initiatives to strengthen governance is voluntary.[261] Box 8 summarizes the main initiatives.

However, a country's lengthy abstention from participation can also send a signal to markets. The Fund has also updated its policies on safeguarding the use of IMF resources to prevent misreporting of information to the Fund (prominent cases are Russia, Ukraine and Indonesia, whose central banks were targeted by the IMF in this respect). The World Bank, its mandate being the promotion of development in member countries, has adopted a framework for combating corruption, which comprises the prevention of fraud in its own projects by improving procurement and project implementation, technical assistance for members' anti-corruption endeavors and the inclusion of governance issues in the formulation of the Bank's country assistance strategies.[262]

Multilaterals' initiatives to combat corruption can only go so far. Evidently, their success depends largely on the willingness of host countries to fulfill their responsibilities in fostering a culture of transparency and also setting the incentive structure right, for instance by raising government officials' salaries appropriately. It has to be kept in mind that corruption has a long history in many emerging markets and is literally an integral part of daily life, in some cases reaching all the way to the top of government.[263] Accordingly, the battle for better governance will be a protracted one. Of course, the total elimination of corruption is not feasible, as doing so would come at prohibitive fiscal costs and require extreme legal changes (i.e. excessive civil rights restrictions and very harsh penalties). As always, an optimal theoretical level would be reached where the marginal social costs of reducing corruption equal the marginal social benefits from that action,[264] e.g. in terms of the marginal value of additional capital inflows.

---

[260] See Wolf and Gürgen (2002), pp. 539, 546-547.

[261] See Abed and Gupta (2002), pp. 4, 9.

[262] Ibid., p. 5.

[263] See Wolf and Gürgen (2002), pp. 559-560.

[264] See Tanzi (2002), p. 50.

Box 8: Standards and Codes, and Other Multilateral Initiatives

The main initiatives initiated by the *IMF* comprise:

- The *Special Data Dissemination Standard* (SDDS), adopted in 1996. It applies to member states that have, or might seek, access to international capital markets. The objective is to improve the quality and integrity of the data as well as their coverage, periodicity, and timeliness.
- The *General Data Dissemination Standard* (GDDS), adopted in 1997, revised in 2001/02. It applies to all member states and guides them in the distribution of comprehensive and reliable economic, financial, and socio-demographic statistics to the public.
- The *Code of Good Practices on Fiscal Transparency*, adopted in 1998 and updated in 2001. Participation in applying this code is voluntary, and existing diversity across member countries is fully recognized. The main objective of this code is the promotion of transparent budget preparation, execution, and reporting.
- The *Code of Good Practices on Transparency in Monetary and Financial Policies*, adopted in 1999. This initiative in the area of good governance calls for central banks and other financial agencies to be accountable, especially when these authorities enjoy a high degree of independence.
- The *Reports on the Observance of Standards and Codes* (ROSCs), adopted in 1999, which publicize the extent to which member states observe certain internationally recognized standards in twelve areas of direct operational concern to the IMF (accounting, auditing, banking supervision, combating money laundering and the financing of terrorism, corporate governance, data dissemination, fiscal transparency, insolvency and creditor rights, insurance supervision, monetary and financial policy transparency, payments systems, and securities regulation). The ROSCs are essentially a by-product of the *Financial Sector Assessment Program* (FSAP, see section 2.3).
- The IMF also carries out *technical assistance* on public expenditure management, tax administration, banking systems, foreign exchange and the quality of statistical data. In the area of public expenditure management, the IMF and the World Bank, recognizing the link between weak public administration and poor governance, have initiated additional work in *heavily indebted poor countries* (HIPC) to make sure that debt relief is used for poverty reduction.

Other initiatives by multilateral institutions are:

- The *OECD Revised Recommendation on Combating Bribery in International Business Transactions* of 1997. Building on an OECD resolution that already in 1994 sought to end the tax deductibility of bribes and to criminalize the bribing of foreign officials, this recommendation represents a concrete and prescriptive guideline that covers broad areas of the conduct of international business and establishes a mechanism for monitoring implementation. Furthermore, the adoption of another anti-corruption initiative, called the *Convention on Combating Bribery of Foreign Officials in International Business Transactions*, obligated participating countries – the 30 OECD member states as well as a growing number of nonmembers – to make bribery a crime under the national laws.
- The *United Nations* adopted in 1996 the *Declaration Against Corruption and Bribery in International Commercial Transactions*. The declaration, while not legally binding, represents the most comprehensive agreement on criminalizing foreign bribery and ending its tax deductibility.

Source: Abed and Gupta (2002), pp. 7, 9-11, and further information taken from the IMF's website: www.imf.org

The role of the IMF and the World Bank in fighting corruption should be guided by the following principles. While the Bank should take the lead in the tackling of more micro-type governance problems such as government procurement systems through technical assistance, the Fund should explicitly interfere in cases where macroeconomic stability or, more generally, achieving the macroeconomic objectives of an IMF-supported program is put at risk by corrupt practices in monetary and fiscal affairs. This would require the IMF to incorporate the implementation of specific governance reforms as strict performance criteria in its conditionality. These reforms should be achieved primarily with the support of the World Bank; the Fund should restrict its consulting activities to areas directly under its mandate, i.e. assisting the monetary and fiscal authorities in rather general restructuring projects. It is hoped that the threat of withholding IMF financing will induce member states to address governance issues at all levels of government, but most importantly at the highest level, and communicate the detrimental effects of corruption openly to the public.

2.3 Promoting Financial System Stability

The IMF's increased focus on the issue of financial market stability led to the 1999 introduction of the *Financial Sector Assessment Program* (FSAP). Currently, a total of up to 24 *Financial System Stability Assessments* (FSSAs) per year are conducted jointly with the World Bank. These new instruments are directed at helping member countries identify and evaluate vulnerabilities in their financial sectors as well as immediate needs for corrective action[265] (i.e. to determine how sources of risk are being managed, ascertain the developmental and technical assistance needs, and set priorities for policy responses). Given the short time of its operation, it is too early to judge whether the FSAP has indeed contributed to making financial systems, notably in emerging markets, more stable and transparent. One may wonder if the relatively standardized approach of the FSSAs does not target primarily the "legal" fulfillment of IMF requirements in this respect. What the assessments do accomplish is to reveal specific parts of the supporting infrastructure that are missing or inadequate. These consist in an "information base" comprised of coherent accounting rules, credible auditing and a credit information industry as well as an impartial judiciary and a well-functioning set of collateral and bankruptcy laws. The mere identification of these structural weaknesses is very instrumental in establishing a firm base for a more resilient financial system.

[265] See Abed and Gupta (2002), p. 10.

Early warnings systems for detecting incipient currency crises – and indirectly, banking crises – are now an established feature in many international financial institutions and large private banks. The sophistication of some systems, notably one proposed by the European Central Bank (ECB), even goes so far as to not only reliably determine the case of a looming crisis but also the time of its conclusion. The ECB multinomial logit model has also been shown to predict 84% of currency crises between 1993 and 2001 correctly, outperforming the two already powerful IMF models[266] whose success rates stand at 70% and 76%. Importantly, the ECB model also features a low rate of "false alarms", i.e. calling a crisis when there was none, and a high conditional probability (50%) of a crisis happening if an alarm occurred.[267] The ECB model therefore strikes a good balance between a broad coverage of transmission channels and a relatively concise set of explanatory variables. As will be explained below, certain crises were not called because exceptional factors not accounted for in the system were at work – Korea: rapid increases in private sector borrowing including both direct borrowing by corporations and bank borrowing to finance corporate investment (the share of short-term debt in total external debt peaked at 58%), Argentina: both a large share of government debt servicing and a large premium to be paid on the debt.[268]

The built-in flexibility of modern early warning systems – the threshold for calling a crisis (ECB: 20%) and the time horizon prior to a crisis scrutinized (ECB: 12 months) are changeable – poses a tradeoff to policymakers. Depending on their loss functions, policymakers will weigh the benefits from receiving a signal relative to the cost of this being a false alarm and the cost of possibly missing a crisis. Someone who is risk averse toward missing a crisis will lower the threshold and lengthen the time period, thus getting more signals but also more false alarms, while a risk-loving policymaker will accordingly favor a higher threshold and shorter time span.[269] Now, if a large number of market players share the same degree of risk-aversion and, accordingly, set similar parameters in their early warning systems, this tacit understanding is likely to cause herd behavior which may actually *precipitate* the outbreak of a crisis at a time when ordinary economic policy measures could still be effective in achieving a turnaround. In this sense the benefit of accessing timely

[266] For an overview of the two IMF models – one developed by the IMF's Developing Country Studies Division (DCSD) and one by Kaminsky, Lizondo and Reinhart (KLR) – and other early warning systems used in a number of private banks see IMF (2002), pp. 49-51.

[267] See Bussiere and Fratzscher (2002), pp. 17-18.

[268] Ibid., p. 30.

[269] Ibid., pp. 32-33.

information on a possible crisis is joined by the danger of greater market volatility, as the proliferation of structurally related early warning systems concurrently seeing the red light may prompt market participants to react in a uniform fashion.

Looking forward, two aspects relevant to emerging markets should be addressed by the next generation of early warning systems. For one thing, they should be able to distinguish between full-blown currency-cum-banking crises and episodes where one type of crisis dominates. So far, early warning systems exclusively for detecting banking crises are clearly underrepresented. Yet it may be the specific risk of a downturn in the targeted foreign banking market, whether joined by a currency crisis or not, that is most critical to banks contemplating entry into emerging markets. The second aspect concerns the inclusion of corporate sector data and is actually related to the first. The IMF itself acknowledges: "Banking crises are intimately linked to corporate financial stress, and new tools developed to estimate forward-looking measures of credit risk of both banks and corporates could be used as part of an EWS."[270] These "third-generation" type of external crisis models focus on both corporate and banking weaknesses caused by incomplete financial markets which lead firms to rely on debt and foreign financing. The vulnerability to external crises thus rises in line with deteriorating corporate balance sheets. This appears to have been the case in many countries affected by the Asian crisis that featured relative macroeconomic stability but also insufficient corporate (and public sector) governance, which encouraged an environment of excessive risk-taking and, consequently, imprudent financial leveraging (including a large fraction of short-term debt) by domestic corporations and banks.[271]

There is now empirical evidence on the predictive power of systems incorporating information on the financial and governance structure of corporations.[272] Mulder et al. (2002) test various measures of corporate sector indicators along with macro institutional indicators and those characterizing legal regimes. From their estimations five variables emerge as particularly significant for affecting the probability of a crisis: (1) the financial leverage of a firm, (2) this leverage divided by the share of the corporate sector in bank lending (composite corporate/banking sector exposure), (3) the combined

[270] IMF (2002), p. 59.

[271] See Ghosh and Ghosh (2003), p. 482.

[272] *Corporate governance* has been defined as "the rules, standards, and organizations that govern the behavior of corporate owners, directors, and managers and that define their duties and accountabilities to outside investors"; see Ghosh and Ghosh (2003), p. 484.

corporate/banking sector's debt as a percentage of exports, (4) the ratio of public debt to total debt as a macro institutional indicator and (5) a corporate governance indicator which depicts shareholder rights.[273] Factors three and five are found to have the greatest explanatory power. This lends further support to the theory that external crises are prompted by weaknesses in corporate balance sheets and an insufficient voice of minority shareholders who are generally considered instrumental in the timely detection and correction of such deficiencies. The authors also show that, in terms of predictive power, their early warning system, accounting for both balance sheet and legal indicators, outperforms for any given threshold the same model without legal factors and the robust macro-variable model by Berg and Pattillo (1999).[274] The empirical findings of Mulder and co-authors suggest that the "banking sector channel" as measured by the highly meaningful composite corporate/banking sector variable is especially important in explaining the *depth* of a crisis.

Another recent study by Ghosh and Ghosh (2003) uses comparable firm-level variables in determining whether structural determinants contributed to "deep" currency crises. Their paper's special contribution to the empirics of early warning systems is the use of a *binary recursive tree* accounting for "context dependence" which, in this framework, refers to complex interactions between governance, macroeconomic, and corporate indicators. For example, given the fact that governance structures differ strongly across jurisdictions, the resilience of countries to either macroeconomic or corporate sector imbalances may also differ greatly. The application of this technique yields results that are especially revealing: countries with a low score on governance and, in addition, with a particularly high corporate debt-equity ratio are seven and five times more likely, respectively, to have a crisis than countries that are found safer in these respects. Therefore, the "danger" threshold depends decisively on the

[273] Even so, the other legal/institutional indicators tested – creditors' rights, contract enforceability, accounting standards and the origin of a host country's legal system – are only slightly less significant than the one chosen for the parsimonious specification and should thus also be considered good determinants of crises; see estimation results in Mulder et al. (2002), p. 23.

[274] Mulder et al. (2002, p. 12) suggest a novel measure of predictive accuracy correcting the popular "noise-to-signal *ratio*" which measures the number of crisis periods called correctly as a percentage of the number of false alarms. As opposed to this ratio, which does not detail how many crises were actually called, the "signal-to-noise *balance*" proposed by the authors measures the difference between the percentage of pre-crisis periods called correctly and the percentage of false alarms, both expressed in terms of the total number of pre-crisis periods.

combination of institutional, macroeconomic and corporate governance indicators present in each country.[275]

2.4 Expropriation Risk and Dispute Settlement

The interesting observation that the section on "nationalization and expropriation" in UNCTAD's 2003 World Investment Report is the only section of relevance to this study that does not elaborate on "options for the future" sheds light on the complexity of this particular issue in FDI regulation. It is not that there is a shortage of ideas – indeed, Mistry and Olesen (2003) make no fewer than 26 suggestions for bilateral donors on how to mitigate expropriation risk and thus unleash FDI flows to least-developed countries – but most proposals are either not far-reaching enough, do not credibly provide the necessary protection or are difficult to agree on at the international level. As is clear from both the theoretical analysis and the empirical results presented in Chapter IV, it is preferable to influence the set of incentives facing host governments such that the likelihood of expropriation is lowered to the extent that FDI takes place in a largely unconstrained manner. This mutually beneficial outcome can be achieved by resorting to the financial power that multilateral development organizations enjoy in the eyes of host country officials.

A related viable alternative that has been cited by some authors[276] is to involve a third party in the host country – a bank or a political risk insurance company – in the financing or securing of FDI projects. As with local banks, foreign investors would have them supply a large part of the debt financing so that if the affiliate is disowned, the banks would take the brunt of the loss and therefore try to persuade the government to leave the venture untouched. Indeed, as debt service is met out of local production, the net worth that is lost in the FDI project would be rather low.[277] The problem with that approach is that in some emerging markets the financial sector is not yet developed enough to provide reliable large-scale financing of FDI projects. In this sense multilateral efforts to foster financial market development may also serve the interests of foreign investors. To involve domestic insurance agencies appears less effective at any rate because the host government might prevent them from paying out the insurance premium.

---

[275] See Ghosh and Ghosh (2003), pp. 496, 500-501.

[276] See, for example, Moosa (2002), p. 156, or Mistry and Olesen (2003), p. 50.

[277] Similarly, using a large share of local labor in the foreign affiliate also lowers the probability of government interference; see Moosa (2002), p. 159.

However, provisions to settle investment disputes must be in place even if the risk of expropriation is lowered. Occasionally, the creation of a new organization for arbitration of investment disputes has been suggested. It appears, however, that the ICSID is widely respected as an independent arbiter of disputes, making fair rulings for the most part. Investors should be given the right to file a claim with the ICSID directly without first having to exhaust the remedies provided by local courts, which are arguably not unbiased. Therefore, efforts should be centered on broadening ICSID's mandate and improving the transparency of its adjudication, thereby further reinforcing its acceptance among developing countries. In determining the outcome of the case, the court could adopt a wider developmental perspective instead of exclusively considering the strictly legal contractual performance of the parties.[278] With respect to exercise of governmental regulation, the definition of what kind of regulatory action aimed at preserving environmental or public health actually constitutes an unlawful taking needs to be rendered more precise by law or legal practice than previous cases have shown it to be currently.

Ultimately, the goal in a conceivable new multinational round on tackling investment barriers must be to define expropriation and determine compensation payments such that foreign investors are afforded appropriate protection without undermining national sovereignty in the conduct of public policy. To assure investors of their rights and remove possible discretion in the national authorities' making a case, clear rules for investor-state dispute settlement, preferably in ICSID or UNCITRAL, should be enshrined in all international agreements.[279] This, however, would require the WTO to change substantially as the Doha Declaration, calling for further clarification, expressly refers only to disputes between member states.

3 Policy Implications and Outlook

The empirical part of this study, along with further theoretical considerations, has illustrated that the astounding intricate linkages between macroeconomic, financial and institutional factors require researchers and policy-makers to look beyond the traditional determinants of foreign direct investment, which means embracing a holistic approach.

---

[278] See Moran (2002), p. 37.

[279] See UNCTAD (2003), p. 116.

As Jeffrey Sachs puts it, using a fitting analogy:

> "Maybe we can think of the institutions in a society like the organelles of a cell: (...) One of the features of a complex interconnected system like a living cell is that when any one of those organelles is misfiring, the whole cell can die. (...) When the body is misfiring, the doctor has to make a *differential diagnosis*. (...) Macroeconomists often fail to make this kind of differential diagnosis. When an economy is collapsing, we try to isolate the problem in the places we know best, whether that is the budget or the tax policy or the exchange rate. We have endless debates about manipulating macroeconomic variables, when the deeper problems in the system – the organelles that are misfiring – may be rooted in completely different institutions, whose failure is being transmitted throughout the entire system, and therefore manifesting itself as a macroeconomic problem as well. In that case, the macroeconomic failures are symptoms, not the primary causes of social and economic collapse."[280]

The multi-faceted nature of barriers to foreign direct investment also necessitates both division of labor and targeted collaboration between international financial institutions at the same time.

Along these lines, the institutional framework for negotiating further liberalization of foreign direct investment should be guided by a "general-to-specific" approach. The order is intuitive: basic rules acceptable to all countries, both industrial and developing, ought to be regulated at the global level. Then there is room for regional agreements in which countries, sharing the same basic goal of promoting their (sub-)continent, agree on eliminating more barriers. Specific issues should be dealt with in bilateral treaties, and, while the use investment incentives should be limited, there is no reason for having reservations about the unilateral informational promotion of FDI.

What is needed in addition is a coherent international architecture for lowering barriers to FDI and settling investment disputes. Essentially, the goal must be to devise a new *multilateral* framework of investment rules and an impartial legal system tasked with judging the legitimacy of temporarily imposed investment barriers. Given that the failure of the OECD-MAI was due in large measure to the exclusion of developing countries in the negotiations, unleashing a wave of protest from these and some NGOs, the appropriate forum for a new bargaining round on breaking down investment barriers would be the WTO. Admittedly, the outcome of such a round might be rather limited, likely comprising only the basic points that the whole range of countries can agree to. Perhaps the

[280] Sachs (2003), pp. 34-35.

aforementioned FDI-related provisions of the GATS could be adopted for the real sector to the effect that, as a rule, host countries must allow entry of foreign firms into all sectors but the most sensitive ones and also the repatriation of profits. Arguably, there would indeed be a fair chance for passing such a ground rule, which can only be suspended if an impartial third party finds an external imbalance to prevail. The cornerstone to such a new system would be the legal framework for collaboration between the WTO and the IMF that is already in place. Article XV:2 of the GATT describes the effect of consultation with the Fund, specifically that the WTO is required to accept certain findings and information that correspond to the legal nature of the Fund's work:

> "In such consultations, the [WTO] shall accept all findings of statistical and other facts presented by the Fund relating to foreign exchange, monetary reserves and balance of payments, and shall accept the determination of the Fund as to whether action by a [WTO member] in exchange matters is in accordance with the Articles of Agreement of the International Monetary Fund, or with the terms of a special exchange agreement between that [WTO member] and the [WTO]."

The phrasing and the specific contents of that article are significant. The term "shall accept" means that the determinations of the Fund are factual findings and are thus to be taken as binding. Hence, the Fund's statement is not merely another expert opinion to be considered or weighted against those of other experts. In other words, the Executive Board of the Fund does not operate as a hired expert but as the authority to which the international community has assigned the special role of making such determinations. A renewed thrust to arrive at a WTO agreement on investment should recognize that fact and thus revamp the WTO's panel system of dispute settlement. In a number of cases, the respective panels did not consult the Fund or, even if they did, also solicited the opinion of other outside experts. In the Argentinean footwear case of 1997 a WTO panel declined to consult the Fund because the case involved an import surcharge that was arguably beyond the areas of expertise of the IMF – foreign exchange, monetary reserves and balance of payments. In the case of India's protracted imposition of trade restrictions, which, being a balance of payments issue, was clearly within the IMF's competence, the panel *chose* to consult the Fund, which amounts to treating the consultation requirement as discretionary. After the panel had accepted the Fund's statement, prompting India to challenge the ruling, the appellate body of the WTO found that the panel had given considerable weight to the views expressed by the IMF, not simply accepting its views but critically assessing these by turning to other sources such as the report of the Reserve Bank of India.[281] While the panels' legal practice may have been broadly in accord with WTO statutes, it renders understandable that not all member states would find their rulings impartial.

The structure of a new WTO dispute settlement system should be as follows: Upon receiving a claim by a litigant, the WTO panel would be *mandated* to consult the Fund "on its matters", and, what is new, the World Bank, which is uniquely positioned to assess "micro"-type issues that are outside the Fund's direct expertise. These issues could comprise, for example, the imposition of import taxes, which penalize foreign investors if they, unlike their domestic competitors, source components needed for local production largely from outside the country, or possibly even the exercise of regulatory power in environmental matters. This way, the Argentinean footwear case could have been reviewed by an independent expert carrying weight. Such a supplement would, of course, require an explicit understanding or even the drafting of a written agreement between the WTO and the Bank. The rulings of either institution on whether or not cases of temporary imposition of certain restrictions are justified would be legally dispositive. An appellate body might even be placed outside the WTO, so perhaps the ICSID as a party normally not involved in the WTO-IMF framework would be the appropriate institution to accept such appeals.

Some member states might be uncomfortable with delegating such far-reaching decision-making powers to the IMF (or, conceivably, the World Bank). It must be kept in mind, though, that the Fund's statement is deliberated and approved by its Executive Board, where potentially all members, even a country that is represented "only" by an executive director responsible for the constituency it is in, have an opportunity to debate the factual description and evaluation of an external imbalance in the country in question, thereby promoting confidence that all views are duly represented. This multilateral forum, where the particular interests of the litigants tend not to aggravate the already complex issues, appears far better suited to arriving at a well-balanced judgment than a panel in which only a fraction of countries are represented. The public acceptance of either Bretton Woods institution as a decision-making body would be strengthened by the requirement, such as the one embedded in NAFTA, that a country invoking a balance of payments exception enter into "good faith" consultations with the IMF (or the World Bank) on economic adjustment measures in order to remove the underlying imbalance causing the difficulties. By linking the declarative statement that a serious imbalance exists and that the

[281] See Siegel (2002), pp. 571-572, 576, 582.

measure taken to address it is deemed lawful with the requirement that a country adopt corrective action as part of a structural adjustment program involving Fund financing, the international community would be led to presume that these restrictions were going to be repealed within a reasonable time period.[282]

This new institutional architecture in the sphere of investment barriers that is based on a refined collaboration between the WTO, on the one hand, and the IMF and World Bank, on the other, represents a proper institutional arrangement, as it builds on the comparative advantage of each institution and allows for a clear separation of powers at the international level.

Finally, an outlook on the latest and some possible future developments in the area of emerging market FDI seems in order. The ongoing economic advancement of several emerging markets, predominantly located in Asia, is already leading to a shift in FDI patterns. Having been almost exclusively net importers of capital in the early days, economies such as China and India are turning into sizable equity investors themselves. Figures show that during the 1990s China invested annually on average US$2.3 billion in companies abroad, which, admittedly, is still low in comparison to the roughly US$50 billion it receives in FDI each year. Indian companies bought 36 foreign firms worth US$800 million in 2003. Small scale as the investment may still be, anecdotal evidence points to a greater outward orientation of these emerging economies. Chinese companies sell automobiles in Arab countries, take over aviation and electronics firms in Germany, and buy oil fields and power plants in Australia and Indonesia – beyond the immediate domestic energy need.[283] This implies that we are seeing a rise in reverse investment, not in terms of foreign affiliates repatriating profits but equity participation of emerging market corporations in other emerging economies and even countries of the industrialized world.

A fresh strand of the literature will therefore investigate the intricacies of emerging-to-emerging country FDI. While most of the previous FDI literature justifiably omitted home country characteristics in the theoretical and empirical work, variables measuring the capacity of emerging economies to carry out FDI projects need to be taken into account when assessing the sustainability of their investments in the developing world. In this respect, it will be intriguing to examine the effect of the still-existing gap between superior headline economic performance and lackluster governance structures on the stability of FDI flows and the associated development outcome.

---

[282] See Siegel (2002), pp. 583-584.

[283] See Frankfurter Allgemeine Zeitung (2004), p. 16.

References

Abed, G.T./Gupta, S. (2002): "The Economics of Corruption: An Overview", in: Abed, G.T./Gupta, S. (Eds.): "Governance, Corruption & Economic Performance", International Monetary Fund, Washington D.C.: 1-16

Agarwal, J.P./Gubitz, A./Nunnenkamp, P. (1991): "Foreign Direct Investment in Developing Countries – The Case of Germany", Kieler Studien No. 238, Kiel Institute of World Economics

Aizenman, J. (1991): "Foreign Direct Investment, Productive Capacity and Exchange Rate Regimes", NBER Working Paper No. 3767

Aizenman, J. (1992): "Exchange Rate Flexibility, Volatility, and Domestic and Foreign Direct Investment", IMF Staff Papers, Vol. 39/4: 890-922

Almus, M./Czarnitzki, D. (2003): "The Effects of Public R&D Subsidies on Firms' Innovation Activities: The Case of Eastern Germany", Journal of Business & Economic Statistics, Vol. 21/2: 226-236

Asiedu, E./Villamil, A.P. (2000): "Discount Factors and Thresholds: Foreign Investment When Enforcement is Imperfect", Macroeconomic Dynamics, Vol. 4: 1-21

Asiedu, E./Villamil, A.P. (2002): "Imperfect Enforcement, Foreign Investment, and Foreign Aid", Macroeconomic Dynamics, Vol. 6: 476-495

Baldwin, R.E. (1989): "Measuring Nontariff Trade Policies", NBER Working Paper No. 2978

Barham, J. (2003): "Feast of the Vultures", LatinFinance (December): 26-27

Barrell, R./Pain, N. (1996): "An Econometric Analysis of U.S. Foreign Direct Investment", The Review of Economics and Statistics, Vol. 78: 200-207

Barrell, R./Pain, N. (1999): "Trade Restraints and Japanese Direct Investment Flows", European Economic Review, Vol. 43: 29-45

Barro, R.J. (1991): "Economic Growth in a Cross Section of Countries", Journal of Economic Perspectives, Vol. 106: 407-443

Barro, R.J. (2001): "Economic Growth in Asia Before and After the Financial Crisis", NBER Working Paper No. 8330

Barro, R.J./Lee, J.-W. (2002): "IMF Programs: Who is Chosen and What are the Effects?", NBER Working Paper No. 8951

Barry, F./Bradley, J. (1997): "FDI and Trade: The Irish Host-Country Experience", The Economic Journal, Vol. 107: 1798-1811

Barth, J.R./Caprio, jr., G./Levine, R. (2001): "The Regulation and Supervision of Banks Around the World – A New Database", World Bank Policy Research Working Paper No. 2588

Bellak, C. (1999): "Kritische Einschätzung der empirischen Erfassung und Verwendung von Direktinvestitionsdaten", in: Döhrn, R./Heiduk, G.: "Theorie und Empirie der Direktinvestitionen", Schriftenreihe des Rheinisch-Westfälischen Instituts für Wirtschaftsforschung (No. 65), Berlin: 103-128

Berg, A./Pattillo, C. (1999): "Are Currency Crises Predictable? A Test", IMF Staff Papers, Vol. 46/2: 107-138

Beyer, J. (2002): "Wie erfolgreich sind Maßnahmen zur Förderung von ausländischen Direktinvestitionen? – Empirische Befunde aus den Transformationsländern", Zeitschrift für Wirtschaftspolitik, Vol. 51/1: 63-83

Birch, M./Braga, C.A.P. (1993): "Regulation in Latin America: Prospects for the 1990s", The Quarterly Journal of Economics and Finance, Vol. 33 (special issue): 119-133

Blandón, J.G. (1998): "The Timing of Foreign Direct Investment Under Uncertainty: Evidence from the Spanish Banking Sector", University of Pompeu Fabra (Barcelona), Economic Working Paper No. 360

Blomström, M./Kokko, A. (2003): "The Economics of Foreign Direct Investment Incentives", in: Herrmann, H./Lipsey, R. (Eds.): "Foreign Direct Investment in the Real and Financial Sector of Industrial Countries", Berlin/Heidelberg/New York: 37-56

Blundell, R./Costa Dias, M. (2000): "Evaluation Methods for Non-Experimental Data", Fiscal Studies, Vol. 21: 427-468

Braunerhjelm, P./Svensson, R. (1996): "Host Country Characteristics and Agglomeration in Foreign Direct Investment", Applied Economics, Vol. 28: 833-840

Brealey, R.A./Kaplanis, E.C. (1996): "The Determination of Foreign Banking Location", Journal of International Money and Finance, Vol. 15/4: 577-596

Brunetti, A./Weder, B. (1997): "Investment and Institutional Uncertainty – A Comparative Study of Different Uncertainty Measures", IFC Technical Paper No. 4

Bubnova, N. (2000): "Governance Impact on Private Investment", World Bank Technical Paper No. 488

Buch, C.M. (1999): "Capital Market Integration in Euroland – The Role of Banks", Kiel Working Paper No. 932, Kiel Institute of World Economics

Buch, C.M. (2000): "Why Do Banks Go Abroad? – Evidence from German Data", Journal of Financial Markets, Instruments and Institutions, Vol. 9/1: 33-67

Buch, C.M./Lapp, S. (1998): "The Euro – No Big Bang for European Financial Markets", Beihefte der Konjunkturpolitik (Zeitschrift für angewandte Wirtschaftsforschung – Applied Economics Quarterly), Vol. 47: 11-78

Buch, C.M./Lipponer A. (2004a): "FDI Versus Cross-Border Financial Services: The Globalisation of German Banks", Economic Research Centre of the Deutsche Bundesbank, Discussion Paper No. 05/04

Buch, C.M./Lipponer, A. (2004b): "Clustering or Competition? The Foreign Investment Behaviour of German Banks", Economic Research Centre of the Deutsche Bundesbank, Discussion Paper No. 06/04

Bulíř, A./Moon, S. (2003): "Do IMF-Supported Programs Help Make Fiscal Adjustment More Durable?", IMF Working Paper No. 03/38

Bussiere, M./Fratzscher, M. (2002): "Towards a New Early Warning System of Financial Crises", ECB Working Paper No. 145

Calvo, G.A. (1996): "Capital Flows and Macroeconomic Management: Tequila Lessons", International Journal of Finance & Economics, Vol. 1: 207-223

Calvo, G.A./Mendoza, E.G. (1996): "Petty Crime and Cruel Punishment: Lessons from the Mexican Debacle", American Economic Review, Vol. 86/2: 170-175

Cardone-Riportella, C./Álvarez-Gil, M.J./Lado-Cousté, N./Sasi, V. (2000): "Going International: Are Financial Services Companies Following Manufacturing Firms?", Centre for International Business Research, Helsinki School of Economics and Business Administration, Working Paper No. Z-8

Chakrabarti, A. (2001): "The Determinants of Foreign Direct Investment: Sensitivity Analyses of Cross-Country Regressions", Kyklos, Vol. 54: 89-113

Chen, Y.-F./Funke, M. (2003): "Option Value, Policy Uncertainty, and the Foreign Direct Investment Decision", HWWA Discussion Paper No. 234

Chennells, L./Griffith, R. (1997): "Taxing Profits in a Changing World", The Institute of Fiscal Studies, London

Claessens, S./Demirgüç-Kunt/Huizinga, H. (1998): "Hoes Does Foreign Entry Affect the Domestic Banking Market?", World Bank Policy Research Working Paper No. 1918

Clarke, G./Cull, R./Peria, M.S.M./Sánchez, S.M. (2001): "Foreign Bank Entry: Experience, Implications for Developing Countries, and Agenda for Further Research", World Bank Policy Research Working Paper No. 2698

Conway, P. (1994): "IMF Lending Programs: Participation and Impact", Journal of Development Economics, Vol. 45: 365-391

Cushman, D.O. (1985): "Real Exchange Rate Risk, Expectations, and the Level of Direct Investment", The Review of Economics and Statistics, Vol. 67: 297-308

Dabla-Norris, E. (2002): "A Game Theoretic Analysis of Corruption in Bureaucracies", in: Abed, G.T./Gupta, S. (Eds.): "Governance, Corruption & Economic Performance", International Monetary Fund, Washington D.C.: 111-134

Demirgüç-Kunt, A./Detragiache, E. (1998): "The Determinants of Banking Crises in Developing and Developed Countries", IMF Staff Papers, Vol. 45/1: 81-109

Desai, M.A./Foley, C.F./Hines, Jr., J.R. (2003): "Chains of Ownership, Regional Tax Competition, and Foreign Direct Investment", in: Herrmann, H./Lipsey R. (Eds.): "Foreign Direct Investment in the Real and Financial Sectors of Industrial Countries", Berlin/Heidelberg/New York: 61-98

Dicks-Mireaux, L./Mecagni, M./Schadler, S. (2000): "Evaluating the Effects of IMF Lending to Low-Income Countries", Journal of Development Economics, Vol. 61: 495-525

Dielman T. (1988): "Pooled Cross-Sectional and Time Series Data Analysis", New York

Dunning, J. (1977): "Trade, Location of Economic Activity and the MNE: a Search for an Eclectic Approach", in: Ohlin, B./ Hesselborn, P./Wijkman, P. (Eds.): "The International Allocation of Economic Activity", Proceedings of a Nobel Symposium held in Stockholm, London: 395-431

Easterly, W./Rebero, S. (1993): "Fiscal Policy and Economic Growth: An Empirical Investigation", NBER Working Paper No. 4499

Eaton, J./Gersovitz, M. (1983): "Country Risk: Economic Aspects", in: Herring, R.J. (Ed.): "Managing International Risk – Essays Commissioned in Honor of the Centenary of the Wharton School, University of Pennsylvania", New York/Melbourne (Cambridge University Press)

Eaton, J./Gersovitz, M. (1984): "A Theory of Expropriation and Deviations from Perfect Capital Mobility", The Economic Journal, Vol. 94 (March): 16-40

Efron, B. (1982): "The Jackknife, the Bootstrap and Other Resampling Plans", Society for Industrial and Applied Mathematics, Philadelphia (USA)

Efron, B./Tibshirani, R.J. (1993): "An Introduction to the Bootstrap", Monographs on Statistics and Applied Probability, Vol. 57, New York/London

Eichengreen, B./Rose, A.K. (1998): "Staying Afloat When the Wind Shifts: External Factors and Emerging-Market Banking Crises", NBER Working Paper No. 6370

Euromoney (1997): "Country Risk – It Could be Worse", December: 60-62

Euromoney (2000): "Country Risk – Commodity Prices Boost Emerging Markets", March: 106-109

Everhart, S.S./Sumlinski, M.A. (2001): "Trends in Private Investment in Developing Countries – Statistics for 1970-2000 – and the Impact on Private Investment of Corrpution and the Quality of Public Investment", IFC Discussion Paper No. 44

Farrell, D./Remes, J.K./Schulz, H. (2004): "The Truth About Foreign Direct Investment in Emerging Markets", The McKinsey Quarterly No. 2004/I: 25-35

Fernández-Arias, E./Hausmann, R. (2001): "Capital Inflows and Crisis: Does the Mix Matter?"; in: OECD (Ed.): „Foreign Direct Investment Versus Other Flows to Latin America", Paris: 93-110

Fernández-Arias, E./Montiel, P. (2001): "Reform and Growth in Latin America: All Pain, No Gain?", IMF Staff Papers, Vol. 48/3: 522-546

Fischer, A. (2000): "Direktinvestitionen", Bern/Stuttgart/Wien

Focarelli, D./Pozzolo, A.F. (2001): "The Patterns of Cross-Border Bank Mergers and Shareholdings in OECD Countries", Journal of Banking and Finance, Vol. 25: 2305-2337

Frankfurter Allgemeine Zeitung (2004): "Chinas Unternehmen drängen ins Ausland", No. 2 (January 3): 16

Froot, K.A./Stein, J.C. (1991): "Exchange Rates and Foreign Direct Investment: An Imperfect Capital Markets Approach", The Quarterly Journal of Economics, Vol. 106: 1191-1217

Galindo, A./Micco, A./Serra, C. (2002): "Better the Devil that you Know: Evidence of Entry Costs Faced by Foreign Banks", IADB Working Paper No. 477

Garibaldi, P./Mora N./Sahay, R./Zettelmeyer, J. (2002): "What Moves Capital to Transition Economies?", IMF Working Paper 02/64

Gaytán, A./Johnson, C.A. (2002): "A Review of the Literature on Early Warning Systems for Banking Crises", Central Bank of Chile Working Paper No. 183

Ghosh, S.R./Ghosh, A.R. (2003): "Structural Vulnerabilities and Currency Crises", IMF Staff Papers, Vol. 50/3: 481-506

Ghura, D./Goodwin, B. (2000): "Determinants of Private Investment: A Cross-Regional Empirical Investigation", Applied Economics, Vol. 32: 1819-1829

Glick, R./Hutchison, M. (1999): "Banking and Currency Crises: How Common are Twin Crises", Center for Pacific Basin Monetary and Economic Studies, Economic Research Department, Federal Reserve Bank of San Francisco, Working Paper No. PB99-07

Goldberg, L.G./Johnson, D. (1990): "The Determinants of US Banking Activity Abroad", Journal of International Money and Finance, Vol. 9: 123-137

Goldberg, L.S./Klein, M.W. (1997): "Foreign Direct Investment, Trade and Exchange Rate Linkages in Southeast Asia and Latin America", NBER Working Paper No. 6344

Goldberg, L.S./Kolstad, C.D. (1995): "Foreign Direct Investment, Exchange Rate Variability and Demand Uncertainty", International Economic Review, Vol. 36/4: 855-873

Goldstein, M./Montiel, P. (1986): "Evaluating Fund Stabilization Programs with Multicountry Data: Some Methodological Pitfalls", IMF Staff Papers, Vol. 33 (June): 304-344

Greene, W.H. (2003): "Econometric Analyses", 5th Edition, Upper Saddle River

Grigorian, D.A. (2003): "On the Determinants of First-Time Sovereign Bond Issues", IMF Working Paper No. 03/184

Grubel, H. (1977): "A Theory of Multinational Banking", Banca Nationale de Lavoro, Quarterly Review (December): 349-363

Hallward-Driemeier, M. (2003): "Do Bilateral Investment Treaties Attract FDI? Only a Bit...and They Could Bite", World Bank Policy Research Working Paper No. 3121

Haque, N.U./Khan, M.S. (1998): "Do IMF-Supported Programs Work? A Survey of the Cross-Country Empirical Evidence", IMF Working Paper No. 98/169

Hausmann, R./Fernández-Arias, E. (2001): "Foreign Direct Investment: Good Cholesterol?" in: OECD (Ed.): "Foreign Direct Investment Versus Other Flows to Latin America", Paris: 19-49

Heckman, J. (1979): "Sample Selection Bias as a Specification Error", Econometrica, Vol. 47: 153-161

Heckman, J.J./Ichimura, H./Todd, P. (1997): "Matching as an Econometric Evaluation Estimator: Evidence from Evaluating a Job Training Program", Review of Economic Studies, Vol. 64: 605-654

Heiduk, G./ Hodges, U.W. (1992): "German Multinationals in Europe: Patterns and Perspectives", in: Klein, M./Welfens, P.J.J. (Eds.): "Multinationals in the New Europe and Global Trade", Berlin

Heritage Foundation (2002): "2003 Index of Economic Freedom", Washington D.C.

Hoekman, B./Saggi, K. (1999): "Multilateral Disciplines for Investment-Related Policies?", World Bank Policy Research Working Paper No. 2138

Honohan, P. (1997): "Banking System Failures in Developing and Transition Countries: Diagnosis and Predition", BIS Working Paper No. 39

Hubert, F./Pain, N. (1999): "Innovation and the Regional and Industrial Pattern of German Foreign Direct Investment", in: Barrell, R./Pain, N. (Eds.): "Investment, Innovation and the Diffusion of Technology in Europe", Cambridge University Press (Massachusetts): 168-194

Ihrig, J. (2000): "Multinationals' Response to Repatriation Restrictions", Journal of Economic Dynamics & Control, Vol. 24: 1345-1379

Ilmakunnas, P./Maliranta, M. (2004): "Foreign Medicine: A Treatment Effect Analysis of the Productivity Effects of Foreign Ownership", Applied Economics Quarterly – Konjunkturpolitik: 41-60

International Monetary Fund (IMF) (1993): "Balance of Payments Manual", 5th edition, Washington D.C.

International Monetary Fund (IMF) (2002): "Global Financial Stability Report – Market Developments and Issues", (March) Washington D.C.

Inter-American Development Bank (2002): "Beyond Borders: The New Regionalism in Latin America – Economic and Social Progress in Latin America", Washington D.C.

International Finance Corporation (2002): "IFC's Strategic Priorities", Washington D.C.

Jost, T. (1997): "Direct Investment and Germany as a Business Location", Economic Research Group of the Deutsche Bundesbank, Discussion Paper 2/97

Jost, T. (1999): "Zur Aussagekraft der Direktinvestitionsstatistiken der Deutschen Bundesbank", in: Döhrn, R./Heiduk, G.: "Theorie und Empirie der Direktinvestitionen", Schriftenreihe des Rheinisch-Westfälischen Instituts für Wirtschaftsforschung (No. 65), Berlin: 129-148

Jost, T./Nunnenkamp, P. (2002): "Bestimmungsgründe deutscher Direktinvestitionen in Entwicklungs- und Reformländern – Hat sich wirklich etwas verändert?", Kieler Arbeitspapiere No. 1124

Judge, G.G./Hill, R.C./Griffiths, W.E./Lütkepohl, H./Lee, T.-C. (1989): "Introduction to the Theory and Practice of Econometrics", New York

Kaminsky, G./Reinhart, C.M. (1999): "The Twin Crises: The Causes of Banking and Balance-of-Payments Problems", American Economic Review, Vol. 89/3: 473-500

Kaminsky, G./Schmukler, S.L. (2003): "Short-Run Pain, Long-Run Gain: The Effects of Financial Liberalization", IMF Working Paper No. 03/34

Kaufmann, D./Kraay, A./Zoido-Lobatón, P. (1999): "Aggregating Governance Indicators", World Bank Policy Research Working Paper No. 2195

Khan, M.S./Knight, M. (1981): "Stabilization Programs in Developing Countries: A Formal Framework", IMF Staff Papers, Vol. 28: 1-53

Khan, M.S./Knight, M. (1985): "Fund-Supported Programs and Economic Growth", IMF Occasional Paper No. 41

Konishi, H./Saggi, K./Weber, S. (1999): "Endogenous Trade Policy under Foreign Direct Investment"; Journal of International Economics, Vol. 49: 289-408

Kosteletou, N./Liargovas, P. (2000): "Foreign Direct Investment and Real Exchange Rate Linkages", Open Economies Review, Vol. 11: 135-148

Krasa, S./Villamil, A.P. (2000): "Optimal Contracts when Enforcement is a Decision Variable", Econometrica, Vol. 68/1: 119-134

Kräussl, R. (2003): "Sovereign Risk, Credit Ratings and the Recent Financial Crises in Emerging Markets", Frankfurt am Main

Leamer, E. (1983): "Let's Take the Con Out of Econometrics", American Economic Review, Vol. 73: 31-43

Leamer, E. (1985): "Sensitivity Analyses Would Help", American Economic Review, Vol. 75: 308-313

Leamer, E. (1988): "Measures of Openness", in: Baldwin, R. (Ed.): "Trade Policy Issues and Empirical Analysis", University of Chicago Press: 147-200

Lehmann, A. (1999): "Country Risk and the Investment Activity of U.S. Multinationals in Developing Countries", IMF Working Paper 99/133

Lehmann, A. (2002): "Foreign Direct Investment in Emerging Markets: Income, Repatriations and Financial Vulnerabilities", IMF Working Paper 02/47

Lehmann, A./Tamirisa, N.T./Wieczorek, J. (2003): "International Trade in Services: Implications for the IMF", IMF Policy Discussion Paper No. 03/6

Levine, R./Renelt, D. (1992): "A Sensitivity Analysis of Cross-Country Growth Regressions", American Economic Review, Vol. 82: 942-963

Lim, E.-G. (2001): "Determinants of, and the Relation Between, Foreign Direct Investment and Growth: A Summary of the Recent Literature", IMF Working Paper 01/175

Lipponer, A. (2003): "A 'New' Micro Database for German FDI", in: Herrmann, H./Lipsey R. (Eds.): "Foreign Direct Investment in the Real and Financial Sectors of Industrial Countries", Berlin/Heidelberg/New York: 215-244

Lipsey, R.E. (2002): "Home and Host Country Effects of FDI", NBER Working Paper No. 9293

Lora, E. (1997): "A Decade of Structural Reforms in Latin America – What Has Been Reformed and How to Measure it", Inter-American Development Bank, Working Paper No. 348

Lora, E. (2001): "Structural Reforms in Latin America: What Has Been Reformed and How to Measure it", Inter-American Development Bank, Working Paper No. 466

Love, J.H./Lage-Hidalgo, F. (2000): "Analysing the Determinants of US Direct Investment in Mexico", Applied Economics, Vol. 32: 1259-1267

Mallampally, P./Sauvant, K.P. (1999), "Foreign Direct Investment in Developing Countries", IMF Finance & Development, Vol. 36/1 (March)

Markusen, J.R. (1990): "First Mover Advantages, Blockaded Entry, and the Economics of Uneven Development", NBER Working Paper No. 3284

Martha, R.S. (1990): "Preferred Creditor Status Under International Law: The Case of the International Monetary Fund", International and Comparative Law Quarterly, Vol. 39: 801-826

Martins, P. (2003): "Wage Differentials and Spillovers of Foreign Firms: Evidence from a Matched Panel", paper presented at the HWWA workshop "Effects of Foreign Acquisitions on Domestic Firms" in Hamburg, October 24-25, 2003Mauro, P. (1995): "Corruption and Growth", The Quarterly Journal of Economics, Vol. 110: 681-712

Mavrotas, G. (2002): "Multilateral Development Banks and Private Sector Financing – The Case of IFC", United Nations University, World Institute for Development Economics Research, Discussion Paper No. 2002/118

Mendoza, E.G., Razin, A./Tesar, L.L. (1994): "Effective Tax Rates in Macroeconomics: Cross-Country Estimates of Tax Rates on Factor Incomes and Consumption", NBER Working Paper No. 4864

Miller, S.R./Parkhe, A. (1998): "Patterns of Expansion of U.S. Banks' Foreign Operations", Journal of International Business Studies, Vol. 29/2: 359-390

Mistry, P.S./Olesen, N.E. (2003): "Mitigating Risks for Foreign Investments in Least Developed Countries", Regeringskansliet – Ministry for Foreign Affairs Sweden, Stockholm

Mody, A./Dasgupta, S./Sinha, S. (1999): "Japanese Multinationals in Asia: Drivers and Attractors", Oxford Development Studies, Vol. 27: 149-164

Mody, A./Murshid, A.P. (2002): "Growing Up with Capital Flows", IMF Working Paper 02/75

Mody, A./Saravia, D. (2003): "Catalyzing Private Capital Flows: Do IMF-Supported Programs Work as Commitment Devices?", IMF Working Paper No. 03/100

Mody, A./Srinivasan, K. (1998): "Japanese and U.S. Firms as Foreign Investors: Do They March in the Same Tune?", Canadian Journal of Economics, Vol. 31: 778-799

Moody's (2003): "Sovereign Bond Defaults, Rating Transitions, and Recoveries (1985-2002)", (February) New York

Moore, M. O. (1993): "Determinants of German Manufacturing Direct Investment: 1980-1988", Weltwirtschaftliches Archiv, Vol. 129: 120-138

Moosa, I.A. (2002): "Foreign Direct Investment – Theory, Evidence and Practice", Houndmills (UK)/New York

Moran, T.H. (2002): "The Relationship between Trade, Foreign Direct Investment, and Development: New Evidence, Strategy, and Tactics under the Doha Development Agenda Negotiations", Asian Development Bank, (September) Manila

Morisset, J. (2003): "Does a Country Need a Promotion Agency to Attract Foreign Direct Investment?", World Bank Policy Research Working Paper No. 3028

Morisset, J./Neso, O.L. (2002): "Administrative Barriers to Foreign Direct Investment in Developing Countries", World Bank Policy Research Working Paper No. 2848

Moshirian, F. (2001): "International Investment in Financial Services", Journal of Banking and Finance, Vol. 25: 317-337

Moshirian, F./Van der Laan, A. (1998): "Trade in Financial Services and the Determinants of Banks' Foreign Assets", Journal of Multinational Financial Management, Vol. 8: 23-38

Mulder, C./Perrelli, R./Rocha, M. (2002): "The Role of Corporate, Legal and Macroeconomic Balance Sheet Indicators in Crisis Detection and Prevention", IMF Working Paper No. 02/59

Myers, S. (1977): "Determinants of Corporate Borrowing", Journal of Financial Economics, Vol. 5: 147-175

Nigh, D./Cho, K.R./Krishnan, S. (1986): "The Role of Location-Related Factors in U.S. Banking Involvement Abroad: An Empirical Examination", Journal of International Business Studies, Vol. 17 (Fall): 59-72

Noorbakhsh, F./Paloni, A./Youssef, A. (2001): "Human Capital and FDI Inflows to Developing Countries: New Empirical Evidence", World Development, Vol. 29: 1593-1610

Nunnenkamp, P. (1998): "German Direct Investment in Latin America – Striking Peculiarities, Unfounded Fears, and Neglected Issues", Kiel Working Paper No. 861, Kiel Institute of World Economics

Nunnenkamp, P. (2001a): "Too Much, Too Little, or Too Volatile? – International Capital Flows to Developing Countries in the 1990s", Kiel Working Paper No. 1036, Kiel Institute of World Economics

Nunnenkamp, P. (2001b): "Foreign Direct Investment in Developing Countries – What Policymakers Should Not Do and What Economists Don't Know"; Kiel Discussion Papers No. 380, Kiel Institute of World Economics

OECD (1996): "OECD Benchmark Definition of Foreign Direct Investment", 3rd Edition, Paris

Pain, N. (2003): "Fiscal Policies, European Integration and the Location of German Foreign Direct Investment", in: Herrmann, H./Lipsey R. (Eds.): "Foreign Direct Investment in the Real and Financial Sectors of Industrial Countries", Berlin/Heidelberg/New York: 99-136

Pallage, S./Robe, M.A. (2003): "Leland & Pyle Meet Foreign Aid? Adverse Selection and the Procyclicality of Financial Aid Flows", CIRPÈE Working Paper No. 03-27, University of Québec at Montreal

Papi, L./Revoltella, D. (2000): "Foreign Direct Investment in the Banking Sector: A Transitional Economy Perspective", in: Claessens, S./Jansen, M. (Eds.): "The Internationalization of Financial Services – Issues and Lessons for Developing Countries": 437-457

Pfaffermayr, M./Bellak, C. (2003): "Firm Performance and Growth After Ownership Change – Empirical Evidence for Austria", Paper presented at the HWWA workshop "Effects of Foreign Acquisitions on Domestic Firms" in Hamburg, October 24-25, 2003

Pfeffermann, G.P./Kisunko, G.V./Sumlinski M.A. (1999): "Trends in Private Investment in Developing Countries and Perceived Obstacles to Doing Business – Statistics for 1970-1997", IFC Discussion Paper No. 37

Pindyck, R.S./Rubinfeld, D.L. (1981): "Econometric Models and Economic Forecasts", 2nd Edition, Singapore

Pistoresi, B. (2000): "Investimenti Diretti Esteri e Fattori di Localizzazione: L'America Latina e il Sud Est Asiatico", Rivista di Politica Economia, Vol. 90: 27-44

Pritchett, L. (1996): "Measuring Outward Orientation in LDCs: Can it be Done?", Journal of Development Economics, Vol. 49: 307-335

Przeworski, A./Vreeland, J.R. (2000): "The Effect of IMF Programs on Economic Growth", Journal of Development Economics, Vol. 62: 385-421

Puhani, P. (2000): "The Heckman Correction for Sample Selection and its Critique – A Short Survey", Journal of Economic Surveys, Vol. 14: 53-68

Ramcharran, H. (1999): "Foreign Direct Investment and Country Risk: Further Empirical Evidence", Global Economic Review, Vol. 28: 49-59

Razin, A. (2002): "FDI Contribution to Capital Flows and Investment in Capacity", NBER Working Paper No. 9204

Razin, A./Sadka, E./Yuen C.-W. (2001): "Excessive FDI Flows Under Asymmetric Information", in: Glick, R./Moreno, R./Spiegel M.M. (Eds.): "Financial Crises in Emerging Markets", New York etc. (Cambridge University Press)

Rosenbaum, P.R./Rubin, D.B. (1983): "The Central Role of the Propensity Score in Observational Studies for Causal Effects", Biometrika, Vol. 70: 41-55

Rubin, D.B. (1974): "Estimating Causal Effects of Treatments in Randomized and Non-Randomized Studies", Journal of Educational Psychology, Vol. 66: 688-701

Rubin, D.B. (1977): "Assignment to Treatment Group on the Basis of a Covariate", Journal of Educational Statistics, Vol. 2: 1-26

Sabi, M. (1988): "An Application of the Theory of Foreign Direct Investment to Multinational Banking in LDCs", Journal of International Business Studies, Vol. 19 (Fall): 433-447

Sachs, J. (2003): "Panel Discussion – Promoting Better National Institutions: The Role of the IMF; Remarks by Jeffrey Sachs", IMF Staff Papers Vol. 50: 21-40, here: 34-38

Sagari, S.B. (1992): "United States Foreign Direct Investment in the Banking Industry", Transnational Corporations, Vol. 1/3: 93-123

Sala-i-Martin, X. (1997): "I Just Ran Four Million Regressions", NBER Working Paper No. 6252

Schneider, F./Frey, B. (1985): "Economic and Political Determinants of Foreign Direct Investment", World Development, Vol. 13/2: 161-175

Schnitzer, M. (1999): "Expropriation and Control Rights: A Dynamic Model of Foreign Direct Investment", International Journal of Industrial Organization, Vol. 17: 1113-1137

Schobert, F. (2003): "Die unilaterale Einführung einer Fremdwährung – Währungswahl, Seigniorage and Zinsprämieneffekte in mittel- und osteuropäischen Ländern", Frankfurt am Main

Seth, R./Nolle, D.E./Mohanty, S.K. (1998): "Do Banks Follow Their Customers Around?", Financial Markets, Institutions & Instruments, Vol. 7/4: 1-25

Sianesi, B. (2001): "Implementing Propensity Score Matching Estimators with STATA", Paper prepared for the UK Stata Users Group VII meeting (May), London

Siegel, D.E. (2002): "Legal Aspects of the IMF/WTO Relationship: The Fund's Articles of Agreement and the WTO Agreements", The American Journal of International Law, Vol. 96: 561-599

Sin, C.Y./Leung, W.F. (2001): "Impacts of Foreign Direct Investment Liberalisation on Investment Inflows", Applied Economic Letters, Vol. 8: 253-256

Singh, H./Jun, K.W. (1995): "Some New Evidence on Determinants of Foreign Direct Investment in Developing Countries", World Bank Policy Research Working Paper No. 1531

Standard & Poor's (2003): "2002 Defaults and Rating Transition Data Update for Rated Sovereigns", (January) New York

Stark, J./Hartenstein, D. (2002): "Strengthening the International Financial System", Deutsche Bundesbank, Frankfurt am Main

StataCorp. (2003): "STATA Base Reference Manual, A-F and S-Z, Release 8", College Station (Texas)

Stehn, J. (1992): "Ausländische Direktinvestitionen in Industrieländern", Kieler Studien No. 245, Kiel Institute of World Economics

Stevens, G. (2000): "Politics, Economics and Investment: Explaining Plant and Equipment Spending by US Direct Investors in Argentina, Brazil and Mexico", Journal of International Money and Finance, Vol. 19: 153-183

Stockman, A.C.J./Vlaar, P.J.G. (1996): "Volatility, International Trade and Capital Flows", De Nederlandsche Bank – Reprint Series No. 453

Sung, H./Lapan, H.E. (2000): "Strategic Foreign Direct Investment and Exchange-Rate Uncertainty", International Economic Review, Vol. 41: 411-423

Tanzi, V. (2002): "Corruption Around the World: Causes, Consequences, Scope, and Cures", in: Abed, G.T./Gupta, S. (Eds.): "Governance, Corruption & Economic Performance", International Monetary Fund, Washington D.C.: 19-58

Tanzi, V./Davoodi, H.R. (2000): "Corruption, Growth, and Public Finances", IMF Working Paper No. 00/182

Thomas, J./Worrall, T. (1994): "Foreign Direct Investment and the Risk of Expropriation", Review of Economic Studies, Vol. 61: 81-108

Thompson, E.R./Poon, J.P.H. (2000): "ASEAN After the Financial Crisis – Links Between Foreign Direct Investment and Regulatory Change", ASEAN Economic Bulletin, Vol. 17/1: 1-14

Tuman, J. P./Emmert, C. F. (1999): "Explaining Japanese Foreign Direct Investment in Latin America 1979-1992", Social Science Quarterly, Vol. 80/3: 539-555

Turner, A.G./Golub, S.S. (1997): "Towards a System of Multilateral Unit Labor Cost-Based Competititveness Indicators for Advanced, Developing, and Transition Countries", IMF Working Paper 97/151

Turner, P./Van 't dack, J. (1993): "Measuring International Price and Cost Competitiveness", BIS Economic Papers No. 39 (November)

UNCTAD (2001): "Host Country Operational Measures", UNCTAD Series on Issues in International Investment Agreements, New York/Geneva

UNCTAD (2003): "World Investment Report 2003", New York/Geneva

Verbeek, M. (2001): "A Guide to Modern Econometrics", Chicester (UK)

Wagner, J. (1991): "Die bundesrepublikanische Industrie auf dem Weltmarkt", Berlin

Wagner, J. (2002): "The Causal Effects of Exports on Firm Size and Labor Productivity: First Evidence from a Matching Approach", Economic Letters, Vol. 77: 287-292

Wei, S. J. (2000): "How Taxing is Corruption on International Investors", Review of Economics and Statistics, Vol. 82: 1-11

Wheeler, M./Mody, A. (1992): "International Investment Location Decisions – the Case of U.S. Firms", Journal of International Economics, Vol. 33: 57-76

Williams, B. (1997): "Positive Theories of Multinational Banking: Eclectic Theory Versus Internalisation Theory", Journal of Economic Surveys, Vol. 11/1: 71-100

Yamori, N. (1998): "A Note on the Location Choice of Multinational Banks: The Case of Japanese Financial Institutions", Journal of Banking & Finance, Vol. 22: 109-120

Studien zu Internationalen Wirtschaftsbeziehungen

Herausgegeben von Prof. Dr. Michael Frenkel

Band 1 Christiane Nickel: Insider und Outsider bei der Osterweiterung der Europäischen Währungsunion. 2002.

Band 2 Georg Stadtmann: Noise-Trader auf Devisenmärkten. Viel Lärm um Nichts? 2002.

Band 3 Wolf-Heimo Grieben: Trade and Technology as Competing Explanations for Rising Inequality. An Endogenous Growth Perspective. 2003.

Band 4 Alexander Mende: Order Flow Analyses and Foreign Exchange Dealing. 2005.

Band 5 Torsten Wezel: Determinants of Foreign Direct Investment in Emerging Markets. An Empirical Study of FDI Flows from Germany and its Banking Sector. 2005.

www.peterlang.de

Peter Lang · Europäischer Verlag der Wissenschaften

Ralph Leonhardt

Foreign Direct Investment, Ownership, and the Transfer of Technology

Frankfurt am Main, Berlin, Bern, Bruxelles, New York, Oxford, Wien, 2004.
164 pp., num. tab.
European University Studies: Series 5, Economics and Management.
Vol. 3085
ISBN 3-631-52558-3 / US-ISBN 0-8204-7302-2 · pb. € 34.–*

Using a survey of more than 1000 German investment projects in Central and Eastern Europe, this study analyses the strategies of international joint ventures. Their risks and, in particular, their innovative potential is investigated. As a statistical tool for the analysis of share equations the conditional Tobit model is introduced. The theoretical base is a continuous time, full information model of a joint venture. Surprisingly, sufficient and necessary conditions for joint venture instability and technology transfer can be derived. The survey is used to apply the introduced concepts and to demonstrate the validity of the approach empirically.

Contents: The Econometrics of Ownership Shares · Conditional Tobit Estimation · International Technology Transfer and the Joint Venture Lifecycle · Spillover and Joint Venture Instability · The Value of Transferred Knowlege · Policy Recommendations · Appendix